Great Meals from the Northwest

A Seasonal Cookbook

Judie Geise

Sumi drawings by George Tsutakawa

J. P. TARCHER, INC.
Los Angeles
Distributed by Houghton Mifflin Company
Boston

I would like to gratefully acknowledge the following: my mother and father, for instilling in me an awareness of good food; my dear friend Roberto Tacchi, for his love of Italian cuisine and his excellent cooking, both of which were an inspiration to me; Warren Hill; Mrs. Joel Ramstad; Shirley Collins, for four wonderful and informative years; Ayame and George Tsutakawa, for their generosity, and especially George for his beautiful paintings; and most of all, my husband, Jonn, for his encouragement and patience.

—J.G.

Library of Congress Cataloging in Publication Data

Geise, Judie, 1945—
Great meals from the Northwest.

Originally published under title: The Northwest kitchen.
Includes index.
1. Cookery, American—Northwest, Pacific. I. Title.
TX715.G318   641.5   82-5475
ISBN 0-87477-227-3   AACR2

Requests for such permissions should be addressed to:
J. P. Tarcher, Inc.
9110 Sunset Blvd.
Los Angeles, CA 90069

MANUFACTURED IN THE UNITED STATES OF AMERICA
V 10 9 8 7 6 5 4 3 2 1

CONTENTS

INTRODUCTION 1

INTRODUCTION

Music has been called "the universal language"; but for me, the title of champion communicator must go to good cooking. Nothing is so easily understood, so quickly assimilated, or so thoroughly enjoyed as fine food.

The twentieth century has seen some strange and paradoxical developments in the realm of food, cooking, and eating. Technology, plus high-speed transportation and communications, have made more foods accessible more of the time to more people than ever before. At the same time, it has become much harder to procure foods that are not processed into anonymity, that are ripe and flavorful, untainted by chemicals and additives. We have easy access to cookbooks featuring cuisines from Armenian to Zulu, but meanwhile most of us have lost touch with the family traditions—the day-to-day practices, the attitudes toward ingredients and their combinations—that created those cuisines in the first place.

I am no exception to these trends. I spent much of my childhood in and around one of those much-envied "old-country kitchens" and appreciated it hardly at all until years later, when I began to cook myself. But it was probably those early experiences that helped me to realize that good cooking is not a matter of how many cookbooks you have on your shelf, or how many pots you have hanging on your wall, but of developing a style of cooking, based on sound tradition but adapted to the region where you live and the kind of life you live there.

This may sound too obvious to be worth mentioning, but think a moment. How often have you had a meal, in a restaurant or visiting friends, that really is in tune with the season, that harmonizes with time and place and company, that has none of the "canned" aroma of the cookbook? The gourmet explosion of recent years has made dining at home fashionable again, and that is all to the good. But often, the food served remains impersonal, uninteresting, unmemorable, however elaborate it may be: edible decor, not the core of the experience.

This book is neither a random collection of favorite recipes nor a text on the "culinary tradition" of the Pacific Northwest (if such a thing exists). Rather it is a sort of kitchen autobiography. It is a record of my own explorations of the foodstuffs available in the Pacific Northwest, where I now live, explorations guided by my own background and inclinations and by the different ethnic cuisines that have become adapted to the region.

The recipes included here will be useful to any cook. I hope that they, and the way that they are arranged, will also encourage the reader to go beyond them — not simply reproducing dishes but developing them in new directions, adding personal touches and serendipitous ingredients, finding an individual style. Many of the recipes given here are "classics," dishes that in one form or other are familiar to anyone with a standing interest in good food. I have reworked these dishes to my own taste, adapting them to the ingredients and the seasons of the Northwest, while trying to keep the essential qualities that make the dish memorable.

It may surprise Northwesterners to find in this book so many dishes whose origins are Mediterranean, Italian, Southern French, and Middle Eastern. They are here partly because these foods suit my tastes for simplicity, directness, and lack of pretense; and partly because the foodstuffs available in the Northwest, particularly the seafoods, are for the most part beautifully adaptable to this style of cooking.

Rather than following the traditional arrangement of a cookbook into chapters of hors d'oeuvres, meats, vegetables, and so forth, this one is organized around the seasons, to encourage you to take advantage of the freshest and most appetizing raw materials available. In addition, each monthly chapter contains menu suggestions, as well as more general thoughts on the specific month and the opportunities it affords. I hope the users of this book will use it one month at a time, concentrating on the recipes appropriate for that month when making plans to shop and to entertain. But of course many seasons overlap — good fresh salmon is available April-September — so you will find in each month many references to other recipes in the book. No one should think that cooking seasonally, as this book is organized to encourage, should be a trap or a constraint. Quite the contrary: it will lead you to discover a cornucopia of new products. For many of the specific wine suggestions that accompany the recipes I gratefully acknowledge the assistance of the knowledgeable Ron Irvine of Pike and Western Winemerchants in the Pike Place Market in Seattle.

I hope this book will be useful to both beginning and experienced cooks. Although there are a number of basic techniques described, some experience is assumed about the fundamentals of kitchen technique. For the really inexperienced, I recommend one of the most useful books to date, James Beard's *The Theory and Practice of Good Cooking*. Cookbooks, including this one, should be taken with several grains of salt. Attitudes are more important than recipes, and I hope these predispositions come out clearly in *The Northwest Kitchen:* an awareness of the importance of using the best-quality ingredients (always, not just for special dishes or occasions); the importance of freshness and seasonal cooking; the superior virtues of simplicity and restraint; and above all a willingness to experiment, adapt, and rethink each dish as skill and familiarity grow. In the long run, the way you cook reflects the person you are, how you think and feel. In a fine restaurant or at home, one of the essential ingredients of good cooking is personality; and no matter how good the cookbook, this is one ingredient that only you can add to the recipe.

—Judie Geise   Seattle, Washington

January, Soups and Stews

Menu 1
Chicken Liver Mousse (December)
Poule au pot with Green Sauce (January)
Mousse aux Mandarines (December)

Menu 2
Potted Salmon (August)
Onion Soup (January)
Green Salad Vinaigrette
Chestnuts Flavored with Fennel Seed (November)

Tsutakawa

Onion Soup
Lamb and Bean Soup
Dutch Pea and Ham Soup
Garbure Basquaise
Potato Leek Soup
Bayou Bisque
Oyster Stew
Pot au Feu
Poule au Pot
Salsa Verde for Poule au Pot
Bigos
Chicken, Shrimp, and Sausage Gumbo
Carbonnades of Short Ribs
Short Ribs of Beef with Carrots
Beef and Pork Chili
Lamb Shanks, Greek Style
Choucroute Garnie
Stracotta alla Fiorentina
Banana Rum Souffle Glace

The subtle aroma of a simmering soup stock becomes for me a gentle reminder of those wintery days in my childhood when these luscious smells wafted from the family kitchen almost daily. All of America has been brought up on soups; fortunately the ones I grew up with did not have their origins in a can but rather in the hearts and minds of some very good cooks. I was fortunate enough to grow up in what is now termed an "Old World" family. Both my maternal and paternal grandparents were born in Middle Europe and immigrated to America in their early twenties.

I was born a second-generation American, but my family's eating habits were still very European. I was unaware of the decidedly foreign influence in the food I was exposed to as a child: it did not become apparent to me until much later in life when I started cooking for myself.

Neither my mother nor my grandmother used cookbooks. Sometimes a handwritten recipe was passed from one generation to another, was used once or twice, and then seemed to disappear into their memories, to emerge when it was needed. I remember the preparation of pate a choux, various cakes, and other pastries being made without the aid of any measuring device whatsoever. All their kitchen equipment was extremely simple and utilitarian, but this did not prevent them from preparing elaborate feasts for the holidays, making their own sausages, or canning vegetables and fruits for the winter.

Among the mainstays of our winter diet were robust soups and stews. Many evenings we sat down to a supper consisting solely of soup: perhaps a rich duck soup studded with prunes and homemade noodles or a delicate broth prepared with both fresh and dried mushrooms. A loaf of rye bread from the neighborhood bakery and a crock of sweet butter completed an extremely satisfying meal.

Today, unfortunately, homemade soups are all but extinct. Time is the missing ingredient. A good soup takes lots of time to prepare: it must be simmered gently to allow each ingredient to give out all of its flavor. Because flavors need time to blend slowly, very often a soup will taste even better on the second or third day, so you should not be apprehensive about making a large pot.

Some of the soups in this chapter depend on a stock for their base, but do not be alarmed. I am baffled why most cooks think that stock-making is a major undertaking. Perhaps it is because of the elaborate stock recipes they find in "gourmet cookbooks." Ingredients such as veal knuckles or marrow bones are wonderful if you can find them, but they are not the main components in a good stock. Ox tails or short ribs, for example, are easy to find and inexpensive; they lend good flavor to rich beef stock and also provide the necessary gelatinous qualities required. A stock is a simple thing: it should depend on what can be found in your larder. Here's another example. Suppose you are planning to serve boned chicken breasts for dinner. Simply reserve the skin and bones, place them in a pot along with an unpeeled carrot, a small onion, and a rib of celery—all cut into thick slices—a pinch of fresh or dried thyme, parsley, and a little salt and pepper; cover all the ingredients with cold water and place over low heat to simmer slowly for about two hours. The result will be about a quart of stock with a lovely and concentrated chicken flavor; nothing out of a can, doctored up or otherwise, could ever approximate its good clean flavor. If you must omit the celery *or* the thyme *or* the carrot, you *still* have a decent stock.

But most of the soups here do not depend on stocks for their flavors: flavors so definite don't require the extra savor a stock would provide. With such ingredients, you will find that the old maxim of "throwing anything and everything into the soup pot" is quite preposterous. Where a certain harmony of flavors is the ultimate goal, care must be taken not to upset the balance. Soup-making for many cooks suffers most from indiscriminate additions of spices and herbs, compatible or not — thus changing the entire character of the dish.

There is something marvelously intimate and homey about soup. You think of sharing it with people you feel close to, people who are, in one way or another, part of your family. The directness and honesty about such a meal is difficult to improve upon. For thousands of years, soup has been nourishing and sustaining mankind with its simple goodness, just as for many of us it nourished our childhood and created our warmest memories.

Onion Soup
serves six to eight

This onion soup depends on a stock flavored primarily with chicken rather than beef, which gives a lighter flavor to the finished dish. I like to serve it in wide, shallow soup plates and float large toasted-cheese croutons in the middle. You can substitute water for part of the vermouth and/or wine, but the stock will be just that much less richly flavored.

You might precede this soup with chicken liver mousse (December) or celery root remoulade (November) if you are planning on it as a main course. The underlying sweetness of the onions demands that the accompanying wine be dry and fruity: a very dry sherry, perhaps, or a fruity muscadet or beaujolais.

1½	pounds beef knuckle or shank bone
1	large onion, peeled and cut in half
4½	cups dry white vermouth and/or dry white wine
5	pounds chicken backs and necks with excess fat removed
3	ribs celery, with leaves
·	bouquet garni
·	salt and freshly ground pepper
·	small handful parsley
2	bay leaves
1	small loaf day-old French bread
3	tablespoons butter
¼	pound salt pork, blanched

and cut into small dice
6 cups onions, cut in half and thinly sliced
2 or 3 cloves garlic, minced
· pinch of sugar
2 tablespoons fresh thyme, minced, or ½ teaspoon dried thyme
½ pound Swiss cheese, grated coarsely
1½ tablespoons flour

Preheat oven to 450 degrees. Place the beef bone and onion in a shallow baking pan and place in the oven. Bake them for 45 minutes or until they are a deep, rich brown. Remove the pan from the oven and place the beef bone and the onion in a large (12- to 14-quart) stockpot. Pour off any fat from the pan used to bake the bone, add ½ cup of the vermouth, and set pan over high heat to deglaze and reduce for a few minutes. Add this liquid to the stockpot. Add the chicken parts, celery, bouquet garni, salt and pepper, parsley, bay leaves, 2 cups vermouth, and enough water to cover all. Bring to a boil, skimming off any foam from the surface, and reduce the heat to simmer. The stock should be simmered for 2 to 3 hours. Take care not to oversalt at the beginning, for as the stock reduces the flavor becomes more concentrated.

While the stock simmers, cut the French bread into slices an inch thick. Place in an oven set at 200 degrees and bake until it is completely dried out, 30 to 45 minutes.

Remove all bones from the stock and strain the liquid through a fine sieve; skim off all fat with a bulb baster. You should have approximately 3 quarts of stock. The soup may be made in advance to this point; any stock not used immediately may be frozen.

In a heavy 5-quart soup pot, melt the butter over medium heat, add the cubed salt pork, and lightly brown. Remove, drain on paper towels, and reserve.

Into the rendered fat put the sliced onions and garlic, sprinkling them with a pinch of sugar, salt, pepper, and thyme. Cover the pot and steam over medium heat for 20 to 30 minutes. Stir the flour into the onions with a whisk and cook for 5 minutes until it is incorporated. Add the remaining 2 cups of vermouth, stirring constantly, and cook for 5 minutes more. Add the prepared stock, bring to a boil, reduce heat, and simmer for 30 minutes. Stir in the reserved pork bits and taste for seasoning.

When you are ready to serve the soup, preheat the broiler, set the croutons on a baking sheet, cover each with some grated cheese, and put under the broiler until the cheese is completely melted. Remove from oven; put 1 or 2 croutons in each bowl of soup and serve.

Lamb and Bean Soup

serves six to eight

A robust winter soup that combines inexpensive but flavorful breast of lamb with aromatic vegetables and white beans. The dried hot peppers lend a slightly spicy overtone. Try a light red wine like an Italian Valpolicella, a young Beaujolais, or a St. Emilion with this soup.

The night before, soak the beans in cold water to cover and marinate the lamb: in a shallow container large enough to hold the meat in one layer, put the lemon juice, oregano, salt, and pepper; mix well and add the lamb. Cover and refrigerate overnight.

1½ cups dry baby lima beans

2 pounds breast of lamb, cut into "ribs" and trimmed of any fat

· juice of 3 or 4 lemons

1 teaspoon dried oregano

· salt and freshly ground pepper

½ cup salt pork, blanched and cut into small cubes

3 tablespoons olive oil

1 large onion, peeled and coarsely chopped

2 carrots, peeled and cut into large dice

3 stalks celery, cut into large dice

2 leeks, cleaned well and coarsely chopped (including 2 inches of green)

4 cloves garlic, peeled but left whole

1 bay leaf

2 dried hot chili peppers

The next day, heat the olive oil in a 4- to 6-quart soup pot; add the salt-pork cubes, and saute them until they have turned brown and crisp and all their fat is rendered. Remove and drain on paper towels. To the rendered fat add the onion, carrots, celery, leeks, and garlic; stir the vegetables to coat them evenly with the fat and saute them over medium heat for 10 minutes without browning. Add the drained beans, the lamb, 2 tablespoons of its marinade, the bay leaf, and the chili peppers. Cover all the ingredients with water and season lightly with salt and pepper. Bring the soup to a boil, reduce heat, and simmer for about 1½ hours, skimming the top during the first half hour of cooking. Adjust the seasoning if necessary and serve with black bread and sweet butter.

Dutch Pea and Ham Soup
serves eight

Traditionally, green split peas are used in this soup; I find the yellow ones more attractive in both color and flavor. Although the cooking time is lengthy, this dish requires little attention after the initial chopping, peeling, and dicing. A spicy but delicate wine such as an Alsatian Riesling is required for this dish.

2   cups dried yellow split peas (1 pound)

2   ham hocks, each about 1 to 1½ pounds

1   small celery root, about 1 pound, peeled and cut into small dice

3   carrots, peeled and cut into small dice

3   leeks, well cleaned and finely chopped (including 2 inches of green)

3   medium boiling potatoes, peeled and cut into small dice

1   medium onion, peeled and finely chopped

·   salt and freshly ground pepper

1   bay leaf

½   teaspoon dried summer savory or marjoram

Place the split peas and the ham hocks in a large, heavy soup pot, add a little salt, and cover with 3 quarts of water. Bring to a boil, skim off any scum rising to the surface, reduce the heat, and simmer for about 2½ hours.

To the stock, add the celery root, carrots, leeks, potatoes, onion, salt, pepper, and bay leaf; continue to simmer for an additional 35 to 45 minutes, or until the vegetables are tender.

Remove the ham hocks from the soup, discard the bones and skin, cut the meat into small pieces, and add them to the soup. Add the summer savory or marjoram, adjust the seasoning if necessary, and serve.

Garbure Basquaise
serves six to eight

Garbure: It's been described as a soup that is not a soup; a stew, rather, so filled with delicious ingredients that a spoon inserted in it will indeed stand up. This dish originated in Bearn, France, the largest of all Pyrenean states and a land of lusty and rugged individuals whose character is reflected in the food they eat.

Although you may have to hunt a bit for it, I have suggested using Savoy cabbage here because its flavor and texture are both so much more delicate than conical or head cabbage. The amount of garlic, which may horrify some, may be adjusted, but the cooking time is so long that the whole cloves melt into the soup, leaving behind only an elusive flavor.

This is a dish that ages beautifully and should be prepared a day or even two in advance. Serve it with plenty of crusty French bread, a crock of sweet butter, a green salad, and a lusty red wine like a young Cotes du Rhone.

1   pound dried baby lima beans
2   bay leaves
1   small onion, peeled and stuck with 2 cloves
1   teaspoon salt
2½ pounds smoked ham hock, cut in half
2-pound head of cabbage (Savoy, if possible)
4   small red bell peppers
1   tablespoon butter (optional)
2   carrots, peeled and cut into large dice
2   turnips, peeled and cut into large dice
3   medium potatoes, peeled and cut into large dice
3   leeks, cleaned and cut into thin slices including 2 inches of the green
1   medium onion, cut into large dice
6 to 8 cloves garlic, peeled but left whole
·   salt and freshly ground pepper
1   teaspoon each of dried thyme and marjoram
3   small dried hot red peppers
½   pound green beans, cut into lengths of 1 inch

The night before, place the dried beans in a bowl, cover them with water to a depth of 3 inches, and allow them to soak. The next day, drain the beans, place them in a 4-quart pot, and add the bay leaves, onion, and salt. Cover with 3 quarts of water, bring to a boil, reduce the heat, and simmer them for 30 minutes, stirring occasionally.

While the beans are cooking, prepare the ham hock: trim off any excess fat and reserve it. Place the hock in a pot and cover with cold water. Bring the water to a boil and cook the ham hock for 5 minutes. Remove and reserve.

Cut the cabbage into thin shreds and put into a large pot of boiling, salted water for 5 minutes to blanch. Pour into a large colander, refresh under cold running water, and drain well.

Place the peppers on a piece of foil under a preheated broiler. Allow them to blacken under the heat, turning them so that each side is charred. This will take about 10 minutes. Remove the peppers when done and wrap in a towel to steam for about 5 minutes. Remove the skins under cold running water, discarding the stem and seeds. Cut the flesh into julienne strips and set aside.

In an 8- to 10-quart enameled pot, render the fat removed from the ham hock, using the butter if necessary to prevent sticking. Remove the pieces of fat and add the carrots, turnips, potatoes, leeks, onion, garlic, and cabbage. Season the vegetables lightly with salt and pepper and add the thyme and marjoram. Add the whole dried red peppers and saute the vegetables for about 10 minutes, turning to coat them with the fat.

Remove the bay leaves and the onion from the beans and add them with their cooking liquid to the vegetables. Add the ham hock and cover all with water. Bring to a boil, reduce the heat, and simmer for about 1 hour, skimming off the foam in the first few minutes. Do not add any salt at this point because the ham will release quite a bit during the cooking process.

Remove the ham hock; discard the bones and gristle. Cut the meat into small pieces and return them to the soup. Add the green beans and simmer for about 10 minutes more, adding the reserved red pepper slices in the last 5 minutes. Taste and adjust the seasoning if necessary. Serve in large soup plates.

Potato Leek Soup
serves four to six

This humble preparation, most enjoyable in itself, can be used as the basis for a myriad of variations. When watercress is in season, reduce the quantity of leeks and add a bunch of the peppery greens with stems removed and proceed as outlined, floating a fresh sprig of watercress in each bowl as a garnish. With the addition of heavy cream, added just before serving, this soup is served chilled as vichyssoise, the creation of Louis Diat, the chef who once made the Ritz-Carlton Hotel in New York a gathering place for those who appreciated fine food. An elegant garnish for this soupe glace is a tiny spoonful of red or black caviar placed on the top of each portion.

There is no reason not to serve this soup as a cool-weather main course, especially accompanied by a first course of Swiss chard tart (November) or terrine of rabbit (October) and followed by chestnuts flavored with fennel (November) as a dessert substitute. A good Riesling would make a fine complement for this soup, or perhaps a California chenin blanc.

6	leeks
4	tablespoons butter
3	cups potatoes, cut into large dice
½	cup onion, coarsely chopped
1	large clove garlic, sliced
·	salt and freshly ground pepper
1	cup dry white vermouth
5	cups chicken stock, mildly seasoned
1	small potato, cut into quarters and thinly sliced (about ½ cup)
·	dash freshly grated nutmeg
½	cup milk (optional)

Cut off and discard all but 2 inches of the green leaves on the leeks. Peel off and discard any discolored outer skin and cut lengthwise, almost in half, to the root end. Wash under cold running water to remove any sand or grit. Cut off the root ends and discard. Put aside one of the smallest leeks and slice the rest into ¼-inch slices.

Melt 3 tablespoons of butter in a 3-quart pot; add the leeks, diced potatoes, onion, and garlic, and season with salt and pepper. Cook over high heat, stirring constantly until the vegetables are coated with butter and are slightly softened, about 5 minutes. Add the vermouth and the stock, bring to a boil, reduce the heat, and simmer for 30 minutes.

While the soup is cooking, cut the reserved leek into pieces about the length and thickness of a wooden matchstick (julienne). Melt the remaining tablespoon of butter in a small skillet; add the leek and the thinly sliced potato. Saute the vegetables over low heat for about 5 minutes and reserve.

Remove the soup from the heat and allow to stand for 10 minutes to cool slightly. Strain off the liquid and reserve. Place the vegetables in the container of a food processor fitted with the steel blade and puree. Rinse the soup pot with hot water, return the stock to it, add the puree, and stir in with a wire whisk. Add the leek and potato garnish with their butter and stir together. Place the soup over low heat and warm it slowly. Add the nutmeg and taste for seasoning. If the soup is too thick for your liking, add the optional half cup of milk and blend in with a whisk.

Serve immediately.

Bayou Bisque
serves six to eight

While the combination of crab and yams must at first glance seem odd, it produces an undeniably delicious taste experience. Live crab is desirable because the difference in flavor and texture is worth the extra effort involved.

This soup is extremely rich: if used as a first course a little cup will suffice for each serving and will make a wonderful prelude to roast beef. Even as a main course, a ladle or two will suffice when accompanied by a simple green salad or vinaigrette. Serve with a moderately priced Burgundy like a Macon Villages, or a Northwest or California Traminer.

1	lemon, sliced
1	small onion, sliced
·	few sprigs parsley
6	small dried red peppers
2	bay leaves
·	few peppercorns
·	salted water sufficient to cover crab
1	live crab, approximately 2 pounds
2	tablespoons butter
4	tablespoons finely chopped shallot or onion
1½	tablespoons flour
1½	cups dry white vermouth or dry white wine
¼	teaspoon sweet paprika
4	cups milk

1½	pounds yams, boiled whole, skinned, and cubed
·	salt
·	pinch cayenne pepper
½	pint heavy cream
2 or 3	drops Tabasco
·	grating of fresh nutmeg
·	French bread cut into small cubes and sauteed in butter until brown

In a large stockpot combine the ingredients for the court bouillon: lemon, onion, parsley, red peppers, bay leaves, peppercorns, and salted water; bring to a boil and cook for 30 minutes.

While the stock is flavoring, boil the yams in their skins until done, about 10 minutes. When they are cool enough to handle, peel them and cut them into large pieces. Add the crab to the boiling stock and cook for about 6 minutes to the pound. (If your crab is an especially lively one, you may find it easier to wrap it in cheesecloth and then toss it into the pot.) Remove the crab, allow it to cool, clean it, and reserve the meat; there should be about a half pound.

Melt the butter in a heavy 5-quart soup pot and saute the shallot or onion over medium heat until golden; add the flour, blending with a whisk, and cook for 5 minutes. Whisk in the wine, add the paprika, and cook a few minutes more. Add the milk, yams, and cayenne and salt to taste, and bring to a boil, stirring occasionally. Simmer for 5 minutes and drain through a colander, reserving all liquid.

Cool the solids for a few minutes and then puree in a food processor fitted with the steel knife blade. Blend the puree into the reserved liquid; set over low heat and add the crab meat and cream, stirring constantly. Simmer the soup for about 10 minutes; season to taste with Tabasco and nutmeg. Serve in soup bowls or large soup plates and top each serving with croutons.

Oyster Stew
serves two

A good oyster stew is one of the world's most simple dishes to prepare. The only essentials are impeccably fresh oysters, butter, heavy cream, and a bit of milk; all other ingredients, including seasonings, are extraneous.

Matching a wine to a dish as delicately flavored as oyster stew is a ticklish problem. The main thing is to get a wine low in acidity, such as a California Riesling, or a French Muscadet from a warm year such as 1976.

1 to 2 dozen fresh oysters in the shell (choose the smallest)
3　tablespoons butter
1　whole shallot, peeled (optional)
1　cup clam nectar
1　cup milk
1/2　cup heavy cream
.　dash Worcestershire sauce
.　pinch each of celery salt and cayenne
.　freshly ground pepper

Shuck the oysters, reserving their juice. Melt the butter in a small enameled saucepan. Add the oysters and their juice and the shallot; cook over low heat until the edges of the oysters curl: 1 or 2 minutes. Add the clam nectar, heavy cream, milk, Worcestershire, celery salt, and cayenne and bring just to the boil over low heat. Remove the shallot and serve immediately, topping each bowl with freshly ground pepper to taste.

Pot au Feu
serves eight

The legendary French boiled beef dinner; the rich bouillon is served as a first course, followed by the meats mounded on a platter and surrounded with the vegetables. Accompany this sumptuous feast with crisp French bread, cornichons, coarse salt, horseradish sauce, and/or mustard. Try a Barbera from Italy with this, or a good Beaujolais; or see how a hearty English ale like Bass suits you.

2	whole fresh tomatoes (do not use canned)
1	large onion, unpeeled
·	pan of boiling water
4	carrots, unpeeled and coarsely chopped
2	celery stalks, coarsely chopped
2	leeks, cleaned and coarsely chopped
1	small turnip, peeled and cut into quarters
4	cloves garlic, unpeeled and left whole
2	bay leaves
4	sprigs parsley
½	teaspoon dried thyme, or 3 sprigs fresh thyme
1	tablespoon salt
6	peppercorns
4	pounds brisket of beef, lean
1½ to 2 pounds ox tails
3- to 3½-pound chicken, tightly trussed
6	carrots, peeled and cut into quarters
1	small celery root, peeled and cut into 1-inch cubes
6	leeks, cleaned and cut into 3-inch lengths
1	cotechino (a large Italian pork sausage) or Polish or farmer's sausage, cooked separately (optional)

Preheat oven to 400 degrees. When hot, cut the tomatoes and onion in half, place them in a shallow ovenproof container, and bake them for 20 to 30 minutes until they are browned. This adds a rich color to the stock.

Place the baked tomatoes and onion in the bottom of an 8- to 10-quart soup pot. Add a cup of boiling water to the baking pan, scrape off any brown particles from the bottom, and add to the large pot. To the baked vegetables add the carrots, celery, leeks, turnip, garlic, bay, parsley, and thyme; sprinkle the salt and the peppercorns over all and place the beef and the ox tails on top. Cover with very cold water and bring slowly to a simmer, skimming off all brown scum from the surface. Keep the liquid barely simmering for 3 to 3½ hours, until the meat is almost tender.

Remove the brisket and the ox tails, reserving the latter meat for another purpose; strain the broth into a large bowl and degrease it thoroughly. Discard the vegetables. Replace the stock in the pot, add the brisket and the chicken, and simmer over low heat. After 45 minutes, add the sliced carrots; cook for 15 minutes more, then add the celery root and the leeks and continue to cook for an additional 15 to 20 minutes, until all the vegetables are tender.

Remove the meats to a platter, add the sausage, and surround with the cooked vegetables. Keep them warm while serving each person a small bowl of broth; then follow with the meats and vegetables.

Salsa Verde (Green Sauce)
for Poule au Pot

A piquant sauce usually served with boiled or poached dishes in Italy. You may want to use it only over the chicken or perhaps stir a small amount of it into the broth, too.

¼ cup coarse fresh
     breadcrumbs
·   chicken broth
½ cup parsley, loosely packed,
     stems removed
2   tablespoons capers
1   large clove garlic
1-inch squeeze anchovy
     paste or 2 flat anchovy
     fillets, finely chopped
½ tablespoon red wine vinegar
¾ cup olive oil
·   salt and freshly ground
     pepper

Soak the breadcrumbs in just enough chicken stock to cover them for 10 minutes. Squeeze out excess moisture and place bread pulp into a small mixing bowl.

Finely chop the parsley, capers, and garlic together; stir into the bread mixture along with the anchovy paste and the vinegar. Stirring constantly, pour in the olive oil slowly until the sauce is of a creamy consistency. If it is too thick for your taste, you may wish to add a bit more oil. Add a few grindings of pepper, taste for seasoning, and add salt if necessary. The sauce may be made hours in advance and held covered until serving time. Refrigerate if to be held overnight.

Poule au Pot
serves four

This dish is composed of a chicken poached whole and served in its own broth with a selection of seasonal vegetables. Such simplicity does not prepare you for the subtleties of flavor the dish contains. It deserves a fine French Graves from Bordeaux or your best California Semilllon or Fume Blanc.

3½ - to 4-pound chicken
½ lemon
4 garlic cloves, not peeled
· a few sprigs of fresh thyme and/or parsley
1 small onion, peeled and sliced
1 carrot, peeled and coarsely chopped
1 celery stalk, coarsely chopped
· white wine or dry white vermouth
2 cups chicken broth (optional)
· salt and a few black peppercorns
1 bay leaf
4 leeks, thoroughly washed but left whole
3 to 4 large carrots, peeled and cut into wedges about 4 inches long
3 small turnips, peeled and cut into quarters
8 small potatoes, peeled and cut into olive shapes
4 stalks celery, each cut into thirds, *or* 1 small celeriac peeled and cut into large cubes

Wash the chicken thoroughly under cold running water, remove any fat found within the cavity, and rub it inside and out with the cut side of a lemon. Stuff the belly with the garlic, thyme, and parsley and truss well. In a 6-quart soup pot put the chopped onion, carrot, and celery; cover the bottom of the pot with an inch of white wine or dry vermouth. Add the chicken stock (optional) and enough water to cover the chicken, add the salt, peppercorns, and bay leaf, bring to a boil, reduce the heat, and simmer for about 40 minutes.

Remove the chicken carefully and put the stock through a sieve. Discard the cooked vegetables, put the stock back into the pot, add the chicken, carrots, potatoes, turnips, leeks, and celery or celeriac, and simmer for 20 to 25 minutes more until all the vegetables are tender.

When done, remove the chicken, skin it completely, and cut into serving pieces. Into large soup plates place a serving of chicken and an assortment of vegetables; ladle some broth over all and serve at once.

Bigos

serves six to eight

This hunter's stew is the national dish of Poland. Every family has its own version. The idea is to add to the pot whatever meat the hunter happens to bring home; here the recipe calls for pork, beef, and sausage, but you could substitute lamb or venison for the beef, duck or goose for the pork if your family has a hunter. The imported mushrooms lend a wonderful flavor to the stew. Look for dried *boletus edulis;* any milder-tasting mushroom would get lost among the other flavors.

Serve this stew with black or rye bread and a crock of sweet butter. A soft but ample wine like a Pomerol or Barolo is indicated.

2   ounces dried imported mushrooms
6   tablespoons butter
¼   pound salt pork, rind removed and cut into small cubes
1   pound fresh mushrooms, cleaned and thickly sliced
·   dash fresh lemon juice
2   medium onions, peeled, cut in half, and thinly sliced
1   large baking apple, peeled, cored, and finely chopped
2   cloves garlic, peeled and finely chopped
3   pounds sauerkraut, rinsed under cold water and drained well

·   salt and freshly ground pepper
·   pinch ground allspice
2   pounds lean pork, cut into 1½-inch cubes
2   pounds beef round or chuck, cut into 1½-inch cubes
1   cup liquid from dried mushrooms
½   cup Madeira
1   pint sour cream
½   pound Polish or farmer's sausage, cut into 1-inch rounds
2   bay leaves

Preheat oven to 350 degrees.

Place the dried mushrooms in a small bowl and cover with boiling water. Let stand for 30 minutes, drain, reserving one cup of the liquid, and chop coarsely.

In a large heavy skillet melt 3 tablespoons butter; add the salt pork cubes and saute over moderately high heat until they are brown and have rendered their fat. Remove with a slotted spoon to paper towels and set aside.

To the fat in the skillet add the sliced fresh mushrooms and the dried mushrooms; sprinkle with a little lemon juice and cook over high heat for 4 minutes, until they are browned. Remove with slotted spoon to a large mixing bowl. To the remaining fat, add the sliced onions, apple, and garlic, and cook over medium heat for about 10 minutes, until the onions have softened. Remove with slotted spoon to large mixing bowl. Put the drained sauerkraut in the bowl with the apple and onion, season with salt, pepper, and a dash of allspice, and mix together well.

Add the remaining 3 tablespoons butter to the skillet; season the pork cubes with salt and pepper and brown them over moderately high heat. Remove, place on top of sauerkraut mixture, and repeat procedure with beef cubes. With the skillet still over high heat, add the reserved mushroom soaking liquid and the Madeira, bring to a boil, and allow to reduce for a few minutes.

Pour the hot liquid over meat and sauerkraut mixture, add the sausage and the sour cream, mix well, and pour all into a heavy 6-quart ovenproof casserole; top with the bay leaves, cover, and bake for 1½ hours. Remove cover and continue to bake for 45 minutes or until the meats are tender. Taste for seasoning and serve.

Chicken, Shrimp, and Sausage Gumbo
serves six

The roux used in this recipe forms the basis of many Creole dishes; unlike its French ancestors, this roux is browned and then cooked a good deal. File powder (ground sassafras leaves) can be purchased in any spice shop; it is used as a thickening agent and care should be taken not to boil the gumbo after it is added or it will become stringy. Ideally the wine to accompany this dish should be light and fragrant like those of Provence or southern Italy: try a Rubesco or a merlot rose.

3-pound chicken
1   medium onion, coarsely chopped
2   carrots, coarsely chopped
2   ribs celery, coarsely chopped
2   garlic cloves, left whole and unpeeled
1   bay leaf
·   salt and 6 or 8 peppercorns
·   few sprigs parsley
½   teaspoon dried thyme
4   cups chicken stock
⅓   cup vegetable oil
1   pound Polish or farmer's sausage, cut into ½-inch slices
1   pound shrimp, shelled and deveined
5   tablespoons flour
1   cup onion, finely chopped
½   cup green pepper, chopped
2   tablespoons sliced scallions with green tops

2   cloves garlic, finely chopped
·   pinch cayenne or dash
    Tabasco
1   cup tomatoes, peeled,
    seeded, and coarsely
    chopped
·   salt and freshly ground
    pepper
1   tablespoon file powder

Wash and truss the chicken.
Place the onion, carrots, celery,
garlic, bay, salt, peppercorns,
parsley, and thyme in a heavy
4-quart Dutch oven. Place the
chicken on top of the vegetables,
add the stock and 2 quarts of
water, and bring to a boil.
Reduce the heat and simmer the
chicken for about 1 hour.

When the chicken is tender,
remove it from the stock, allow
it to cool slightly, and remove
the meat from the bones. Put
the bones and skin back in the
pot and continue to cook for
another hour. Cut the chicken
into bite-size pieces and reserve.
Drain the stock, discarding the
vegetables; there should be
about 2 quarts.

Rinse the Dutch oven with hot
water and dry. Add the oil and
heat it; add the sausage meat
and brown it over moderate
heat, stirring frequently. When
done, remove with a slotted
spoon and reserve. Add the
shrimp to the pot, saute for 3 to
4 minutes until pink, remove
with a slotted spoon, and
reserve.

Make the roux with the
remaining oil: over low heat
blend in a tablespoon of the
flour at a time, stirring
constantly with a wire whisk;
when the flour has been
absorbed, raise the heat slightly
and allow the roux to brown
until it takes on a medium-
brown color.

When this stage is reached, stir
in the onion, green pepper,
scallions, garlic, and tomatoes
and continue to cook over low
heat for about 10 minutes, until
the vegetables are tender. Stir in
the stock, 2 cups at a time;
season lightly with the salt and
pepper and simmer over low
heat for 30 minutes. Add the
reserved chicken, sausage, and
shrimp and allow them to heat
through. Stir in the file powder,
remove from heat, and serve in
soup plates over a mound of
steamed or boiled rice.

Carbonnades of Short Ribs
serves four

This beef and beer stew, a
specialty of Belgium, is usually
made with boneless meat. The
bones from the short ribs,
though, add an amazing
amount of flavor to the sauce
and also aid in thickening the
stew. The dish is served

classically with boiled or steamed potatoes; buttered noodles are also a good accompaniment.

Accompany this with the watercress and walnut salad (October) and a not-too-sweet beer: Mexico's Dos Equis is a good example.

¼ pound bacon, cut into small dice
2 tablespoons butter
4 to 6 pounds beef short ribs ("English style"), trimmed of any excess fat
· flour for dredging meat
· salt and freshly ground pepper
2 pounds mild onions, peeled, cut in half, and thinly sliced
2 or 3 cloves garlic, minced
2 tablespoons flour
3 cups dark beer
1 cup beef stock
2 tablespoons red wine vinegar
½ tablespoon brown sugar
½ teaspoon each dried thyme and tarragon
1 bay leaf

Preheat oven to 350 degrees.

Melt the butter in a 4- or 5-quart ovenproof casserole with lid; add the bacon and saute over high heat until it is crisp and the fat is rendered. Remove bacon and drain on paper toweling.

While the bacon is cooking, dry the ribs and coat them with the flour, salt, and pepper, shaking off any excess. Brown them in the rendered fat over high heat. Remove them and reserve.

To the remaining fat, add the onions and garlic and cook them slowly over low heat for about 15 minutes. Stir in the flour and cook for 3 or 4 minutes, stirring constantly, until it is thoroughly incorporated. Pour in the beer and the beef stock, stirring until the liquid has thickened. Add the vinegar, sugar, and herbs and simmer for about 5 minutes.

Immerse the ribs in the liquid, sprinkle with the reserved bacon bits, cover, and bake for 2 hours until the meat is tender and is separating from the bones.

Short Ribs of Beef with Carrots
serves four

Look for short ribs labeled "English cut"; they contain very little fat and are more meaty. A watercress and walnut salad (October) would go nicely after this main dish; serve a big soft wine like a Pomerol or the Casarsa "Strevecchio" from northeast Italy.

2 tablespoons butter
½ cup salt pork, cut into small cubes and blanched
4 to 5 pounds beef short ribs
· flour for dredging meat
· salt and freshly ground pepper
4 medium onions, cut in half and thinly sliced
· small pinch sugar
4 cups beef stock
½ cup Madeira
¼ teaspoon tarragon
14 to 16 small "French-style" carrots, about 3 inches long, peeled and cut lengthwise into quarters

Preheat oven to 350 degrees.

Melt the butter in a large skillet; add the salt pork cubes and saute them over medium heat until their fat is rendered and they are brown and crisp. Drain them on paper towels and reserve.

Trim any excess fat from the ribs, dry them well, and sprinkle them lightly with flour, salt, and pepper. Put them in the skillet containing the rendered pork fat, set over high heat, and brown on all sides.

Remove the ribs, set them aside, and add the onions to the pan. Sprinkle them with a tiny pinch of sugar, salt, and pepper and cook them till they are lightly browned. Remove the onions from the skillet, add the beef broth, and reduce the liquid over high heat to half its original amount.

While the broth is reducing, place the browned ribs in a 4- or 5-quart ovenproof casserole, sprinkle them with the reserved pork bits, and cover them with the browned onions. Add the reduced stock and the Madeira and sprinkle with the tarragon.

Cover and bake for 1 hour and 45 minutes. Add the carrots, pushing them down into the liquid. Cover again and bake another 45 minutes until ribs and carrots are tender.

Beef and Pork Chili
serves six

Both the beef and pork ideally should by cut into small cubes rather than ground, but if you must use ground try to obtain a coarse rather than a fine grind. This will give the chili a richer flavor and more interesting texture. The chilies called for here are whole, dried Mexican anchos: rounded pods 2 to 2½ inches in diameter, their rich red-black outside skin a mass of tiny wrinkles. Ancho chilies may be found at shops specializing in Latin foods. Although not traditional, I find that a bit of sour cream stirred into chili tames most of its heat, but the sour cream should be passed separately to each individual. Serve with corn tortillas or cornbread and a good Mexican beer.

6   dried whole Mexican ancho chili peppers
¼   cup vegetable oil or rendered bacon fat
3   medium onions, cut in half and thickly sliced
4   cloves garlic, coarsely chopped
1   pound lean beef (chuck, rump, round), cut into small cubes
1   pound lean pork (shoulder or country-style ribs, with bones removed), cut into small cubes
·   salt and freshly ground pepper
1-pound, 12-ounce can Italian plum tomatoes, drained and coarsely chopped
2   cups beef broth
1½ cups beer
1½ teaspoons cumin seed, lightly ground with a mortar and pestle
1   teaspoon ground coriander
½   teaspoon celery seed
½   teaspoon marjoram
2   bay leaves
·   large pinch powdered allspice
·   small pinch powdered cloves
½   teaspoon Tabasco
1½ cups cooked kidney beans

Place the chilies in a bowl and cover them with boiling water; allow them to stand for 30 minutes. Drain the chilies; remove and discard the seed pod inside. Chop them into a fine paste with a knife.

Heat the vegetable oil in a 10-inch skillet, add the onions, and saute them over moderate heat for 10 minutes. Add the garlic and saute for 1 to 2 minutes more. Remove the onions and garlic with a slotted spoon and put them into a 4- or 5-quart Dutch oven; reserve.

Season the beef and pork lightly with salt and pepper. Brown them well in the oil remaining in the skillet. Remove the meat with a slotted spoon and add it to the onions.

Add the chili paste to the oil remaining in the skillet and saute it over moderate heat for 5 minutes, until the paste becomes dry and fragrant. Stir in the chopped tomatoes and cook for 10 minutes more. Add the tomato and chili mixture to the onions and meat.

Add all other ingredients except the kidney beans to the pot and combine well. Bring the chili to a boil, reduce the heat, and simmer for 2 hours. Skim off any fat that may rise to the surface during the first 30 minutes of cooking.

When the beef and pork cubes are tender and the sauce reduced and slightly thickened, add the cooked kidney beans and continue cooking only long enough to heat them through.

Serve immediately, passing sour cream separately.

Lamb Shanks, Greek Style
serves four

Lamb shanks braised in a tart, lemony sauce seasoned with oregano and thyme, all flavors redolent of the Mediterranean. To complete the menu, serve with a rice pilaf and caponata. If you have access to a good Greek retsina, try it with this dish; otherwise a full-flavored French Graves, though rather expensive, would be just the thing.

4	lamb shanks
·	flour for dredging meat
·	salt and freshly ground black pepper
3	tablespoons olive oil
1	cup finely minced onion
1	clove garlic, finely minced
½	tablespoon each oregano and thyme
½	cup dry white vermouth or dry white wine
⅓	cup fresh lemon juice
3	cups lightly seasoned chicken stock
2	bay leaves
⅛	teaspoon Bovril or other meat extract (optional)
·	large pinch allspice

Preheat the oven to 350 degrees.

Dredge the lamb shanks with flour; shake off any excess and season with salt and pepper. Heat the oil in a large skillet over high heat, add the meat, and brown evenly on all sides. Remove the shanks and place in a lidded ovenproof casserole wide enough to hold the meat in one layer.

To the oil left in the skillet add the onion and garlic and saute over medium heat till almost melted, about 10 minutes. Add the herbs and stir in the wine, 1 cup of the chicken stock, and the lemon juice. Raise the heat to high and boil briskly till the liquids are slightly reduced. Pour this mixture over the lamb, add the remaining stock and the bay leaves, cover, and bake for 1 hour and 45 minutes. (The recipe can be completed ahead to this point.)

Take the casserole out of the oven, remove the lamb shanks, and set them aside. Skim all fat from the surface of the sauce and discard. Set the casserole over high heat and reduce the sauce to about 2 cups. Add the Bovril and allspice, blend thoroughly, and taste for seasoning. Replace the lamb in the casserole, cover, and put back in the oven to bake for 30 to 45 minutes, or until the meat is almost falling off the bones.

Choucroute Garnie

serves six

This is a specialty of Alsace, the region of France that borders on Germany. Choucroute is an excellent cold-weather dish; it is ideal for a large group, and it can be prepared a day in advance and gently reheated.

Purchase the sauerkraut bottled or from a specialty store if possible; the tinned variety is often too acidic. An Alsatian Riesling is a natural with this dish, but you might consider something a little more unusual: a Riesling from the Pfalz region of Germany.

3	pounds good sauerkraut
2	tablespoons goose or duck fat (substitute butter if unavailable)
½	pound salt pork, blanched and cut into small cubes
1	cup onion, finely chopped
1	large baking apple, peeled, cored, and coarsely chopped
2	cloves garlic, finely chopped
10	juniper berries wrapped in cheesecloth, or ¼ cup gin
2	cups dry white Alsatian wine
2	bay leaves
·	freshly ground pepper
6	smoked pork chops, thick-cut
1	large Polish or farmer's sausage
8 to 10	knackwurst

Rinse the sauerkraut under cold running water. Put it in a colander to drain thoroughly.

Melt the fat in a heavy 6-quart Dutch oven or casserole. Add the salt pork cubes and saute them over moderately high heat until they are brown and have rendered their fat. Remove and drain on paper towels. Add the onion, apple, and garlic to the remaining fat and saute for about 10 minutes.

Stir in the sauerkraut. (Pull clumps apart with your fingers.) Add the juniper berries or gin, cover, and cook over low heat for 20 minutes, stirring occasionally. Add the wine and the bay leaves and season lightly with freshly ground pepper. Mix in the reserved salt pork bits, cover, and simmer over low heat for 2 hours.

Add the smoked pork chops, cover again, and cook for 20 minutes. Add the Polish or farmer's sausage and cook another 15 minutes. Finally, add the knackwurst and cook for 10 minutes more.

To serve, mound the sauerkraut on a large serving platter, top with the chops and the sausages, and surround with boiled potatoes. Accompany with a variety of mustards, pickles, and an imported beer.

Stracotto alla Fiorentina

serves six

Some of the finest beef in the world is raised in Tuscany and while most of it is simply grilled, this specialty of Florence, akin to a pot roast, is extremely popular. Serve some of the sauce spooned over a sturdy pasta first and follow with the meat, sliced and covered with the remainder of the sauce and accompanied by a seasonal green vegetable. Serve a wine to match the ingredients: a Chianti Classico or Barolo, or perhaps a fine dry California Grignolino or Zinfandel from Heitz or Fetzer.

½ ounce dried Italian mushrooms

3½ pounds beef pot roast, rump, chuck, eye of round, or shoulder (arm)

· salt and freshly ground pepper

3 or 4 sprigs fresh rosemary or 1½ teaspoons dried

3 large cloves garlic, peeled and thinly sliced

3 tablespoons olive oil

1 cup carrot, peeled and cut into small dice

1 cup onion, peeled and finely chopped

½ cup celery, cut into small dice

1 clove garlic, minced

1 teaspoon finely grated lemon peel

1½ cups dry red wine (Chianti, Classico, Barolo, or Barbera)

1 cup tomatoes, peeled, seeded, and finely chopped

8-ounce can Progresso tomato sauce

· pinch allspice

1 cup beef stock (optional)

Place the dried mushrooms in a small bowl and cover them with boiling water. Allow them to stand for 30 minutes and drain, reserving 1 cup of liquid; chop the mushrooms into coarse pieces and set aside.

Dry the meat well and season with salt and pepper. Cut small slits in the meat; insert a piece of garlic and a little rosemary into each cut. Heat the olive oil in a 4-quart heavy casserole, add the beef, and brown well on all sides over high heat; remove and reserve. Pour out all but 1 tablespoon of the oil and add the carrot, onion, celery, garlic, and lemon peel. Sprinkle lightly with salt and pepper and saute over medium heat, stirring, for 5 minutes. Add the reserved chopped mushrooms and continue to cook for 1 to 2 minutes. Turn up the heat, add the wine, and allow to reduce for 1 to 2 minutes. Add the tomatoes, tomato sauce, allspice, a good grinding of black pepper, and the meat. Add the reserved mushroom liquid to the pot. The meat should be halfway covered by sauce; if it is not add the optional beef stock.

Cover the pot and simmer for about 3 hours or until the beef is tender. Serve as suggested. May be prepared a day in advance.

Banana Rum Souffle Glace
serves six

A cold dessert souffle is one of the most refreshing endings for any winter meal. Since it is frozen, it has the added advantage that it can be prepared a day or two in advance.

2 small bananas
5 egg yolks
⅔ cup sugar
¼ cup dark rum
1 teaspoon lemon juice
2 cups heavy whipping cream
· unsweetened cocoa powder or finely ground amaretti

Peel and slice the bananas and puree them in a food processor. Beat the egg yolks with the sugar until thick and lemon-colored. Stir in the banana puree, rum, and lemon juice and blend together.

Beat the whipped cream until stiff. Gently fold in the banana mixture with a rubber spatula. Pour the souffle into a 1-quart souffle dish fitted with a 2-inch collar (made of either foil or waxed paper). Cover the top with plastic wrap and freeze for at least 4 hours.

Before serving, remove collar and dust the top and sides of the souffle lightly with the cocoa powder or the ground amaretti to give a "browned" effect.

February, Quick Meals

Menu 1
Bianco e Nero (February)
Saltimbocca (February)
Broccoli with Caper Vinaigrette (February)
Crema Romano di Caffe (February)

Menu 2
Curried Scallops (February)
Steamed Rice Flavored with Lime
Carrottes Rapees (February)
Cassis Omelette Souffle (February)

Italian Bean and Tuna Salad
Carrottes Rapees
Cucumber Salad
Cucumbers with Sour Cream
Broccoli with Caper Vinaigrette
Broccoli Puree
Pasta Carbonara
Bianco e Nero (Capellini with Caviar)
Scallops Nicoise
Curried Scallops
Scallop and Cream Saute
Sole Meuniere
Veal and Pepper Saute
Chinese Pepper Steak
Beef Stroganoff
Chicken Scallops Piccata
Saltimbocca
Breast of Chicken Parmigiana
Crema Romano di Caffe
Cassis (Black Currant) Omelette Souffle
Omelette Souffle with Apples and Rum
Bananas Foster

Growing up in an old-country family with a heritage of good cooking, as I did, was a rare and valuable thing. Unfortunately, I did not realize that at the time. When I moved downstate to New York City at the tender age of eighteen, I did not know how to boil the proverbial egg.

But it is difficult to live in New York, especially in Greenwich Village, without becoming aware of the importance of good food and becoming more and more involved in its preparation. You can't walk down the streets without being assaulted by the aromas of the neighborhood: felafalel, mo shu pork, paella, moussaka, zuppa di pesce. Soon I heeded their subtle beckonings and began to eat my way through the city's varied cuisines.

The desire to eat well in my own home naturally followed, and I began to do a little cooking, very simple things just for myself and my friends. I had to learn all the basics by trial and error, with a tight budget and no equipment worthy of the name.

It is amazing what you can do with a bit of imagination and a two-burner hotplate. I remember a curry dinner for four prepared in under an hour with the assistance of the myriad food shops in my neighborhood. I stopped at a favorite deli on my way home from work to purchase an immense just-roasted turkey drumstick and the condiments; then visited the grocery for vegetables, a ripe melon, and some good imported beer; then raced home to prepare the sauce, steam the rice, cut the melon and turkey into bite-sized pieces, assemble, and serve.

Balducci's, the Tiffany's of greengrocers, was a particular inspiration. Its staff of delightful Italian men in big green aprons was ready to supply you with tiny bouquets of fresh herbs in any season, spinach selected leaf by leaf, raspberries and melon in December, and Italian pinecones which, baked, popped open to release their pignoli nuts. Near Balducci's there was a cheese shop where you could select from 500 cheeses, dozens of pates and quiches, scores of sausages and breads.

I learned something very important during those days. Because my mother and grandmother had spent a great deal of time in the kitchen, I had grown up believing that hours of preparation were necessary for any good meal. Now I realized that wasn't true. The preparation of an excellent, irreproachable meal need not take up the better part of a whole day. These days, when many cooks also work outside the home, that's a particularly important lesson. And even if you don't work, it's essential to have at least a handful of good, quick, dependable recipes in your repertoire for particularly busy or tiring days, or in case of guests' unexpected arrival.

It's a great boon that eating habits seem to be changing. Large and complicated meals, even for formal occasions, don't please as much as they once did, for the trend is toward lighter food, fresher food, quickly and simply prepared dishes, and fewer courses per meal.

Many delicious meals can be prepared in an hour or so, simply by taking advantage of foods that take very little time to cook. Numerous vegetables can and should be served raw—indeed, they taste far better that way than cooked—but that doesn't mean you should just chop them into a bowl. Carrottes rapees, for instance, grated raw carrots dressed with oil and vinegar, appear on every crudites platter in France. Cucumbers, tomatoes, celery, fennel, and bell peppers can all be very pleasing in composed salads, too. Even the tired old canned cooked bean will turn into a fresh delight mixed, for example, with finely chopped red onion, flaked tuna and herbs, and a bit of good vinegar and olive oil: it's just as good as a separate first course as it is on an antipasto platter.

Another aid to quick meals is to have your larder well stocked with an assortment of food items, such as beans, that lend themselves to quick preparation. Canned tomatoes, the Italian plum variety especially, are essential; so are anchovy fillets, tuna packed in oil or water, vegetables such as chickpeas (garbanzo beans), cannolini beans, and so on.

The quickest-cooking meat is veal; but quite apart from its astronomical price, good veal is very difficult to obtain in most parts of this country. For quick meat dishes, therefore, I suggest poultry; chicken and even turkey are effective and far less costly replacements for veal in many dishes, and their cooking times are nearly identical.

It's also important to seek out the shops in your area that market ready-dressed and ready-to-cook meat entrees. This is no more "cheating" than a Frenchwoman's running down to the charcutier for a pate or a fowl in aspic. These shops provide an invaluable service, and they should be encouraged: shops like A & J Meats in Seattle, with its stuffed lamb breasts, chicken Kiev, rouladen, and special sausages. Small neighborhood bakeries, apparently a dying breed, also need encouragement: they can provide you with the usual fresh breads and pastries as well as raw dough to use as the basis for your own pizza or pissaladiere.

Happily, there has been a definite increase in food specialty shops and delis handling everything from imported pates to good homemade potato salads. DeLaurenti's Italian Market in Seattle's Pike Place Market is a superior example. Here you can find not only imported Italian specialties like virgin olive oil, prosciutto, and pancetta, but also foods and condiments from all over the Middle East, Mexico, China, and India; plus an enormous variety of canned goods, including tins of biscuits, crackers, and other crisp and crunchy delicacies. In such stores only the "meals" or appetizers in cans are to be approached with suspicion: they are always expensive, usually disappointing, so leave them to the "gourmets" they're designed for. Just remember the cardinal rule: cheap or expensive, plain or elaborate, food has just one aim—to taste good. If it doesn't, no amount of fancy labels or gold medals earned in 1909 can save it.

Italian Bean and Tuna Salad
serves four to six

Of Tuscan origin, this simple salad makes a lovely first course or can become part of an antipasto platter.

15-ounce can cannellini beans
3 tablespoons mild onion, finely chopped
1 small garlic clove, finely chopped or put through a press
6-ounce can tuna, packed in olive oil, drained
· salt and freshly ground pepper
1 teaspoon dried oregano, summer savory, or thyme chopped together with

2 tablespoons fresh parsley
· juice of ½ lemon
. dash of red wine vinegar
⅓ cup fruity olive oil

Refresh the beans under cold running water and drain thoroughly. Place the beans in a mixing bowl and add the onion and tuna, separating the tuna into large flakes. Season with salt and pepper to taste, sprinkle with the herbs, and toss all together gently. Dress with the lemon juice, vinegar, and oil, mixing well. Chill slightly or serve immediately.

Carrottes Rapees
serves four

This salad is dressed with sherry wine vinegar (available at wine and specialty shops), which intensifies the natural sweetness of the carrots. If you use sherry vinegar in another preparation, take care to add less than usual because of its intense flavor.

5 medium carrots
1 shallot, peeled
½ teaspoon grated lemon peel
2 tablespoons parsley, chopped
1 tablespoon sherry wine vinegar

6 tablespoons olive oil
· salt and freshly ground pepper

Peel and coarsely grate the carrots; place in a serving bowl. Chop together the shallot, lemon peel, and parsley, place in a small mixing bowl, and add the vinegar, olive oil, and salt and pepper to taste. Blend this dressing well, pour it over the carrots, and toss all together. Chill for 30 minutes before serving.

Cucumber Salad

serves four

Both the rice wine vinegar and the sesame oil are available in shops that specialize in Oriental foods.

3	medium cucumbers
·	sea salt
2	tablespoons lemon juice
1	teaspoon rice wine vinegar
1	teaspoon sugar
3	tablespoons peanut oil (or other tasteless vegetable oil)
1	tablespoon sesame oil
·	salt

Peel the cucumbers; cut them in half and remove their seeds; then cut each half in two again. Sprinkle with a light coating of sea salt and allow to stand for 10 to 30 minutes. Rinse them under cold running water, dry well, and cut into thin slices.

Mix the dressing: in a small bowl combine the lemon juice, vinegar, sugar, vegetable and sesame oils, and a small pinch of salt. Pour over cucumber slices and chill for half an hour or longer.

Cucumbers with Sour Cream

serves four

3	medium cucumbers
1½	cups sour cream
1	tablespoon mild vinegar
·	pinch each of sugar and salt
¼	teaspoon dried dill

Peel the cucumbers and slice them crosswise very thinly.

Combine the sour cream, vinegar, sugar, salt, and dill, mix well, and pour over the cucumbers. Toss the cucumber slices with the dressing and chill for an hour or so until they have wilted.

Broccoli with Caper Vinaigrette
serves four

I owe the inspiration of blending the aromatic flavor of capers with broccoli to Craig Claiborne. This treatment, with a spicy hot vinaigrette, is a bit more dressy and elaborate than his: it's well worth the extra bit of trouble.

2 pounds broccoli
· the juice of ½ lemon
· pinch dry mustard
2-inch squeeze of anchovy paste
· salt
1 small shallot, peeled and minced
1 tablespoon capers, minced
4 tablespoons olive oil
· dash Tabasco
· freshly ground pepper

Cut off and discard the bottom inch of the broccoli stalks. Peel the tough outer skin from the stalks with a vegetable peeler. Cut the stalks off near the flowers, slice the stalks in half lengthwise, and then slice them into 2-inch lengths. Separate the blossoms into bite-size pieces.

Bring enough water to cover the broccoli to a boil. Add salt and the stalks and cook them uncovered for about 5 minutes, or until they can just be pierced with a thin knife and offer no resistance. Add the blossoms and cook for about 5 minutes more, just until tender. Pour into a colander, refresh with cold water, and drain well.

While the broccoli is cooking, prepare the sauce: place the lemon juice in a small bowl, add the mustard, anchovy paste, and salt, and mix together. Add the shallot, capers, olive oil, and Tabasco and stir well. Taste for seasoning and add the pepper just before pouring the sauce over the broccoli. Place the broccoli in a serving dish, pour the sauce over it, and toss gently. Serve immediately.

Broccoli Puree
serves four

Vegetable purees, because of their lack of texture, can remind one of baby food. However, I have found some quite palatable: this one is my favorite.

2 pounds broccoli
3 tablespoons butter
2 tablespoons onion, finely minced
3 tablespoons freshly grated Parmesan cheese
· salt and freshly ground pepper
· pinch of freshly grated nutmeg

Cut off and discard the last inch of the broccoli stalks. Peel the tough outer skin from the stalks with a vegetable peeler or a very sharp paring knife. Cut the stalks off near the flowers and slice them into 1-inch lengths. Place them in boiling, salted water and allow them to cook for 3 or 4 minutes. While the stalks are cooking, separate the flowers into bite-size pieces. Add them to the boiling water with the stalks and continue to cook for about 5 minutes, or until the broccoli is just tender. Remove, refresh under cold running water, and drain well.

While the broccoli is draining, melt the butter in a small saucepan and add the onion. Cook over low heat until the onion is softened, about 5 minutes. Place the broccoli in the container of a blender or food processor fitted with the steel knife blade and puree. Remove the puree and add it to the onion in the saucepan, season with the cheese, salt and pepper, and nutmeg, and cook over medium heat till the broccoli is heated through, stirring often. Serve at once or keep warm in a double boiler.

Pasta Carbonara
serves four to six

For the pasta, use small shells, riccini, rotelle, or any other that will "catch" the sauce. A deliciously quick meal; accompany with a tossed green salad and a light red Italian wine such as Grignolino.

6 to 8 rashers of bacon, cut into small dice
4 tablespoons onion, finely minced
½ cup dry white vermouth
1 whole egg plus 2 egg yolks
1 cup heavy cream
½ cup freshly grated Parmesan or Romano cheese (or combination of both)

· salt
· large pinch of cayenne pepper or dash of Tabasco
1 pound pasta
3 tablespoons butter, cut into small pieces
¼ cup fresh parsley, minced

Put a large pot of salted water on the heat and bring to a full boil. While the water is heating, place the bacon in a skillet and saute over medium heat until just crisp around the edges. Add the onion and continue to saute for another 6 to 8 minutes until the onion is softened. Drain all but a thin film of fat from the skillet and pour the vermouth over the bacon and onion. Simmer this mixture for about 10 minutes or until the liquid is reduced to half its original amount. While this is cooking, place in a small mixing bowl the eggs, cream, grated cheese, salt, and cayenne or Tabasco and mix well. When the water is boiling, drop in the pasta and cook it until just *al dente;* drain well and put back in the pot. Add the butter and parsley and blend; over the pasta pour the egg-cheese mixture, then the hot bacon mixture, tossing with forks till mixed. Place pot over very low heat, stirring constantly, until the sauce has thickened slightly. Serve at once. No additional cheese is necessary as the sauce is quite rich in itself.

Bianco e Nero (Capellini with Caviar)
serves four

I have suggested using imported pasta because its flavor and texture are superior; the Fratelli De Cecco brand is one of the finest. The butter used must be sweet (that is, unsalted), because the salt content in caviar is so high.

The more expensive the caviar, the lower its salt content will be: since only a small amount of caviar is called for, you should choose the best you can afford. When using a pasta as fine as capellini or fedelini, time is of the essence; cook it quickly and add the sauce immediately when it is ready. If you are doubling the recipe, increase the amount of caviar to three ounces rather than four. Resist the obvious temptation to serve champagne: instead try a very dry, very chilled Manzanilla sherry or icy Russian vodka.

1	tablespoon olive oil
1	tablespoon salt
½	cup heavy cream
2	ounces caviar, unchilled
6	tablespoons sweet butter, at room temperature
·	freshly ground black pepper
½	pound imported capellini or fedelini, very fine spaghetti

Place a pot filled with 3½ quarts of water on high heat, add the olive oil, and bring to a boil.

Whip the heavy cream lightly; it should not be stiff. Fold in the caviar and set aside. Cut the butter into small pieces.

When the water begins to boil, add the salt and the pasta. Cook for no longer than 4 minutes, drain into a colander, shake off excess water, and place immediately back in the pot. Working quickly, add the

softened butter bits, the cream and caviar mixture, and a good grinding of pepper. Toss the pasta gently, allowing the sauce to coat each strand. Serve immediately in heated soup plates. Grated cheese should not be served with this dish.
Note: The only salt in this dish is in the pasta water; the caviar will add sufficient salt to the final preparation.

Scallops Nicoise
serves four

The tomato and garlic sauce in this dish is the perfect foil for the succulent sweetness of the scallops. Try a tangy, fragrant Anjou wine with this, or a true Tavel rose.

3   tablespoons butter
1   tablespoon olive oil
2   tablespoons onion, minced
2   large garlic cloves, peeled and minced
1-pound, 12-ounce can whole tomatoes, seeded and finely chopped (reserve juice)
·   pinch of sugar
·   pinch of saffron or curry powder
¼   teaspoon dried thyme chopped together with
2   tablespoons fresh parsley
·   salt and freshly ground pepper
2   tablespoons dry white vermouth
6   imported black olives, pitted and cut into small dice
1½   pounds scallops; if sea scallops are used, cut each into 2 or 3 pieces

First prepare the sauce. Melt 1 tablespoon butter with the olive oil in a skillet, add the onion, and saute over medium heat for 5 minutes or until it is golden. Add the garlic and the tomatoes, sprinkle with sugar, saffron or curry powder, herbs, salt and pepper, and vermouth. Bring to a boil over high heat, reducing the liquids to a light glaze. Add the reserved tomato juice, reduce heat, and simmer for about half an hour, adding the olives during the last 5 minutes of cooking.

Melt the remaining 2 tablespoons of butter in a 10-inch skillet, add the scallops, and saute them for 2 to 3 minutes over high heat. Add them with the pan juices to the tomato sauce, allowing the flavors to mingle for a few minutes. Serve with steamed or saffron rice.

Curried Scallops
serves four

The flavor of this quickly prepared dish depends on the quality of the seasonings used. Curry paste gives a richer and more savory taste than dry powder. Fresh ginger root is specified; an excellent way to keep fresh ginger handy is to wrap the whole unpeeled root tightly in foil and keep it in the freezer. Then, when it is needed, simply take it out and grate what you need directly into the dish you are preparing. Black mustard seed is found in shops specializing in East Indian foods; do not substitute the larger yellow mustard seed.

This is a mild curry; serve it with steamed rice mixed with butter and a little lime juice. The carrottes rapees (this chapter) makes a refreshing side dish. Try a fruity Northwest Chardonnay with this meal.

3½ tablespoons vegetable oil
½ teaspoon black mustard seeds
1¼ cup onion, finely chopped
1 teaspoon curry paste (or to taste)
1½ tablespoons flour
1 cup clam juice or lightly seasoned fish stock
½ cup heavy cream
1 teaspoon fresh ginger root, grated
2 tablespoons sour cream or unflavored yogurt
1½ pounds scallops (if sea scallops are used, cut each in two)
· pinch of sugar (optional)

Heat 2 tablespoons oil in a heavy 10-inch skillet; add the black mustard seeds and stir to coat them with oil. Immediately add the onion and saute over medium heat for about 5 minutes. Add the curry paste, blending it with the onion, and cook for 1 to 2 minutes; then add the flour, stir well, and cook over low heat for 5 minutes.

When the flour has browned lightly, add the clam juice or fish stock and stir till the liquid thickens. Pour in the heavy cream, add the ginger, and cook the sauce over low heat for about 10 minutes.

While the sauce is cooking, heat the remaining 1½ tablespoons oil in a skillet over high heat; add the scallops and saute them briefly, 3 to 4 minutes—only long enough to just cook them. Add the scallops with their pan juices to the curry sauce, stir in the sour cream or yogurt, taste for seasoning, and add a small pinch of sugar if desired. Serve at once.

Scallop and Cream Saute

serves four

Bay scallops are suggested in this recipe because they are more succulent and slightly sweeter. Sea scallops can be substituted, but they should each be cut into two or three pieces because of their larger size.

This dish will serve six as a first course; it is rich enough to stand as a main dish with just a green salad, good French bread, and a not-too-dry Northwest or Alsatian Riesling.

2	tablespoons butter
1	teaspoon vegetable oil
1½	pounds bay scallops
·	salt and freshly ground pepper
·	freshly grated nutmeg
¼	cup dry white vermouth
½	teaspoon dried tarragon
⅓	cup heavy cream

Heat the butter and the oil in a skillet just large enough to hold the scallops in one layer. When the butter has stopped foaming, add the scallops and saute over moderately high heat for 2 to 3 minutes. Season them with salt, pepper, and a light dusting of nutmeg and remove them with a slotted spoon; reserve.

Pour the vermouth into the skillet and reduce over high heat until a glaze is formed. To this add the scallops, tarragon, and heavy cream and saute over high heat until the cream is slightly reduced and thickened, about 5 minutes. Taste for seasoning and serve at once.

Sole Meuniere

serves two

One of the most delicious (and simplest) of all fish dishes. The secret of moist flesh with a slightly crisp outer layer lies in the fact that the fillets are thoroughly dried and only dredged with flour just before going in the pan; this also prevents the sole from sticking. The recipe can be prepared with small whole fish such as smelt or trout as well.

The classic French accompaniment for this dish is steamed potatoes; for a little color and flavor on the side I recommend the fresh asparagus with ginger if asparagus is in season. If not, try the broccoli puree (this chapter) or leeks vinaigrette (November). A light French Chardonnay such as a Macon Blanc is ideal.

1	pound very fresh sole fillets
·	salt and freshly ground pepper
·	flour for dredging
2	tablespoons butter

2 tablespoons olive or other vegetable oil
· small handful chopped parsley
· lemon wedges

Dry the fillets well with paper towels and sprinkle them with salt and pepper. Place them close to the cooking area along with a shallow bowl of flour.

In a 10-inch skillet melt 1 tablespoon of the butter over moderately high heat with the olive or vegetable oil. When the oil is hot, dust each fillet lightly with flour and put it in the pan. Saute each side until lightly brown, about 2 minutes, turning with a wide spatula and taking care not to break the fillets apart.

Remove the fish to a hot platter, discard the oil remaining in the skillet, wipe it out with a paper towel, and melt the remaining 1 tablespoon butter, allowing it to turn a light brown. Pour the butter over the fillets, sprinkle with parsley, and garnish with lemon wedges. Serve at once.

Veal and Pepper Saute
serves four

The veal and peppers are combined with a light tomato sauce, and since very few of us are likely to have on hand a good homemade sauce, I have recommended using canned: Progresso makes a good one.

Although the tomato sauce is traditional, this dish may be served with a lighter sauce: simply use the recommended amount of vermouth, omit the tomato pulp, and substitute chicken stock for the tomato sauce. An inexpensive Bordeaux or an Italian Bordolino would go well with this dish.

1¼ pounds veal round steak, boneless
· flour seasoned with salt and freshly ground pepper
4 tablespoons olive oil

2 large cloves garlic, peeled and cut in half
2 green bell peppers, seeded and cut into 1-inch squares
½ cup onion, sliced
¾ cup dry white vermouth or chicken stock
½ cup tomato pulp (tomatoes, peeled, seeded, and coarsely chopped)
¾ cup tomato sauce
· pinch of sugar
· pinch of dried oregano
· grated Romano or Parmesan cheese

Trim away and discard any fat on the veal; cut the meat into 1-inch cubes. Heat the olive oil in a heavy 12-inch skillet, add the garlic, and saute until it turns golden (do not brown); remove and discard. Raise the heat to moderately high, add the veal cubes, and brown them on all sides. Add the pepper squares and saute for 3 minutes; add the onion and continue to cook for another 3 minutes.

Pour in the vermouth (or chicken stock), scraping up any brown particles on the bottom of the pan, and reduce the liquid until it lightly glazes the veal and peppers. Add the tomato pulp and tomato sauce and season with a small pinch of sugar, oregano, salt, and pepper.

Reduce the heat to low, cover the skillet, and simmer for 10 minutes. Taste and adjust the seasoning, if necessary, and serve over steamed rice. Sprinkle the top of each portion with freshly grated Romano or Parmesan cheese.

Chinese Pepper Steak
serves four

An important part in preparing any dish that must be quickly cooked is having all ingredients ready and as close as possible to the cooking area. This is especially true of Chinese cooking, where a minute wasted looking for the sherry could mean the ruination of the dish.

A seasoning rather unorthodox in Western cooking is used here. Five-spice powder is a mixture of pulverized anise, fennel, clove, cinnamon, and Szechuan pepper that goes particularly well with beef. Serve with an egg-flower soup using your best chicken stock for a first course, fruit for dessert, and a fine dry beer like Pilsner Urquell instead of wine.

1¼ pounds flank steak
1   egg white
1   tablespoon sherry or gin
3   tablespoons soy sauce

1   tablespoon sugar
2   teaspoons cornstarch
1½ teaspoons Chinese five-spice powder
4   tablespoons peanut oil
2   medium red or green bell peppers, seeded and cut into 1-inch squares
1   medium onion, peeled and cut into wedges, ½-inch wide
1   large garlic clove, cut into slices
½   cup beef stock
1   tablespoon cornstarch mixed with 2 tablespoons water or beef stock
1   teaspoon Oriental sesame-seed oil

Trim away and discard any fat from the flank steak. Cut the meat lengthwise into strips about 2 inches wide, then cut each strip diagonally against the grain into slices ¼-inch thick.

Mix thoroughly the egg white, sherry, soy, sugar, cornstarch, and five-spice powder in a small bowl; add the meat slices, mix, and marinate for 30 minutes to 1 hour.

Meanwhile place the peppers, onions, oil, garlic, stock, cornstarch mixture, and sesame-seed oil within easy reach of your stove. Set a wok or a large heavy skillet over high heat for about 1 minute. Add 1 tablespoon peanut oil, turn heat down slightly, and put in the peppers and onions. Stir-fry (tossing frequently) for 4 minutes or until just tender;

remove with a slotted spoon. Add to the wok or skillet the remaining 3 tablespoons oil and heat until almost smoking. Add the garlic slices and stir for a few seconds, removing them before they turn brown. Discard. Immediately add the meat in its marinade and stir-fry for 3 minutes or until the meat shows no sign of pink on the surface. Add the peppers, onions, and beef stock; cook for 1 minute. To this add the cornstarch mixture, stirring constantly until the sauce is thickened. Pour over all the sesame-seed oil, mix well, taste for seasoning, and serve immediately over rice.

Beef Stroganoff
serves four

Traditionally this dish is prepared with tenderloin of beef, an extraordinarily expensive cut of meat, but it also can be prepared with flank steak that has been marinated briefly and cut on the bias against the grain. This technique, borrowed from the Chinese, produces very tender meat if it is cooked quickly over high heat. The traditional accompaniment for this dish is buttered noodles; a young Burgundy or dry California Zinfandel would suit as long as they are full-flavored and round.

1½	pounds flank steak
2	tablespoons Madeira
·	salt and freshly ground pepper
6	rashers thick-sliced bacon, cut into large dice
½	pound mushrooms, cleaned and sliced
·	squeeze of lemon juice
½	cup onion, finely minced
1	clove garlic, finely minced
¼	cup dry white vermouth
1½	cups sour cream
·	small handful parsley, finely chopped

Trim away and discard any fat from the flank steak. Cut the meat lengthwise into strips about 2 inches wide, then cut each strip diagonally against the grain into slices ¼-inch thick.

Place the slices in a small bowl, add the Madeira, salt, and pepper, and mix.

In a heavy 10- or 12-inch skillet saute the bacon over medium heat until brown and crisp; remove and reserve. To the remaining fat add the mushrooms, sprinkle with a little lemon juice, salt, and pepper, and brown quickly over high heat (about 3 minutes); remove with a slotted spoon and reserve.

Set the skillet over high heat and add the flank steak with its liquid and saute in the hot fat very quickly. This will take only 4 or 5 minutes. Remove to a hot platter and keep warm.

To the fat remaining add the onion and garlic and cook for about 5 minutes over medium heat. Add the vermouth, turn up the heat, and reduce the liquid briefly. Add the sour cream, mushrooms, and bacon bits; reduce heat and simmer long enough to heat all ingredients through. Taste for seasoning, pour over meat slices, garnish with parsley and plenty of freshly grated pepper, and serve over rice or buttered noodles.

Chicken Scallops Piccata
serves four

Here breast of chicken substitutes for costly (and in many areas difficult-to-find) veal. This tangy dish goes well with a simple dish of pasta dressed in butter and cheese and a green salad. An inexpensive Bordeaux such as an Entre-Deux-Mers is suggested.

- breasts of two chickens, split, skinned, and boned
- flour seasoned with salt and freshly ground black pepper
2 tablespoons butter
1 tablespoon olive oil
3 tablespoons dry white vermouth
- juice of ½ lemon
- finely chopped parsley and lemon slices

Cut each chicken piece diagonally against the grain into ¼-inch-thick slices. Pound the slices lightly to a uniform thinness. Dredge these scallops lightly with the seasoned flour, shaking off any excess. Heat the butter and oil in a heavy skillet large enough to hold all the scallops in one layer; when the foam subsides add the scallops and brown them over high heat for 2 to 3 minutes per side;

remove them to a heated platter.

Pour off all but a thin film of fat from the pan and add the vermouth and lemon juice. Reduce this over high heat for 2 to 3 minutes, taste for seasoning, pour over the scallops, and garnish with parsley and lemon slices.

Saltimbocca
serves two

Saltimbocca, literally translated, means "jump in the mouth," perhaps because the dish is so delicious that it seems to disappear without any assistance from the eater. Classically it is prepared with veal—delicate pink scallops cut from the leg and pounded to transparency— but veal of this character is almost impossible to find in the Northwest so I have substituted chicken breast instead. Before cooking, soak the chicken in milk to achieve a lighter, more delicate meat (I also use this technique very often with fish to "clean up" the flavor). A fine dry German wine, like a Rheingau "Kabinett," would complement this, or a good Graves or Sancerre.

1	chicken breast, boned, divided in two, and lightly pounded
·	milk to cover
·	flour
·	salt and freshly ground pepper
·	powdered sage
1	tablespoon butter
1	teaspoon olive oil
2	slices prosciutto
2	slices Mozzarella
¼	cup chicken stock
¼	cup Marsala wine
·	lemon juice to taste

Preheat oven to 450 degrees.

Cover the chicken breast fillets with milk and soak for about ½ hour. Remove, dry thoroughly, dredge with flour, and season on both sides with salt, pepper, and a small pinch of sage. In a 10-inch skillet melt the butter with the olive oil; when the foam subsides, add the chicken and saute over moderately high heat for 5 or 6 minutes till golden brown and slightly crisp on both sides.

Remove the chicken to an ovenproof platter, reserving the pan juices in the skillet. Cover each piece of chicken with a piece of prosciutto folded to fit, then with a slice of cheese trimmed to fit. Place in oven.

Working quickly, add the stock to the reserved pan juices in the skillet and reduce it slightly over high heat; add the Marsala and reduce to a light glaze. Add the lemon juice to taste and taste for seasoning, adding salt and pepper if desired. The whole deglazing process should take no longer than 3 to 4 minutes, in which time the cheese on the chicken should be melted and lightly browned.

Remove the platter with the chicken from the oven, pour pan sauce over, and serve.

Breast of Chicken Parmigiana
serves four

If you have everything on hand, a very quick and elegant main dish; even the cream sauce is very quick to make. Serve with the raw mushroom salad (April) or the broccoli with caper vinaigrette in this chapter. If you're in no hurry with this meal, it goes delightfully with a good risotto, like those in Giuliano Bugialli's *The Fine Art of Italian Cooking* (New York Times Books). Drink an Italian Soave or a California Chardonnay with this dish.

- breasts of two chickens, split, skinned, and boned
- flour seasoned with salt and freshly ground pepper
- 1 egg, lightly beaten
- 2 cups unseasoned fresh breadcrumbs (homemade if possible)
- 2 tablespoons butter
- 1 tablespoon oil
  Sauce:
- 2 tablespoons butter
- 2 tablespoons flour
- 1 cup chicken stock
- ¼ cup heavy cream
- scant ¼ cup grated Parmesan cheese
- dash each cayenne pepper and fresh grated nutmeg
- salt

Place the flour, egg, and breadcrumbs in three different shallow bowls. Take the pieces of chicken and dip them, one by one, first into the flour, shaking off any excess, then into the egg, and finally into the crumbs, pressing them firmly into the meat. If you have time, the chicken may be refrigerated: this will help the crumbs to adhere.

Heat the butter and oil in a skillet large enough to hold the chicken pieces in a single layer. When the foam subsides, add the meat, turn the heat to high, and saute each side for about 3 minutes until golden brown and slightly crisp. Remove the chicken to a heated platter and place in a 200 degree oven to keep warm.

Prepare the sauce: in a small saucepan heat the butter. When it has melted add the flour, stirring in with a wire whisk. Cook over medium heat, whisking continuously for 3 to 4 minutes, but do not allow the roux to brown.

Add the chicken stock, turn up the heat a bit, and stir constantly until the sauce thickens. Add the cream and all but 1 tablespoon of the grated cheese and mix in with the whisk. Season with the cayenne, nutmeg, and salt.

Remove the platter of chicken from the oven, pour the sauce over it, and sprinkle the last tablespoon of grated cheese over the top. Place under a hot broiler for 1 to 2 minutes to glaze lightly and serve immediately.

Crema Romano di Caffe
serves four

A light, coffee-flavored confection made from ricotta cheese and whipped cream, the texture much resembling that of a mousse. An extremely simple dessert to prepare that can be made hours or a day in advance.

1   cup (½ pound) ricotta cheese
¼   cup finely granulated sugar
1   tablespoon instant espresso coffee
1   tablespoon boiling water
1   teaspoon unsweetened cocoa powder (optional)
2   tablespoons cognac or good brandy
1   cup heavy cream, whipped

·   sliced almonds

Put the ricotta through a sieve to remove its grainy texture, or place in the container of a food processor fitted with the plastic knife blade. Blend the ricotta until smooth, add the sugar, instant espresso (dissolved in the boiling water), cocoa powder, and cognac; blend together. Fold this mixture into the whipped cream until thoroughly mixed. Spoon into serving dishes, small wine glasses, or individual souffle dishes and chill for at least an hour. Just before serving, garnish with sliced almonds.

Cassis (Black Currant) Omelette Souffle
serves two

Another variation on the omelette souffle using black currant preserves to flavor the yolk mixture and reinforcing the flavor with creme de cassis, also made from black currants. Any preserve or jelly may be used; the rather tart flavors of orange or ginger marmalade are also most interesting. Although this dish is thought of mainly as a dessert, it is most pleasing when served for a festive late breakfast.

3 egg yolks
½ cup black currant preserves
3 tablespoons creme de cassis
3 egg whites
· pinch of salt
½ cup heavy cream, lightly whipped

Preheat the oven to 350 degrees.

Beat the egg yolks with the preserves and 1 tablespoon of the creme de cassis until well combined.

Beat the egg whites in a stainless-steel or copper bowl until frothy; add the pinch of salt and continue to beat until stiff. (The egg whites will not build sufficiently if beaten in ceramic, glass, or porcelain.)

Fold the beaten whites into the yolk mixture carefully; pour this into a well-buttered #24 omelette pan or a 9½-inch skillet. Bake the omelette in the middle of the oven for about 20 minutes; do not open the oven door while baking or the omelette may collapse. Remove from oven, fold omelette in half, and turn out onto a serving plate. Garnish the top with whipped cream and drizzle the remaining 2 tablespoons creme de cassis over all. Serve at once.

Omelette Souffle with Apples and Rum
serves two

This is a dessert souffle baked in an omelette pan; the end result is a deliciously light confection. The fruit filling can be changed to suit your whim or the season at hand.

1 tablespoon butter
1 large baking apple, peeled, cored, and sliced
3½ tablespoons finely granulated sugar
2 tablespoons dark rum
3 large eggs
· pinch of salt

Preheat the oven to 325 degrees.

In a small skillet, heat the butter; add the apple slices, sprinkle them with ½ tablespoon sugar and 1 tablespoon dark rum, and saute over moderate heat for 5 to 7 minutes or until tender, stirring occasionally.

Separate the eggs. Beat the yolks with 1 tablespoon sugar and 1 tablespoon rum until frothy. Beat the whites with a pinch of salt until they are almost stiff, add the remaining 2 tablespoons sugar, and beat them until they form stiff peaks. Fold the whites into the yolk mixture carefully and pour into a well-buttered #24 omelette pan or a 9½-inch skillet. Bake in the middle of the oven for 20 minutes; do not open the oven door while baking or the omelette souffle may collapse.

Remove from oven, place apple filling on one side of the omelette, and fold the other side over it. Turn out onto a warm plate and serve at once.

Bananas Foster
serves four

This elegant and quickly prepared dessert is a specialty of Brennan's in the heart of the French Quarter in New Orleans. The bananas are usually sliced in half lengthwise, but they may be cut into half-inch rounds if desired.

4   bananas, peeled and cut in halves lengthwise
6   tablespoons butter
6   tablespoons brown sugar
½   teaspoon powdered cinnamon
2   teaspoons lemon juice
½   cup dark rum

4   scoops French vanilla ice cream

Melt the butter in a large heavy skillet; stir in the sugar, cinnamon, and lemon juice. Add the pieces of banana and saute over low heat, spooning the sugar syrup over them occasionally. Pour in the rum and allow it to warm for 1 to 2 minutes, then flame. Shake the skillet back and forth until the flames die out; then arrange 2 pieces of banana around each serving of ice cream and pour over each a quarter of their syrup. Serve immediately.

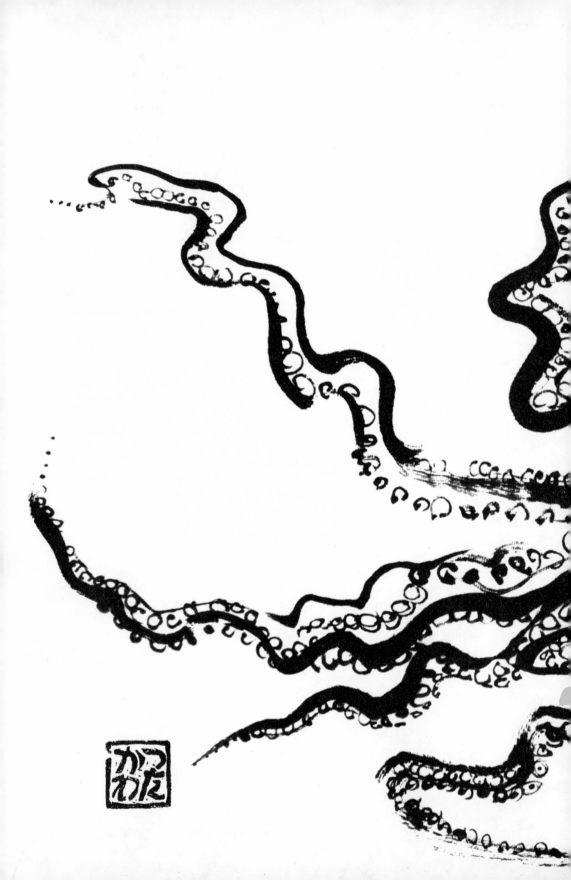

Menu 1
Crab and Oyster Jambalaya (March)
Cornbread
Dandelion Salad Mimosa (April)
Bananas Foster (February)

Menu 2
Roquefort Cheese Strudel (October)
Matelote of Sturgeon (March)
Steamed and Buttered new Potatoes
Asparagus with Egg-Lemon Sauce (April)
Apples Baked in Meringue (October)

Octopus in Tomato Sauce
Baked Smelt
Bouillabaisse Northwest Style
Matelote of Sturgeon
Fish and Cucumber Saute
Clam Pie
Pate of Sole and Shrimp
Turbans of Sole Stuffed with Salmon Mousse
Fillets of Sole Dieppoise
Jambalaya
Squid Salad
Squid and Fish Stew Mediterranean Style
Fried Squid
Plain Steamed Mussels in Their Broth
Stuffed Mussels
Linguini with Mussel Sauce
Mussel Chowder
Paella
Spaghetti Bucaniera

My involvement with cooking became more intense when I moved to the Northwest. After living in New York and becoming thoroughly spoiled by its rich urban diversity, Seattle seemed far less richly endowed. After being pampered by the wonderful little Italian men at Balducci's, would I ever get used to the slapdash ways of the Pike Place Market? It didn't take long.

I naturally began to investigate the rich variety of seafood available in the Northwest. I was familiar for the most part with Northwest fish, most of them being similar to those found on the East Coast, with the notable exceptions of the many different kinds of salmon and the excellent-tasting Columbia River sturgeon. There are, however, some creatures indigenous to this area that came as a total surprise to me: particularly the geoduck—an enormous clam of voluptuous shape and proportions—and the razor clam.

A great abundance of seafood is available to us in the Northwest in

March: Dungeness crab, Alaska king crab, and oysters are all plentiful and familiar, but for the most part the delicious possibilities of mussels, squid, and octopus are being ignored, so I would like to focus on these last three in the recipes for this month.

Mussels, one of the most plentiful of all shellfish on our shores, have for years been shunned by all but a few gourmets. Recently, cultivated mussels have been appearing in our markets at a very reasonable price. They are virtually free of barnacles—not a small point in their favor—and have a more delicate flavor than the uncultivated variety. Because cultivated mussels are so much cleaner, the long process of purifying them of sand is not necessary.

It is not difficult to understand why the singularly unattractive squid is usually overlooked in the fish markets. But since their cost per pound is usually around sixty to eighty cents, they are not to be dismissed lightly these days. Early spring is the best time for squid, whether fresh or frozen. Its flavor is delicate and slightly sweet when properly cooked, and its flesh is much more tender than that of our local clams. The art of preparing squid is probably more advanced in the countries on the Mediterranean rim than anywhere else in the world; therefore, the squid recipes in this chapter are culled from those areas.

The octopus seems to be appreciated only by the Japanese and, again, the people of the Mediterranean. In our markets it is usually found cooked and ready to use; most of it, oddly enough, is imported from outside the country. The enormous population of octopuses in Puget Sound are all much too large to make good eating. The price of octopus, at this writing, is not low, but I feel that it is a delicacy not to be overlooked.

On the matter of purchasing seafood: look for fish with clear, not clouded, eyes, bright color, and a clean sweet smell; reject any fish or shellfish with unpleasant or even a strong odor. Oysters, clams, and mussels must be tightly closed; if when pinched together there is still a slight gapping, reject them. You should depend primarily on the integrity of a trusted fishmonger. If you are not a frequent shopper at any one fish market, a good rule of thumb is to head directly for a market that is owned or operated by Japanese, a people who are notorious for their love of raw, and therefore extremely fresh, fish. There are many of these shops in our area but perhaps the finest is Mutual Fish, a shop that insists on keeping its clams, oysters, etc., under cold running water in their natural state.

No seafood stores well: unfrozen whole fish or fish fillets should not be kept longer than two days; cooked crab and shrimp meat should be used the day of purchase. There is nothing more disappointing than to sit down to a dish of dried and tasteless fish; almost always the problem is overcooking. Take care to cook seafood quickly enough so that its natural moistness is retained. In short: know the seasons, buy fresh, cook lightly.

Octopus in Tomato Sauce
serves four

This is delicious served with steamed rice and a green salad; it is also very good chilled, served in individual portions as a first course. Give the Greek retsina a try with this dish: Demestika is a good brand.

4	tablespoons olive oil
2	pounds cooked octopus, cut into ¼-inch slices
1	cup onion, finely chopped
2	cloves garlic, peeled
1	teaspoon grated lemon rind
4	sprigs parsley
2	cups tomatoes, peeled, seeded, and coarsely chopped
·	pinch sugar
·	pinch allspice
·	salt and freshly ground pepper
¼	cup dry white vermouth or dry white wine
2	tablespoons Pernod

Heat the olive oil in a heavy 12-inch skillet; add the octopus and saute quickly over moderately high heat until lightly browned. Remove and reserve. To the remaining oil, add the onion and saute for 5 minutes.

While the onion is cooking, finely chop together the garlic, lemon rind, and parsley. Add this to the skillet and cook together with the onions for 1 to 2 minutes; do not brown. Add the tomatoes, sugar, allspice, salt, pepper, and vermouth.

Raise the heat and reduce the sauce for 5 minutes. Reduce the heat to simmer and cook for an additional 30 minutes, adding the Pernod during the last 5 minutes. Taste the sauce and adjust the seasoning, if necessary; add the octopus. Cook only long enough to heat the octopus through.

Baked Smelt

serves four

I prefer to bone these small fish; it is a tedious job but one that is well worth it in the end. Serve with boiled potatoes or steamed potatoes with parsley sauce (April), and drink a Sancerre or a California fume blanc.

5	tablespoons butter
2	pounds onions, thinly sliced
·	salt and freshly ground pepper
·	pinch dried thyme
2	pounds Columbia River smelt, cleaned
3	tablespoons dry white vermouth or dry white wine
¼	cup bread crumbs

Preheat oven to 400 degrees.

Melt the butter in a heavy enameled pan; add the onions and season with salt, pepper, and thyme. Cover and steam over low heat for 20 minutes, stirring frequently.

Place half the onions in a shallow, well-buttered ovenproof container; place the smelt on top, sprinkling them with the vermouth or wine. Cover with the remaining onions and sprinkle the top with breadcrumbs.

Bake in the middle of the oven for 10 to 15 minutes, until the fish are just cooked through. If you wish, the dish may be run under the broiler briefly to brown the crumbs.

Bouillabaisse Northwest Style

serves six to eight

There are many arguments against attempting to make a true bouillabaisse outside the south of France, but there is no reason that we can't produce a superb fish soup from local products. The stock for this version is made from crayfish and ocean perch (though any such inexpensive, light-flavored fish would do as well) along with a selection of aromatic vegetables. When fresh fish is not available at reasonable prices for stock-making, frozen will do quite well; the main thing is that the stock be fragrant and highly seasoned. Toasted rounds of French bread and a sauce rouille (made, for the sake of lightness, with a bread rather than an egg-yolk base) are necessary accompaniments. Bouillabaisse is nearly a pungent meal in itself; you might begin with an antipasto of red peppers and feta cheese (July) and close with a light, tangy strawberry souffle or lemon ice (August). Though it would be nice to keep the Northwest theme throughout the meal, the fact is that a Northwest white wine is likely to be too fruity to go with this kind of dinner. Stick to a good inexpensive Bordeaux or Bordeaux Superieure.

Stock:

4 tablespoons olive oil

1½ medium onions, peeled and coarsely chopped

1 small fennel bulb, coarsely chopped (substitute 2 or 3 stalks celery, if unavailable)

3 garlic cloves, peeled but left whole

2 or 3 small leeks, cleaned and coarsely chopped

1 carrot, peeled and coarsely chopped

1 small boiling potato, peeled and coarsely chopped

· salt and freshly ground pepper

2- to 2½-pound whole ocean perch, cleaned and cut into large chunks (including bones and head)

1 pound crayfish in the shell

4 large ripe tomatoes, peeled, seeded, and coarsely chopped

2 cups dry white wine or dry white vermouth

½ teaspoon fennel seeds, bruised with a mortar and pestle

3-inch piece of dried orange peel

2 bay leaves

1 teaspoon saffron leaves

Bouillabaisse:

1½ pounds Columbia river sturgeon, trimmed of skin and bones, cut into 2-inch cubes

1½ pounds sea bass fillets, cut into 2-inch cubes

1½ pounds halibut cheeks (or cod fillets) cut into 2-inch cubes

12 to 14 small shrimp, peeled if you wish

1½ pounds mussels, scrubbed with beards removed

· toasted rounds of French bread

Sauce Rouille:

2 small dried hot red peppers (each about 2 inches long)

1 small piece pimento (optional)

1 piece of French bread, about 2 inches thick

6 large garlic cloves, peeled and put through a press

3 tablespoons olive oil

½ cup fish stock

· salt

Heat the olive oil in a 6- to 8-quart heavy enameled soup pot. Add the onions, fennel or celery, garlic, leeks, carrot, and potato and sprinkle lightly with salt and pepper. Saute over medium heat for about 10 minutes, stirring occasionally to coat the vegetables with oil.

Add the pieces of perch and the crayfish and saute for another 10 minutes; then add the tomatoes, white wine or vermouth, fennel seeds, orange peel, and bay leaves. Add enough water to cover all, bring to a boil, reduce heat, cover, and simmer for about an hour.

With a slotted spoon skim off about 2 cups of the vegetables—removing any bones or crayfish—and puree them in a food processor. Pour the rest of the stock through a fine sieve; discard the vegetables, bones, and crayfish. Rinse the pot with hot water and replace the stock, keeping aside 1 tablespoon, and mix in the pureed vegetables. Add the saffron to a tablespoon of the stock and allow to steep for 10 minutes; add this to the pot. The bouillabaisse may be made ahead to this point.

Make the rouille sauce: put the dried red peppers into a small Pyrex bowl and cover with boiling water; allow them to soften for 5 minutes. Drain and place in a blender or food processor with the pimento. Soak the bread briefly in fish stock, squeeze out excess moisture, and add to the peppers along with the pressed garlic. Blend for a few seconds until a paste is produced. Add the olive oil slowly with the blender at "low"; remove to a serving bowl and stir in half a cup of fish stock; taste for seasoning and add salt if necessary.

Bring the stock pot to a boil, taste and correct seasoning if necessary; add the sturgeon, sea bass, halibut cheeks (or cod), and simmer for about 5 minutes; then add the shrimp and mussels and cook for another 5 to 8 minutes until all the fish and shellfish are tender. Serve immediately in large shallow bowls over rounds of toasted French bread topped with a spread of sauce rouille.

Matelote of Sturgeon
serves four

A specialty of the province of Touraine in France, this dish, usually prepared with eel, is sauced with a rich blend of red wine, cognac, small white onions and mushrooms. The Columbia River sturgeon, with its dense texture and meaty flavor, responds beautifully to the same treatment. This is a very substantial dish; with fennel soup (November) as a first course, steamed potatoes, and lemon ice (August) for dessert, you have a complete meal. The wine should be young and earthy, like a Chinon or Bourgeil; a light Bordeaux or Cote du Rhone will also serve.

1½ pounds fresh Columbia
      sturgeon
3   tablespoons butter
1   teaspoon vegetable oil
¼   cup blanched salt pork, cut
      into small dice
1½ cups whole, tiny white
      onions, boiled for 5
      minutes, skins removed
½   pound mushrooms, thickly
      sliced
·   squeeze of lemon juice
·   salt and freshly ground
      pepper
·   seasoned flour for dredging
¾   cup onion, finely chopped
1   large garlic clove, finely
      chopped
¼   cup cognac or other good
      brandy
1¼ cups young, earthy red wine
¼   cup parsley, finely chopped
·   toasted slices of French
      bread

Preheat oven to 325 degrees.

Remove skin from the sturgeon
and discard. Cut the flesh from
the bones and slice it against the
grain into rectangles 2 inches
long by ½ inch wide. Set aside.

In a large heavy skillet, melt 2
tablespoons of the butter with
the oil, add the salt pork cubes,
and saute over moderately high
heat until they have browned
and rendered their fat. Remove
them to paper towels to drain.

To the rendered fat, add the
small white onions and brown
on all sides, shaking the skillet

occasionally so they do not stick.
Remove them when done and
place in a shallow ovenproof
container.

To the same skillet add the
mushrooms, seasoning lightly
with salt, pepper, and a little
lemon juice; saute over high
heat for about 3 minutes until
golden brown. Remove and
place in the container with the
onions.

Assemble the pieces of fish and
a shallow bowl of flour (seasoned
with salt and pepper) for
dredging near the stove. Add
the remaining tablespoon of
butter to the fat in the skillet
and set over moderately high
heat. When the fat is hot, coat
each piece of fish lightly with
flour and put it in the skillet to
brown on all sides. When the
fish is browned, scatter the
chopped onion and garlic over
it, reduce the heat and cook for
about 3 minutes, stirring
occasionally. Pour cognac over
the fish and allow it to heat for
a minute; then flame. When the
flames have subsided,
immediately add the wine and
cook for a few minutes more.
Remove the fish and place in
the dish containing the onions
and mushrooms; scatter the salt
pork bits over all.

Reduce the sauce over moderate
heat for about 10 minutes,
adding the parsley during the
last 5 minutes. Add salt, pepper,
and a bit of lemon juice to taste.

Pour the sauce over the fish, onions, and mushrooms and place in the oven just long enough to heat through. Serve over thin slices of toasted French bread.

Fish and Cucumber Saute
serves four

Sauteed cucumbers often accompany fish; when both are combined within the same dish the results are uncommonly pleasing. Firm-fleshed fish fillets must be used here; they will keep their shape better than the more delicate varieties. You may substitute heavy cream for half the wine called for, adding it after the wine has reduced a bit in the skillet. Serve with a green salad, or, if it is in season, asparagus with ginger (April). The wine should be a white Bordeaux or a good Muscadet.

2   small cucumbers
3   tablespoons butter
¼   cup onion, finely chopped
·   salt and freshly ground pepper
2   pounds firm fish fillets (cod, sea bass, snapper, halibut cheeks, striped bass, etc.)
·   flour seasoned with salt and pepper
4   tablespoons vegetable oil
¾ to 1 cup dry white wine
·   squeeze lemon juice
1   tablespoon parsley, finely chopped

Peel the cucumbers, cut each in half, and remove the seeds. Cut the flesh into cubes ½ inch square. Melt the butter in a small skillet, add the onion, and saute 1 to 2 minutes until it begins to take on color. Add the cucumber cubes, sprinkle lightly with salt and pepper, and saute for about 5 minutes, stirring occasionally, until just tender. Set aside.

Cut the fish fillets into strips about 3 inches wide. Flour the fish lightly, shaking off any excess. Immediately place in a skillet containing the hot vegetable oil. Quickly fry the fish over moderately high heat, about 1 minute to a side, removing each piece as it finishes cooking. When all the fish is done, pour off any excess oil from the pan, taking care not to disturb the browned particles on the bottom. Pour in the wine and stir constantly until it begins to thicken. Add the fish and the cucumber and onion mixture to the skillet and mix gently until all is coated with sauce. Season with salt, pepper, and lemon juice to taste, stir in the parsley, and allow to cook for an additional minute or two until the fish is heated through. Serve immediately.

Clam Pie

ten-inch pie; serves six

Steamed clams, sauteed mushrooms, and aromatic vegetables bound together with a cream sauce and topped with a crisp crust: a delightful presentation. Asparagus with egg-lemon sauce (April) would make a fine first course or accompaniment. The right wine is crucial: a fine Buena Vista Chardonnay, or one from the Northwest: Eyrie Vineyards, perhaps. Or how about a real Chablis?

3	dozen steamer clams, thoroughly washed
½	cup dry white vermouth or dry white wine
1	whole garlic clove, unpeeled
1	thick slice onion
1	bay leaf
·	few sprigs parsley
·	pinch dried thyme
6	tablespoons butter
½	pound mushrooms, cleaned and thickly sliced
·	squeeze lemon juice
½	cup onion, finely chopped
¼	cup celery, finely chopped
·	salt and freshly ground pepper
¼	cup flour
1	cup heavy cream
·	pinch dried mustard
·	dash Tabasco
1	tablespoon cognac
½	recipe pate brisee (see "Strawberry Tart"), rolled to ¼-inch thickness
1	egg yolk mixed with 1 teaspoon water

Preheat oven to 375 degrees.

Place the clams in a large pot with 1 cup of water, the vermouth or wine, garlic, onion, bay, parsley, and thyme; cover the pot and steam over high heat for about 8 minutes or until the clams open.

Remove and drain clams, reserving 1 cup of the steaming liquid. Remove the clams from their shells and cut each in two; reserve.

In a 10-inch skillet, melt 2 tablespoons of the butter. Add the mushrooms, sprinkle with a little lemon juice, and saute over high heat for 5 minutes, or until brown. Remove them with a slotted spoon and reserve. Add the onions and celery to the butter remaining in the skillet, season lightly with salt and pepper, and saute over moderate heat for 10 minutes.

While the vegetables are sauteing, prepare the sauce. In a heavy enameled saucepan, melt the remaining 4 tablespoons butter; add the flour, stirring constantly with a wire whisk, and cook for 5 minutes. Stir in the reserved clam broth, whisking until the mixture thickens; then add the heavy cream. Season the sauce with mustard, Tabasco, cognac, salt, and pepper to taste; cook for an additional 5 minutes over low heat until the flavors blend. Add the clams, mushrooms, onion, and celery to the sauce, taste, and adjust the seasoning if necessary.

Pour the mixture into a 10-inch pie plate; place the prepared pastry on top, securing it to the rim of the plate by crimping. Cut vents in the pastry and brush lightly with the egg yolk mixture. Bake for 25 to 30 minutes, or until the pastry has browned.

Pate of Sole and Shrimp
serves eight

A seafood pate makes a delightful fish course but all too often such pates are disappointingly bland in flavor and color. One doesn't want to overpower the natural flavor of the fish, but it can be complemented by certain carefully thought out additions.

The fish mousse (or base) of this recipe is made with fillet of sole, bound together with egg white and heavy cream. It is seasoned with a *very* small amount of chopped spinach, a little onion, and a dollop of Pernod (Pernod's anise flavor having a natural affinity for both the fish and the spinach).

This dish can be served warm or chilled, and the choices of sauces to accompany it are numerous. For the warm pate, a fish-stock-based veloute sauce or a sauce Normande using fish stock, creme fraiche, and egg yolk, or perhaps a sauce Nantua.

When the pate is chilled, a mayonnaise sauce is a fine choice, a good homemade mayonnaise flavored with a dash of sherry wine vinegar, a bit of tomato paste, and a soupcon of cognac or good brandy (a variation of sauce Doree).

Another interesting choice is this delicate and quickly prepared cucumber sauce: blanch a peeled and seeded cucumber in boiling water for 5 minutes. Remove, refresh under cold water, and puree in a food processor or food mill. Allow the puree to drain in a fine sieve for 10 minutes. Whip about ¼ cup heavy cream until almost stiff. Salt lightly, fold in the cucumber puree, and season with a dash of Tabasco and lemon juice. Serve this sauce very cold.

A dish this rich and luscious deserves to play first course to something equally elegant: I recommend it with the stuffed breast of veal (September), the chicken Marengo, the Spanish pork roast, and the boned stuffed chicken roll (all August). Pull out the stops with the wine, too: a really dry Alsatian Riesling, a good expensive Graves—Haut Brion blanc would not be too good.

2   pounds fresh sole fillets
4   egg whites
1½   cups heavy cream
·   salt and freshly ground pepper
·   half of a 10-ounce package frozen chopped spinach
1   tablespoon butter
1½   tablespoons onion, finely chopped
·   dash freshly grated nutmeg
1½   tablespoons Pernod
6   ounces tiny Pacific shrimp, cooked (do not use canned)
·   squeeze lemon juice

Preheat oven to 325 degrees.

Cut the fillets of sole into large pieces. Place half of them in the container of a food processor fitted with the steel knife blade. Blend for 1 or 2 seconds to achieve a coarse paste; add 2 of the egg whites and half the heavy cream while the machine is running and blend into a fine paste.

Remove to a mixing bowl and repeat the process with the remaining sole, egg whites, and heavy cream. Season the mixture lightly with salt and pepper.

Cook the spinach as directed on the package and drain well (you should have about ¼ cup). Melt the butter in a small skillet, add the onion, and saute until golden. Add the spinach and cook for 1 or 2 minutes over moderately high heat until all moisture is evaporated. Add this to the sole mousse, season with nutmeg and Pernod, and blend well.

Butter a 6-cup loaf pan and spread half the mousse on the bottom and sides of the mold. Add the shrimp meat sprinkled with a little lemon juice. Fill the mold with the remaining sole mixture. Cover the top of the pate with a buttered piece of waxed paper; on top of this place a layer of foil and seal tightly.

Place the loaf pan in a large baking pan filled with water to reach halfway up the sides of the pate (a bain marie). Place in the middle of the oven and bake for about 1 hour. To test for doneness, insert a metal skewer into the center of the pate; if it is clean when withdrawn the pate is ready.

Allow to stand for at least 10 minutes before unmolding. Slide a thin knife or metal spatula around the sides to loosen and unmold. Serve with your choice of sauce.

Turbans of Sole Stuffed with Salmon Mousse

serves six

The Spanish shrimp is a type of langoustine that is bright lobster-red even before it is cooked; it has a flavor that is quite special. It forms the basis for the sauce used to nap these turbans of sole. If this particular type of shrimp cannot be found, you may substitute crayfish or crab.

This dish makes a sumptuous first course for a main dish such as beef tenderloin with Bearnaise sauce. A broccoli puree (February) would make a good vegetable dish. Serve lemon ice (August) or banana-rum souffle for dessert, depending on your guests' capacity for more rich food. The wine should be the best full-flavored white Burgundy you can afford: perhaps a Meursault.

¾ pound salmon fillet
2   egg whites
1   cup heavy cream
·   salt and freshly ground pepper
6   fillets of sole
2   tablespoons finely chopped shallots
3 to 4 tablespoons dry white vermouth
    Sauce:
3 to 4 Spanish shrimp
1   small carrot, finely sliced
1   thick slice onion
2   shallots, peeled but left whole

·   small sprig of fresh parsley
·   small sprig of fresh thyme or ½ teaspoon dried thyme
½   bay leaf
·   few peppercorns
1   tablespoon wine vinegar
2   tablespoons butter
1½ tablespoons flour
½   cup heavy cream
·   salt
·   pinch each of cayenne pepper and fresh grated nutmeg

Remove skin from the salmon; cut fillet into small pieces and place it in a food processor fitted with a steel knife blade. Run the machine for a few seconds until the fish is just minced, then add the egg whites and blend. While the machine is running add the heavy cream, salt, pepper, and cayenne and continue to blend until the mixture is smooth. Spoon the mousse into a bowl and chill for at least 3 hours. (The dish can be prepared to this point the night before.)

While the mousse is chilling, make the court bouillon: place the shrimp, carrot, onion, shallots, parsley, thyme, bay leaf, peppercorns, and vinegar in a small enameled saucepan and cover with water. Bring to a boil; after 3 or 4 minutes remove the shrimp and shell them, reserving the meat for another use. Return the shells to the broth and cook at a simmer until the broth is reduced to about one cup. Strain the liquid and discard the solids.

Melt the butter in a small enameled saucepan. Add the flour to make a roux; cook for 5 minutes, but do not brown. When the roux is done add the reduced bouillon, blending with a whisk. When the bouillon is completely mixed into a roux and the sauce has thickened, add the heavy cream and seasonings and cook for another 10 minutes, stirring constantly. Keep the sauce warm in a bain marie.

Preheat oven to 350 degrees.

Spread an equal amount of the salmon mousse in the middle of each sole fillet and roll them up. In a shallow, lightly buttered ovenproof container, place the chopped shallots and the vermouth, put in the assembled turbans, and cover with aluminum foil. Bake for about 15 minutes or until the sole is cooked through. Place 1 turban on each serving plate and spoon over each a bit of sauce. The remainder of the sauce may be passed separately.

Fillets of Sole Dieppoise

serves four

This dish would go well with steamed buttered rice, dressed up with chopped parsley for some color. For a tangier accompaniment, try hot leeks in vinaigrette (November). A Sancerre would do nicely with this; or you might want to risk a dry French cider: Cidre Bouche is a safe brand.

4   fillets of sole
½   cup dry white vermouth or other dry white wine
½   cup water
½   bay leaf
4   thin slices onion
2   pounds mussels, steamed and shelled (about 1 cup mussel meat)
½   cup reserved mussel broth
1   cup tiny Pacific shrimp, cooked (do not use canned)
4   tablespoons butte

2   shallots, finely chopped
2   tablespoons flour
½   cup heavy cream
·   salt and freshly ground pepper

Preheat oven to 350 degrees.

Fold each fillet in half and place in a shallow, well-buttered ovenproof container. Pour the vermouth or wine and water over them. Scatter the onion slices on top, add the bay leaf, and cover tightly with foil.

Poach in the oven for about 15 minutes or until the sole is tender. Remove from the oven; pour off and reserve the liquid. Discard the onion and bay leaf. Leave the sole in the dish and set aside.

Combine the mussels with the

shrimps. Melt 2 tablespoons of the butter in a small skillet, add the mussels and shrimps, and place them over low heat. While they are warming, prepare the sauce: melt the remaining 2 tablespoons of butter in a small saucepan. Saute the shallots for 2 minutes, stir in the flour, and cook for 5 minutes over low heat, stirring constantly with a wire whisk. Stir in the combined mussel and sole broths, stir until thickened, add the heavy cream, and season to taste. Scatter the mussels and shrimps over the sole, pour the sauce over them, and put back into the oven to warm through. Run the dish under the broiler for a minute to glaze the top: serve immediately.

Jambalaya
serves six

Jambalaya is a lovely one-dish meal, great for entertaining. Don't be afraid to serve wine, though; a Muscadet or a very dry California French Columbard like Enz would be perfect.

1½ tablespoons butter
1 pound mild Italian sausage (casings removed), coarsely chopped
1½ cups onion, finely chopped
2 medium green peppers, seeded and cut into julienne
1½ cups short-grain white rice (Italian rice is excellent)
1 pound, 12-ounce can plum tomatoes, thoroughly drained and coarsely chopped
2 cloves garlic, minced
½ teaspoon dried thyme
· small pinch powdered cloves
½ teaspoon chili powder
· small pinch of cayenne pepper or 2 to 3 drops Tabasco
small pinch allspice
· small pinch powdered saffron (optional)
· salt and freshly ground pepper
2 cups lightly seasoned chicken or fish stock
¾ pound cleaned crab meat
2 dozen medium oysters, shucked (reserve liquor and add to stock)

In a heavy casserole (I prefer cast iron with enamel) heat the butter, add the sausage meat, and cook over medium heat till all fat is rendered. There should be about 3 tablespoons; if there is more, remove it and discard.

Add the onions and green pepper and saute over medium heat till the onions are limp and golden.

Heat the stock in a saucepan. While it is warming, add the rice to the onions and green pepper and cook it, stirring constantly, until it turns lightly brown—about 5 minutes. This coats each grain of rice with the fat, sealing it so that it keeps its shape and texture during the cooking, as in the technique used in preparing Italian risotto.

Add the tomatoes, garlic, all spices, salt, and pepper to taste and cook for a few minutes until the excess liquid from the tomatoes is absorbed into the rice.

Add the stock, ½ cup at a time, stirring lightly with a fork. Cover the casserole partially and lower the heat to simmer. The rice must totally absorb each addition of stock before any more is added, and a close watch must be kept so that it does not dry out and stick to the bottom of the pot. The dish can be done ahead to this point.

When the rice is done, taste for seasoning; then add the crab and oysters, cover, and cook over medium heat till the crab meat is warmed through and the edges of the oysters have just begun to curl — approximately 10 minutes. Serve immediately, garnished with lemon wedges.

Squid Salad
serves six

Cleaning squid is not difficult, although it does take a little time: the ink sac is usually removed by the fishmonger, making the rest a simple procedure.

Hold the squid in one hand; with the other grasp the head and tentacles and pull. The head will come away with the contents of the body. (If it does not, simply grasp the body at the pointed end and squeeze out the excess with your thumb and fingers.)

Pull out the transparent, quill-like backbone and discard. There are two flaps or "wings" on the body; pull these off under cold running water and all of the outside rosy-colored skin will come off easily, leaving behind a pearly white cone of flesh. Cut the tentacles from the head just behind the eye: restrain yourself from the impulse to discard the wormy things, for when they are cooked, they will firm and spread out like delicate pink flowers.

Rinse both the body and the tentacles under cold running water. Keep the flesh of the squid in a bowl of cold water until you are ready to use it; then drain and dry thoroughly.

This would make a fine first course for a meal whose main dish is sauteed, like chicken parmigiana, scallopine, piccata, or perhaps a saltimbocca.

3 pounds squid, cleaned
1½ cups thinly sliced celery (or fennel)
· salt and freshly ground pepper
1½ teaspoons dried oregano
· dash Tabasco
1½ tablespoons red wine vinegar
¼ cup fruity olive oil

Select the smallest possible squid available. Slice the cleaned bodies into rings of no more than 1 inch wide. Cut the tentacles in half, if they are large. Poach both rings and

tentacles in lightly simmering salted water for about 30 minutes or until they are tender. Remove, drain well, and put in a serving bowl.

Add to the squid the celery, oregano, Tabasco, vinegar, and olive oil and toss together until all are blended. Season to taste with salt and pepper. Let the mixture marinate at room temperature for at least one hour. Before serving, mix well again, drain off any excess moisture, and serve as a first course.

Squid and Fish Stew Mediterranean Style
serves six

Served with an antipasto of roasted red and green peppers with feta cheese, good crusty bread, and a green salad, this makes a real Mediterranean feast. Keep the Provencale theme with a big Hermitage white.

3 pounds squid, cleaned (see "Squid Salad")
4 tablespoons olive oil
3 tablespoons onion, finely chopped
3 tablespoons fennel, finely chopped
2 garlic cloves, minced
¼ cup parsley, finely chopped
1 cup dry white vermouth
2 cups Italian plum tomatoes, drained and coarsely chopped
· salt and freshly ground pepper

· small pinch hot red pepper flakes
½ teaspoon dried oregano
· pinch powdered saffron or curry powder (optional)
2 pounds firm-fleshed fish fillets: red snapper, cod, halibut, or striped bass
· thick toasted slices of French or Italian bread

Cut the bodies of the squid into rings, 1 inch wide; cut the tentacles in half if they are large. Reserve.

Heat the olive oil in a 4-quart soup pot; add the onion and fennel and saute over medium heat until the onion is golden. Add the garlic, parsley, and vermouth, raise the heat to high, and reduce the mixture for about 4 minutes. Add the tomatoes, squid, herbs, and spices, cover, reduce the heat, and simmer for about 30 minutes, or until the squid is tender.

Add the fish fillets, cut into bite-sized pieces; cover again and simmer for about 10 minutes, until the fish is just flaky. Taste for seasoning and serve over thick, toasted slices of Italian or French bread.

Fried Squid

serves four

Anyone who has been on the Adriatic coast of Italy will certainly remember an incredible delicacy: tiny squid no more than an inch and a half long dipped in a seasoned flour and quickly fried whole in hot oil until meltingly golden. While the squid available locally is quite a bit larger than the Mediterranean variety, it is just as delicious prepared in this manner. Serve with a hearty pasta dish like bianco e nero (February).

3 pounds squid, cleaned (see "Squid Salad")
·   peanut or safflower oil
·   flour, seasoned with salt, pepper, and a tiny grating of nutmeg
·   lemon wedges

Cut the bodies of the squid into rings ¾ inch wide; cut the tentacles into 2 or 3 pieces if they are large. Dry all the pieces thoroughly.

Fill a large heavy skillet (preferably cast iron) 1 inch deep with oil and place over high heat until the oil is hot but not smoking. Have close at hand a shallow bowl filled with the seasoned flour.

When the oil is ready, dip the pieces of squid in the flour, shaking to remove any excess, and put into the skillet, covering immediately with a spatter shield. Do not crowd the squid; fry only enough to just cover the bottom. As soon as the squid is a golden brown (it will need to be turned occasionally), remove and drain on paper towels. Keep the cooked portion warm in the oven while the rest is cooking. Serve immediately with plenty of lemon wedges.

Plain Steamed Mussels in Their Broth

This recipe and those that follow are all based on steamed mussels.

Mussels must be well cleaned before they are used. Remove the barnacles that often encrust them with with a sturdy, short-bladed knife, then wash under cold running water, rubbing the shells together with your hands.

Pull off the "beards" with your fingers or using a knife. While removing the beards, squeeze each shell; if it does not close tightly, discard it.

Put the mussels into a large bowl, cover with water, and add a bit of sea salt. Sprinkle the top of the water with a handful of cornmeal or flour and allow to stand a few hours or overnight. This last process may be omitted when using cultivated mussels.

2   pounds mussels
3   slices lemon
2   thick slices onion
1   bay leaf

·   sprig each of thyme and parsley
1½ cups water
¼   cup dry white vermouth
·   few peppercorns
·   pinch of salt

In a pot large enough to hold all the mussels, put the lemon, onion, bay leaf, thyme and parsley, water, vermouth, peppercorns, and salt. Bring to a boil and cook a few minutes. Add the cleaned mussels, cover, and steam over high heat for 5 to 8 minutes, until all the mussels have opened.
Remove mussels from pot, put into soup plates, and strain broth over all.

Stuffed Mussels

serves six as first course

These mussels go very nicely with linguini; you can use some of their broth in making the sauce. They also make a good first course for game hens or any of the grilled items in the July chapter. Serve a Fume blanc or a white Bordeaux (Graves for preference).

2   pounds mussels, cleaned as above
1   tablespoon olive oil
4   shallots, minced
1½ teaspoons grated lemon rind
2   tablespoons parsley, minced
1   cup freshly made breadcrumbs
4   tablespoons grated Parmesan cheese

·   dash dried hot red pepper flakes
2   egg whites, lightly beaten
·   salt

Preheat oven to 350 degrees.

Steam the mussels not longer than 5 minutes, remove from pot, extract meat, chop coarsely, and reserve. Reserve the empty shells, also. While mussels are steaming, saute the shallots in the olive oil for 3 or 4 minutes.

Put the chopped mussels into a bowl and add the sauteed shallots with their oil, lemon rind, parsley, breadcrumbs, 2 tablespoons grated cheese, pepper flakes, and egg whites; mix thoroughly, tasting for salt.

Separate the shell halves, stuffing each with a bit of the mussel mixture. Place the stuffed shells in a shallow ovenproof dish. Sprinkle the tops of the mussels with the remaining 2 tablespoons grated cheese and bake for 15 minutes, running under the broiler for the last few minutes to brown the tops lightly.

Linguini with Mussel Sauce
serves four to six

Linguini is a particular kind of pasta, made famous by Neil Simon's *The Odd Couple*. This dish is a fine first course, but with leeks in vinaigrette (November) or broccoli with capers vinaigrette (February) and a green salad, it serves as a main dish as well.

2 pounds mussels, cleaned
1 tablespoon butter
1 tablespoon olive oil
2 large shallots, minced
3 garlic cloves, minced
1½ tablespoons flour
½ cup dry white vermouth
1 tablespoon fresh thyme, minced, or ½ teaspoon dried thyme
1 pound linguini, cooked al dente

Steam 2 pounds of mussels for not longer than 5 minutes; extract the meat. chop coarsely, and reserve. Reduce the mussel cooking liquid over high heat to ½ cup and reserve it too.

In a skillet melt the butter with the olive oil and saute the shallots and garlic for a few minutes, taking care not to brown them. Stir in the flour with a wire whisk and cook for 5 minutes. Add the reserved broth and dry white vermouth and bring to a boil, stirring constantly until the sauce thickens. Reduce the heat, add the thyme and the chopped mussels, and cook just long enough to heat them through. Spoon some sauce over each individual bowl of pasta and pass a mixture of grated Romano and Parmesan cheeses.

Mussel Chowder
serves six to eight

With curried stuffed eggs (August) as the first course and broccoli as a vegetable, this hearty, rich soup makes a meal.

2 pounds mussels, cleaned

1 tablespoon butter
¾ cup salt pork, blanched and cut into small dice
2 leeks, including 2 inches of the green top, cleaned and finely chopped.

¾ cup celery cut into small dice

1½ cups potatoes, cut into small dice

· pinch cayenne pepper

¼ teaspoon powdered saffron or ¼ teaspoon turmeric

½ teaspoon salt

3½ cups milk

½ pint heavy cream

3 tablespoons parsley, minced

Steam the mussels for not longer than 5 minutes, extract the meat, chop coarsely, and reserve. Reduce the cooking liquid over high heat to 1 cup and reserve it too.

Melt the butter in a 5-quart heavy pot; add the salt pork and saute until crisp and golden brown. Remove the pork bits, drain on paper towels, and reserve.

In the rendered fat left in the pot, saute the leeks, celery, and potatoes over high heat for 5 minutes. Sprinkle the vegetables with the cayenne, saffron or turmeric, and salt; add the reserved broth, bring to a boil, and cook for a few minutes.

Remove the pot from the heat and add the milk and heavy cream, stirring well. Over low heat cook the chowder for about ½ hour till the potatoes are soft; then add the reserved mussels and pork bits and simmer for a few minutes to warm the shellfish and blend the flavors.

Serve immediately, topping each bowl with parsley. If the chowder is to be reheated, do not boil or it will curdle.

Paella
serves eight to ten

The technique used in this recipe for cooking the rice is similar to that used for risotto. In a departure from tradition, the tomatoes are omitted and the dish is seasoned with saffron, paprika, and Pernod. Serve with a green salad on the side, and follow perhaps with a frozen cheese bombe (August). White Burgundy is practically a must here, if the wine is to stand up to the seasoning.

¼ pound salt pork or bacon (blanched), cut into small dice

·1 tablespoon olive oil

1½ pounds shrimp, shelled

1½ pounds scallops (if sea scallops are used, cut each in two)

8 hot Italian sausage links, cut into half-inch rounds

10 chicken drumsticks

1 medium onion, coarsely chopped

3 cups Italian rice (a short-grain rice)

3 cloves garlic, finely chopped

¼ teaspoon powdered saffron

¼ teaspoon sweet paprika

- pinch of cayenne pepper or dash of Tabasco
- ½ cup dry white vermouth
- 5 to 6 cups chicken broth
- ½ cup cooked chickpeas
- 15 small steamer clams, well cleaned
- 15 fresh mussels, cleaned and bearded
- 1 to 1½ tablespoons Pernod
- ¼ cup finely chopped parsley
- 2 tablespoons whole capers
- lemon slices

Place the salt pork or bacon with the olive oil in a 6-quart heavy enameled soup pot or paella pan with the olive oil. Saute over high heat till the pork is crisp and the fat is rendered. Remove the pork bits and reserve them. In the remaining fat, saute the shrimp for about 3 minutes over medium heat until just done; remove and reserve them. Do the same with the scallops, then the sausage and the chicken, adding more olive oil if needed.

In the remaining fat, saute the onion for about 5 minutes. Add the reserved salt pork or

bacon, rice, garlic, saffron, paprika, and cayenne or Tabasco; stir with a wooden spoon until the grains of rice are coated with the oil and spices and have become slightly opaque.

Pour in the vermouth and 1 cup of the chicken broth and cook over medium heat until the liquid is absorbed, stirring all the while with a fork. Add the remaining broth as needed, 1 cup at a time, stirring frequently until the rice is almost cooked. The dish may be done ahead to this point.

Preheat oven to 350 degrees.

Gently mix the cooked and reserved shrimp, scallops, sausage, chicken, chickpeas, steamer clams, mussels, and Pernod into the cooked rice. Cover the pot with a lid (if using a paella pan, cover with foil) and place in the oven for 10 to 15 minutes or until the shellfish open. Remove from oven and sprinkle the top with parsley and capers. Rim the dish with lemon slices.

Spaghetti Bucaniera

serves four to six

This peppery tomato sauce (pirate-style, as the name suggests) is filled with the bounty of the sea: mussels, octopus, shrimp, and scallops. In Italy, grated cheese is rarely used over a seafood sauce for

fear it will overpower the delicate flavors of the fish. In this dish, however, an exception can be made. Celery root vinaigrette (November) would make a good vegetable accompaniment. A slightly spicy wine is required: a California Grignolino or an Italian Barbera.

4½ tablespoons olive oil
2 garlic cloves, peeled but left whole
1 small dried hot red pepper
¼ cup pancetta (rolled Italian bacon), cut into small dice
¼ cup onion, finely chopped
1-pound can Italian plum tomatoes, drained and coarsely chopped.
½ cup cooking liquid from mussels
4 ounces cooked octopus, cut into bite-size pieces
4 ounces shrimp, shelled and cut into bite-size pieces
4 ounces scallops, cut into bite-size pieces
1 pound mussels, steamed for 5 minutes, shelled, and coarsely chopped
· salt and freshly ground pepper
¼ cup parsley, minced
1 pound spaghetti, cooked al dente

In a soup pot, heat half the olive oil; add the garlic and pepper and saute over high heat until both have browned. Remove and discard them.

Add the pancetta and onion to the pot and saute over medium heat for 5 minutes. Add the tomatoes and the cooking liquid from the mussels; partially cover the pot and simmer for about 20 minutes.

Meanwhile, heat the remaining olive oil in a skillet, add the octopus, shrimp, and scallops, and saute over high heat for 3 or 4 minutes. Remove from heat and set aside.

When the tomato base has thickened slightly, add the sauteed octopus, shrimp, scallops, and mussels, taste for seasoning, and add salt and pepper if desired. Simmer for 10 minutes more, add the parsley, and serve over pasta.

April, Flavors of Spring

Menu 1
Linguini Primavera (April)
Abbaccio alla Cacciatoria (April)
Braised Peas with Mint (May)
Chocolate Truffles Italienne (December)

Menu 2
Crostini Roberto (April)
Spit-Roasted Baby Lamb (April)
Caesar Salad (May)
Roast Potatoes with Rosemary and Sage (May)
Lemon Ices (August)

Crostini Roberto
Raw Mushroom Salad
Dandelion Salad Mimosa
Watercress and Snow Pea Salad
Sweet Pea Salad
Cream of Lettuce Soup
Grated Zucchini Saute
Asparagus Wrapped in Prosciutto
Asparagus with Fresh Ginger
Asparagus with Egg-Lemon Sauce
Saute of Potatoes and Hazelnuts
Steamed Potatoes with Parsley Sauce
Spit-Roasted Baby Lamb
Abbaccio alla Cacciatoria
Pan-Fried Lamb Steaks with Anchovy Sauce
Saute of Lamb with Artichoke Hearts
Linguini Primavera

Spring brings heady delights of the first young greens: the smooth-leaved butter or Bibb lettuce, curly endive, and escarole, the saw-toothed dandelion and spinach. Fresh herbs begin to appear in local gardens and on the greengrocer's tables, along with tiny radishes, scallions, and new potatoes.

The vegetable that most typifies early spring for me is asparagus. Today we have available a steady supply of asparagus from early March through June, shipped from California, then New Jersey, Massachusetts, and Washington. Although it travels far, it remains one of the few vegetables still harvested by hand, so special care is taken to preserve its freshness.

Because asparagus is extremely perishable, it should be used as soon as possible after purchase. When selecting this vegetable, look for firm stalks that are green for at least two-thirds of their length, with tightly closed buds of a dark green to violet color. I prefer the French method of peeling the stalks to remove their tough outer skin. This allows the vegetable to cook evenly throughout when placed in a skillet filled with boiling, salted water. Testing for doneness is much the same as for pasta: remove a stalk, cut a bit off the stem end, and taste. The entire cooking process should take no longer than four to eight minutes, depending on the thickness of the stalk. This elegant spring vegetable is best served as a separate first course.

Another food for this season is lamb. "Genuine Spring Lamb," a designation made by the Department of Agriculture, is stamped on animals that are five to six months old. The leg of such a lamb should weigh no more than five to seven pounds; the meat should be a light pink in color. The texture of the meat will be fine, the fat very white, firm, and waxy.

In the past, the season on this "specialty" ran from March to October, but in today's markets tender young lamb may be found almost throughout the year. Because lamb is raised all over the country, the climate factors in various areas cause the crop to come to market at different times. For instance, in the milder climates of California and the Northwest, lambs are born in the fall and early winter and are ready for market in the early spring. In most of the country, however, lambs are born later in the winter and spring; this produces the late crop that is ready for marketing in mid-summer.

Although this meat has always been more popular in Europe and the Middle East, our seeming national prejudice against it is being overcome: many have discovered the versatility of lamb and now prefer it to beef. You can make an interesting comparison. Steak tartar, even made with the best tenderloin of beef, does not possess the fineness of flavor that is to be found in kibbeh, a Middle Eastern dish composed of ground raw lamb and a small amount of bulgur (cracked wheat).

Crostini Roberto
serves four to six

Crostini are Italian canapes; this excellent version made of chopped chicken livers is a specialty of Tuscany. The livers are blanched for two reasons: to rid them of any bitterness and to make them easier to chop. The chopping must be done by hand to obtain the correct consistency: tiny, but still recognizable pieces of liver. A food processor or meat grinder will turn the liver into too fine a paste.

The vodka used in this recipe is a deviation from the classic style: it gives the dish a lift without adding any flavor. Cognac, Marsala, or Madeira may be substituted, but the quantity should be reduced. The crostini should be served on rounds of sturdy bread, Italian or French, which are neither fried nor toasted. This allows the liver mixture to soak lightly into the bread.

Crostini are a first course, but they are rich: be careful not to overburden your guests with good things later in the meal. A light main dish like the veal and pepper saute (February) is ideal. Serve with a good inexpensive sparkling wine such as Prosecco (or Veuve Cliquot, if you can afford it); or stick to icy vodka.

¼	cup olive oil
2	tablespoons carrot, finely chopped
1	cup onion, finely chopped
1	small stalk celery, finely chopped
1	tablespoon each fresh rosemary and sage, finely chopped, or ½ teaspoon each dried
1	clove garlic, finely chopped
½	pound chicken livers, cleaned and cut in half
3	tablespoons capers
3	tablespoons anchovy paste
1	tablespoon tomato paste mixed with 2 tablespoons water
.	freshly ground pepper
⅓	cup vodka

Heat the olive oil in a deep 10-inch heavy skillet, add the carrot, onion, celery, and herbs; saute over moderate heat for 10 minutes until golden; do not brown.

Meanwhile bring a small saucepan of lightly salted water to a boil, add the chicken livers, and allow them to blanch for 4 to 5 minutes. Drain immediately, run under cold water, and dry thoroughly. Chop very finely together with the capers.

Add the garlic to the sauteed vegetables and continue to cook 2 to 3 minutes. Add the chicken liver and caper mixture to the vegetables; stir in the remaining ingredients, blending well. Do not add any salt at this point.

Saute this mixture for about 15 minutes or until all excess moisture is absorbed and the mixture resembles a thick paste. Taste for seasoning, adding salt if necessary. Remove mixture from the heat and immediately spread onto thin rounds of Italian or French bread. This mixture may also be allowed to cool and gently reheated later, but it should be kept covered.

Raw Mushroom Salad
serves four

This recipe is an adaptation of a dish served at the Four Seasons restaurant in New York. The dressing used is also very complementary to strong-flavored greens such as romaine, watercress, or spinach.

Dressing:
¾ cup heavy cream
1 tablespoon fine French mustard (Pommery, L'Ancienne, or Dijon)
½ tablespoon red wine vinegar
3 tablespoons olive oil
· salt and freshly ground pepper
· dash Tabasco

Vegetables:
½ pound mushrooms, cleaned and thinly sliced
2 stalks celery, cut into julienne strips 2 inches long
¼ cup grated raw radish

Prepare the dressing: combine the heavy cream with the mustard, vinegar, olive oil, salt, pepper, and Tabasco and mix well. Taste the mixture for seasoning; the dressing should be tangy, which depends on the type of mustard used. You may wish to add more than is called for.

Place the mushrooms, celery, and radish in a serving bowl, pour the dressing over them, and toss well. Serve immediately or marinate at room temperature for an hour or two.

Dandelion Salad Mimosa
serves four

Young dandelion leaves have a pleasing piquant flavor; they should be picked before the plant has flowered to be at their most tender. The piquancy of this salad particularly suits dishes featuring lamb.

1 pound young dandelion leaves
4 rashers thick-sliced bacon, cut into small dice
2 tablespoons lemon juice
· pinch dried mustard
1 shallot, finely minced
· dash Tabasco
· salt and freshly ground pepper
⅓ cup fruity olive oil
1 hardboiled egg

Gently wash the dandelion leaves, tear into bite-size pieces, and refrigerate for at least 30 minutes to crisp. Saute the bacon until browned and crisp; remove to paper towels to drain.

Combine the lemon juice, dried mustard, minced shallot, Tabasco, salt, pepper, and olive oil mixing well. Place the chilled dandelion leaves in a serving bowl, sprinkle with the bacon, and toss with only enough of the dressing to just moisten the leaves. Sieve the white and yolk of the egg separately and sprinkle both on top of the salad. Serve at once.

Watercress and Snow Pea Salad
serves four

An elegant green salad served with a slightly sweet-sour dressing that may be served with almost any meat, poultry, or fish dish.

2   bunches watercress
¼   pound fresh snow peas, smallest possible, ends trimmed off
4 to 6 scallions
    Dressing:
·   juice of ½ lemon
¼   teaspoon dry mustard
1-inch squeeze anchovy paste
1   teaspoon honey
·   dash Tabasco
5   tablespoons olive oil
·   salt and freshly ground pepper

Wash and trim the watercress and place it in a salad bowl. Bring 2 quarts of salted water to a boil, add the snow peas, and cook them for 3 to 5 minutes until tender but still crisp. Run under cold water, drain, and dry thoroughly. Add the blanched snow peas to the watercress. Thinly slice the scallions, including the green tops, and add them to the salad bowl. Cover with a dampened paper towel and chill until serving time.

Prepare the dressing: in a small mixing bowl, combine the lemon juice with the dry mustard, anchovy paste, and honey and stir well. Add the Tabasco and the olive oil, stirring constantly. Season with salt to taste and add a liberal grinding of black pepper.

Stir the dressing well before using, pour over the watercress and snow pea mixture, toss gently but thoroughly, and serve at once.

Sweet Pea Salad
serves four

A most refreshing spring salad composed of fresh new peas, crisp julienne of bacon, sauteed mushrooms, and thinly sliced scallions dressed with olive oil and vinegar. With a rich dish like crostini Roberto (also this month), this is a light but full meal.

2   pounds (unshelled weight) fresh young peas
1   teaspoon sugar
4   rashers thick-sliced bacon, cut into thick julienne
8   small mushrooms, cleaned and thickly sliced
4 or 5 scallions, thinly sliced (including the green tops)
1½ tablespoons red wine vinegar
6   tablespoons olive oil
·   dash Tabasco
·   salt and freshly ground pepper

Place a little water in a saucepan (just enough to cover the peas), add the sugar, and bring to a boil. While the water is heating, shell the peas; add peas to the water and cook them for 5 to 7 minutes, until just tender. Remove peas and run under cold water, drain, and dry thoroughly.

Saute the bacon in a small skillet until crisp and brown; remove and drain on paper towels. Quickly saute the mushroom slices in the hot bacon fat until lightly browned; remove with a slotted spoon.

In a serving bowl, combine the peas, bacon, mushrooms, and scallions. Add the vinegar, oil, Tabasco, and salt and pepper to taste. Toss the salad well and serve at once, or chill for an hour or two.

Cream of Lettuce Soup
serves four

A soup with the delicate taste of springtime. Do not substitute another variety of lettuce or the entire character of the dish will change. This soup would make a light and elegant first course for kulebiaka (May).

3   large heads Boston, butter, or Bibb lettuce
4   tablespoons butter
2   tablespoons shallots, finely chopped
1   small new potato, peeled and finely chopped
4   cups chicken stock, lightly flavored
·   salt and freshly ground pepper
1   cup heavy cream
·   pinch fresh grated nutmeg
·   squeeze of lemon juice
·   toasted croutons

Wash the lettuce and dry it thoroughly. Cut into fine shreds. Melt the butter in a heavy enameled saucepan, add the shallots and potato, and saute over moderate heat for 10 minutes. Add the shredded lettuce and stir until it is coated with butter; cook over low heat for 5 minutes. Add the chicken stock, season lightly with salt and pepper, and simmer for 30 minutes.

Allow the soup to cool slightly and strain the solids into a fine sieve, reserving the broth. Place the vegetables in a food processor fitted with the steel knife blade and puree them. Stir the puree back into the broth, add the cream, and place over low heat. Season with nutmeg and a little lemon juice to taste. Cook the soup for 10 minutes more, stirring occasionally. Serve immediately, topped with toasted croutons.

Grated Zucchini Saute
serves four

The zucchini is salted to release its excess moisture, then very quickly sauteed with a bit of garlic in butter. This dish suits simple roasts of chicken or lamb, as well as sauteed meats.

4   medium zucchini
·   salt
2   tablespoons butter
1   teaspoon olive oil
2   large cloves garlic, finely chopped
·   freshly ground pepper

Grate the zucchini coarsely, salt it lightly, and place it in a colander to drain for 15 minutes. Squeeze out all excess moisture from the vegetable and dry it thoroughly.

Melt the butter with the oil in a heavy 10-inch skillet. Add the garlic and stir it around in the oil for a minute, taking care not to brown it. Add the zucchini and saute it over moderately high heat for 6 to 8 minutes, until tender but still crisp. Season with pepper and serve immediately.

Asparagus Wrapped in Prosciutto
serves four

Nearly everyone has a particular method of cooking asparagus and to suggest that any one way is better than another is to invite argument. However, after much experimentation, I always return to the French method: peeling the asparagus to remove the

tough, stringy outer skin on the stalk, which allows the vegetable to cook evenly all the way through. The following dish makes a dressy first course or accompaniment for a simple dish like roast chicken with rosemary and garlic (May).

32 asparagus spears
8   thin slices prosciutto
3   tablespoons melted butter
¼   cup grated Parmesan cheese

Preheat the oven to 450 degrees.

Prepare the asparagus: break or cut off and discard 2 to 3 inches of the stalks; using a vegetable peeler, peel the outer skins from the stalks.

Bring a 10- or 12-inch skillet filled with water and seasoned with salt to a boil, add the asparagus, and cook over high heat for 4 to 7 minutes, depending on the thickness of the stalks. (Pull one out of the water after a few minutes, cut off a bit of the end, and taste it, just as you would do for pasta.) Remove the asparagus when done and drain well. Divide into 4 groups of 8 each. Wrap each group in 2 slices of prosciutto, place on a serving platter, drizzle with melted butter, and sprinkle with the grated cheese. Place in oven just long enough to allow cheese to melt and serve at once.

Asparagus with Fresh Ginger

serves two

The Chinese technique of stir-frying may successfully be applied to fresh asparagus; here it is seasoned lightly with fresh ginger root, chicken broth, dry sherry, and sesame oil. Do not substitute the dried spice for the fresh ginger root: the flavor will not be the same. The small amount of sesame oil, a classic Chinese touch, lends the finished dish a subtle and slightly nutlike taste that is most pleasant. Try this with fish and cucumber saute (March).

1   pound fresh asparagus
2   tablespoons dry sherry
¼   cup chicken stock
½   teaspoon cornstarch
1½   tablespoons vegetable oil
     (peanut, safflower, corn)
10   paper-thin slices fresh,
     unpeeled ginger root
·   salt
·   pinch finely granulated
     sugar
½   teaspoon sesame oil

Cut off and discard the tough white end of the stalks. Skin the stalks with the aid of a vegetable peeler. Cut the spears on the bias into 1½- to 2-inch lengths.

Combine in a small bowl or cup the sherry, stock, and cornstarch and stir well. Place all the ingredients ready and close to your cooking area.

Heat the vegetable oil in a heavy 10-inch skillet or wok; add the ginger slices and stir them in the oil for a few seconds; do not allow them to brown. Add the asparagus, seasoning stalks lightly with salt and a bit of sugar. Toss them about in the oil for about 3 minutes. Pour in the sherry-cornstarch mixture and stir constantly until it thickens (this will happen almost immedi ately). Stir in the sesame oil, blend thoroughly, and serve at once.

Asparagus with Egg-Lemon Sauce
serves two

Egg-lemon sauce is of Greek origin. It is an extraordinarily light concoction that somewhat resembles a hollandaise, but without the addition of butter. It can be successfully prepared in a cast-iron enameled saucepan if you are careful not to overheat it. If you have no such pan, substitute a double boiler and allow a few minutes more for the sauce to thicken. You will find the sauce just as delightful on green beans or broccoli. This will make a wonderful vegetable accompaniment to the pan-fried lamb steaks (this month) and other sauteed meats.

1   pound asparagus
     Sauce:
2   large eggs
¼   teaspoon dry mustard
.   dash Tabasco
4 or 5 tablespoons lemon juice
1   teaspoon cornstarch
6   tablespoons chicken stock
.   salt and freshly ground
     pepper

Break off and discard the tough, woody end of the stalks and peel the remainder with the aid of a potato peeler. Bring a large skillet filled with salted water to a boil and add the asparagus. Allow the vegetable to cook for 4 to 7 minutes, depending on thickness. (Remove a stalk, cut a bit off the end, and taste to check for doneness.)

Meanwhile, in an enameled cast-iron saucepan place the eggs, mustard, Tabasco, and lemon juice. Combine the cornstarch with the chicken stock in a small bowl and mix thoroughly: add to the saucepan, season lightly with salt and pepper, and blend all together with a wire whisk. Place the saucepan over moderate heat and allow the sauce to thicken slowly, whisking continuously; this should take no longer than 3 to 5 minutes. Remove from heat immediately when done.

When the asparagus has cooked, drain it and dry thoroughly on paper towels. Place in a serving dish, pour the sauce over, and toss gently. Serve at once.

Saute of Potatoes and Hazelnuts
serves four

This unusual combination makes a delicious accompaniment for any simple roasted meat or poultry.

1½ pounds new potatoes
4 tablespoons butter
2 tablespoons vegetable oil
· salt and freshly ground pepper
2 tablespoons toasted hazelnuts, coarsely chopped
4 tablespoons grated Pamesan cheese

Peel and cut the potatoes into ½-inch cubes. Heat the butter with the oil in a heavy 10- or 12-inch skillet, add the potatoes, and season to taste with salt and pepper. Saute over moderate heat, stirring frequently, for about 25 minutes. Sprinkle the nuts and cheese over the potatoes, stirring to coat, and continue to cook for another 5 minutes until the cheese is melted and the potatoes are tender.

Steamed Potatoes with Parsley Sauce
serves four

A simple dish, easily prepared, that makes a wonderful accompaniment for any roast meat, poultry, or fish.

1½ pounds small new potatoes, unpeeled
6 tablespoons butter
3 tablespoons onion, finely minced
¼ cup parsley, finely chopped
· salt and freshly ground pepper

Steam the potatoes over low heat until they are tender: the timing will depend largely on their size. While the potatoes are cooking, prepare the sauce. Melt the butter in a small saucepan, add the onion, and saute over moderate heat for 5 minutes or until tender. Stir in the parsley and cook for another 1 to 2 minutes.

When the potatoes are ready, season with salt and pepper, pour the sauce over them, and toss until they are well coated. Serve at once.

Spit-Roasted Baby Lamb
serves twelve to fourteen

Spit-roasted baby lamb, done in the Mediterranean style, is not so much a dish as a feast: a celebration of spring. The lamb is larded throughout with rosemary and garlic, spitted over an open fire, and slowly roasted to a luscious golden brown. Since it is difficult to find a lamb, baby or not, under 20 pounds, the spit used must be a large one, and it must be turned manually—a laborous task but one that will produce most delicious results.

Because much of the lamb in the Northwest is locally raised, obtaining a whole baby lamb is not as formidable a task as one might imagine. The majority of our local lamb is readied for market around Easter-time and you should contact your butcher a few weeks beforehand to obtain the smallest possible animal, ideally around 20 pounds.

The lamb will already be dressed when you get it, and what remains to be done requires more time than skill. Make small, deep cuts all over the fleshy parts of the body and legs and insert into each a few fresh leaves of rosemary and a small slice of garlic. If you have no access to the fresh herb, you may wish to crush dried rosemary with garlic and use the resulting paste in the same way.

The front legs must be securely tied to the body: use thin wire rather than string. The back legs, also tied together, must be stretched away from the body. Insert a large spit into the neck and through the body; secure it tightly to the hind legs. Next, lightly salt and pepper the meat and baste with a coat of olive oil; then place the lamb 20 to 25 inches above about 15 pounds of hot coals. Turn the spit a quarter turn every 15 or 20 minutes, basting when the meat apears to be too dry. More coals (4 or 5 10-pound bags may be used in all) should be added as needed to retain an even temperature. A baby lamb of the size mentioned will take about 7 hours for the meat to be well done and falling off the bone as the Italians and Greeks prefer it; for medium-rare meat, 5 to 6 hours will suffice. To test for doneness, insert a sharp knife or fork into the breast meat and the leg: meat is well done when very little juice runs out. Using a thermometer that gives an instant reading, allow 175 degrees for well done and 145 degrees to 150 degrees for medium-rare.

A feast of this kind does not lend itself to a lot of hostessy fripperies. It's best to plan a group of accompaniments that can be done ahead, will keep well over a long dining period, and will allow you to socialize as much as your guests. Lots of fragrant roast potatoes with rosemary would complement the lamb. For lighter eaters and for salad course, set out bowls of Caesar salad (May), dandelion salad (this month) and raw mushroom salad (this month): a sort of crazy grand buffet in honor of the spring.

Abbaccio alla Cacciatoria
serves four

A celebrated Roman dish served at Easter-time. The lamb used is traditionally one month old and milk fed: although it may be impossible to find lamb of this quality in our country, this dish can be successfully prepared with any very young lamb of good quality. It is classically served with peas. Try a delicate vegetable course like risi e bisi (May) or braised peas (May). Serve with a light but fine Burgundy: a Savigny-les-Beaune or a non-estate-bottled Gevrey-Chambertin.

3   tablespoons olive oil
2½ pounds very young lamb,
      cut from the leg, boned,
      and cut into 1½-inch cubes
·   flour seasoned lightly with
      salt and freshly ground
      pepper
1   sprig each fresh rosemary
      and sage (or ½ teaspoon
      each dried)
2   cloves garlic
1   tablespoon red wine vinegar
1   cup chicken stock
3   anchovy fillets, finely
      chopped

Preheat the oven to 325 degrees.

Dredge the lamb cubes in the seasoned flour, shaking off any excess. Finely chop together the herbs and the garlic. Heat 2 tablespoons of the olive oil in a small Dutch oven, add the lamb cubes, and brown them over moderately high heat. Sprinkle with the finely chopped herb and garlic mixture, stirring to coat the meat, and continue to cook for 1 to 2 minutes. Pour the vinegar into the pot, immediately cover, and allow it to evaporate. Remove the cover, add the chicken stock, cover again, and place in the oven to cook for about 1 hour or until the lamb is very tender. (This depends on the age of your lamb.)

Meanwhile, heat the remaining tablespoon olive oil in a small skillet, add the anchovy, and cook for a few minutes until the mixture resembles a paste. Stir this paste into the lamb 10 minutes before it has finished cooking.

Pan-Fried Lamb Steaks with Anchovy Sauce
serves four

The flavor of anchovy is most complementary to lamb; this combination is found very often in Provence. Pan-frying any steaks, beef or lamb, produces meat that is very flavorful and juicy provided it is done properly; this takes practice. It is difficult to give exact timing for pan-frying: you must rely on your own judgment. Accompaniments depend on how substantial a meal you are planning: for lighter appetites, try risi e bisi (May), or a Caesar salad (May). Robust alternatives are the potato and artichoke gratin (May) or potatoes with hazelnuts (this month). Try a mature Zinfandel or an Italian or California Barbera: Sebastiani makes a good inexpensive one.

4	anchovy fillets
1	teaspoon grated lemon rind
1	garlic clove
¼	cup parsley
4	tablespoons olive oil
4	lamb steaks, each about ¾ pound, trimmed of excess fat
½	cup heavy cream
·	squeeze lemon juice
·	salt and freshly ground pepper

Chop very finely the anchovy fillets, lemon rind, garlic, and parsley.

Season the lamb steaks lightly with salt and pepper. Heat the olive oil in a large heavy skillet; when the oil is very hot but not yet smoking, add the lamb. Brown the steaks quickly on one side, turn them over, and brown the other side. Reduce the heat and cook the meat for 5 minutes on one side. Turn the steaks over and give them another 4 to 5 minutes. Test for degree of doneness by making a deep cut near the bone to see the color. When the steaks are done to your satisfaction, remove them to a platter and keep warm in an oven set at low heat.

Pour off all but a thin coating of the fat from the skillet, set over moderate heat, and add the chopped anchovy mixture. Stir this into the remaining fat, taking care not to brown it, for 1 to 2 minutes. Add the heavy cream and allow the sauce to reduce slightly. Stir in a bit of lemon juice, taste, and correct the seasoning if necessary.

Pour the sauce over the lamb steaks and serve immediately.

Saute of Lamb with Artichoke Hearts
serves four

This savory saute combines the best of the season: tender, young lamb with artichoke hearts in a lemony sauce. Serve it with a risotto, roast potatoes with rosemary (May) or steamed potatoes with parsley sauce (this month). Serve a robust Chardonnay: a Puligny-Montrachet or a Spring Mountain from California.

2	pounds boned leg of lamb
·	flour, seasoned lightly with salt and freshly ground pepper
4	tablespoons olive oil
½	cup onion, finely chopped
2	cloves garlic, finely chopped
·	finely grated rind of 1 lemon
½	cup dry white vermouth
1	cup chicken stock
1	sprig fresh rosemary or ½ teaspoon dried
½	bay leaf
3	large fresh artichoke hearts, each cut into 6 pieces (see "Artichoke Hearts") for method of trimming) in acidulated water
·	lemon juice

Trim off and discard any fat and gristle from the meat. Cut into 1-inch cubes. Flour the meat, shaking off any excess. Heat the oil in a heavy 10- or 12-inch skillet and add the lamb; brown over high heat and remove. To the remaining oil in the skillet, add the onion, garlic, and lemon rind. Saute the vegetables for about 5 minutes, stirring frequently. Pour in the vermouth and reduce over high heat until it is just a glaze. Put the lamb back into the skillet and add the chicken stock, rosemary, and bay leaf; season lightly with salt and pepper. Simmer the lamb for 1 hour, stirring occasionally.

Drain the artichoke hearts and dry thoroughly. Add them to the lamb and continue to simmer for 25 to 35 minutes until they are tender. Add a bit of lemon juice and season to taste. Serve at once.

Linguini Primavera
serves four to six

A version of springtime pasta with a sauce composed of sauteed onion, julienne of prosciutto, tips of fresh asparagus, heavy cream, and grated Parmesan cheese: hence, despite the delicate name, a substantial dish—too substantial for most appetites as a first course. With a green salad, it is a good light spring meal; a cool, soft Graves will turn it into a feast.

5	tablespoons butter
¼	pound lean prosciutto, cut into julienne
¼	cup onion, minced
·	tips of 1½ pounds asparagus (reserve stalks for another use such as soup)
½	pint heavy cream
·	salt and freshly ground pepper
¼	cup freshly grated Parmesan cheese
1	pound linguini

Melt 2 tablespoons of the butter in a small skillet; add the prosciutto and toss over medium heat for 2 minutes. Add the onion and saute for about 5 minutes until is is soft but not brown. Add the asparagus tips and saute briefly till they are coated with butter; pour in the heavy cream, reduce the heat, and simmer for about 5 minutes. Stir in the cheese just before pouring over the pasta.

Cook the linguini al dente, drain, and put back into the cooking pot with the 3 tablespoons of butter cut into small pieces. Toss the pasta until the butter has melted and put in individual heated soup plates. Stir the grated cheese into the warm sauce and pour some over each serving. Serve with additional grated cheese if desired.

Menu 1
Eggplant Caviar (September)
Cream of Lettuce Soup (April)
Kulebiaka (May)
Cucumbers with Sour Cream (February)
Green Bean Vinaigrette.
Strawberry Fool (June)

Menu 2
Herbed Cheese (May)
Roast Chicken with Rosemary and Garlic (May)
Baked Artichoke Hearts (May)
Italian Rice Salad (August)
Chocolate Truffles Italienne (December)

Caesar Salad
Salad Nicoise
Artichoke Hearts
Artichoke Heart and Cauliflower Salad
Baked Artichoke Hearts
Fried Artichoke Hearts
Stuffed Artichokes
Gratin of Potatoes and Artichoke Hearts
Roast Potatoes with Rosemary and Sage
Braised Peas with Mint
Risi e Bisi
Gravlax
Herbed Cheese
Seviche
Medallions of Pork with Potatoes and Herbs
Roast Chicken with Rosemary and Garlic
Kulebiaka

One of the qualities that marks a fine cook is the ability to season foods well. I use the word "well" rather than "correctly" because seasoning is a highly personal skill, one that is developed slowly as the individual cook becomes acquainted with the flavors of various herbs and spices. Everyone knows a cook who is a whiz at technique, someone who gives a fine performance in the kitchen and whose table settings are divine but whose dishes simply do not taste that good. What is missing is that bit of magic that will transform an ordinary dish into something extraordinary—an adept hand at seasoning.

One of the best ways to learn about seasoning is through experimentation with a variety of ethnic cuisines. Every people has developed preferences through the ages for certain herbs and spices. The Middle Eastern countries favor aromatics like allspice, cinnamon, clove, and mint. The Chinese rely on pungent spices unusual in our Western culture: licorice, star anise, coriander, Szechwan pepper.

The Japanese prefer subtle flavors like those from fresh ginger root and sesame seed. The East Indians lean toward the savory flavors of mustard seed, hot chilies, turmeric, fenugreek, and tamarind. The Spanish employ piquant capers, saffron, orange peel. The Italians favor green herbs like rosemary, sage, oregano, fennel. France makes use of the more delicate chervil, thyme, savory, and tarragon. The Scandinavian countries are fond of the sharp tastes of dill, cardamom, caraway. Very often, the seasonings used in a certain area of our country clearly reflect the national origins of its inhabitants; an excellent example of this is in Louisiana, where the combined influence of France, Spain, Africa, and the West Indies can be felt in the cooking techniques and in the use of a myriad of spices in Creole and Acadian cuisines.

It is a challenge for the budding cook to discover the natural affinities betwen herbs and various foodstuffs; and this study will lead ultimately to the realization that nothing dried or frozen can ever compare in taste or aroma to the fresh herb. It is a pity that only a limited variety of herbs can be purchased fresh, even in large urban centers; and even these are often available only for a short time in the summer. Because of this, most avid cooks have decided to grow their own — not as difficult a task as one might assume. If you do not have access to any plot of ground, remember that herbs grow beautifully in pots. A small, sunny space on my porch is filled with pots of rosemary, summer savory, sage, Italian parsley, dill, basil, three different types of mint, and two of thyme.

In the process of learning the art of seasoning, the obvious combinations must first be utilized. Dill goes with salmon, tarragon with chicken, basil with tomatoes, and so on. Once the reason for these marriages is learned, why one flavor works well with another, you can begin to experiment and to develop your own tastes. When grilling a salmon, use fennel as the major seasoning; its aniselike flavor is most complementary to fish. When roasting a chicken, stuff its belly with a sprig of rosemary and a clove or two of garlic; the resulting flavor is ambrosial. Sprinkle a fresh tomato salad with summer savory or lemon mint in lieu of basil for a refreshing change.

When using fresh herbs, remember that less is more: food should be enhanced and not overpowered by its seasonings. If the only recourse open to you is the use of dried herbs, first taste them; if they have no aroma or very little flavor, omit them from the recipe.

Caesar Salad
serves four

Romaine lettuce, fresh garlic croutons, grated Parmesan cheese tossed with an egg and anchovy dressing, and a whisper of fresh mint.

1   cup fresh bread cubes cut into ½-inch dice (French or sourdough bread)
4   tablespoons olive oil
2 or 3 garlic cloves, peeled but left whole
1   large head romaine lettuce, cleaned and broken into bite-size pieces
1   egg yolk
·   pinch salt
½   teaspoon dry mustard
2   inch squeeze anchovy paste
·   juice of ½ lemon
4   tablespoons olive oil
·   dash Tabasco
·   freshly ground pepper
1   tablespoon fresh mint, chopped
4   tablespoons freshly grated Parmesan cheese

Heat the olive oil in a skillet over medium heat, add the bread cubes and the garlic cloves, and saute, turning the cubes until they are browned and crisp. Drain on paper towels.

Place the romaine in a salad bowl, cover with a dampened paper towel, and chill.

Prepare the dressing: in a small mixing bowl put the egg yolk, a small pinch salt, the dry mustard, and the anchovy paste and stir with a fork or a small whisk. Mix in the lemon juice and add the olive oil slowly, blending well. Season with Tabasco and pepper; taste and add more salt, if necessary. This can be made well in advance of serving time. Remove the salad bowl from the refrigerator and sprinkle with the chopped mint, Parmesan cheese, croutons, and freshly ground pepper. Mix the dressing well and pour only enough of it over the salad to moisten the leaves. Toss gently and serve.

Salad Nicoise
serves four

There must be hundreds of recipes purporting to be the "true" Salad Nicoise. This is definitely not one of them; it is merely a tantalizing combination of the best the

season has to offer. Serve it with crisp French bread and a crock of sweet butter. A crisp Vouvray or a California Chenin Blanc would round out the meal.

98

Vinaigrette dressing:

1   egg yolk
½   teaspoon dry mustard
·   pinch of salt
2-inch-squeeze anchovy paste
2   tablespoons lemon juice
·   dash red wine vinegar
¾   cup fruity olive oil
·   dash Tabasco
1   small garlic clove, put
     through a press
·   freshly ground pepper

Salad:

2   cups new potatoes, peeled
     and sliced
2   large green or red bell
     peppers, roasted (see
     "Roasted Sweet Peppers")
2   large fresh artichoke hearts,
     prepared for cooking (see
     method this month)
2   cups green beans, cut into
     2-inch lengths
1   small red onion, peeled and
     thinly sliced
2   cans (7 ounces each) tuna,
     packed in olive oil and
     drained
2   large ripe tomatoes, cut into
     wedges
4   hardboiled eggs, cut into
     wedges
2-ounce can anchovy fillets,
     drained and separated
½   cup imported black olives

First, prepare the dressing: in a small mixing bowl, place the egg yolk, the dry mustard, a small pinch of salt, and the anchovy paste; mix well. Add the lemon juice and vinegar, stirring, then the olive oil, Tabasco, and pressed garlic; mix again. Season with a few grinds of pepper; taste and adjust if necessary. Set aside.

Cook the potato slices until just tender, drain them thoroughly, and dress while still hot with a little of the vinaigrette. Cut the roasted bell peppers into thick strips and dress them with a little of the vinaigrette.

Cut the artichoke hearts into 8 pieces each, cook in acidulated water until just tender, drain well, and dress with a little vinaigrette.

Cook the green beans until just tender, run them under cold water to stop the cooking process, and drain thoroughly. Dress them with a little vinaigrette.

To assemble: line a large platter with the lettuce leaves, arrange on top of them first the potatoes, then the bell pepper strips, then the artichoke hearts, then the green beans. Scatter the onion rings over the top and mound the tuna over them. Surround this with alternating wedges of tomato and egg, garnish the wedges with anchovy fillets, and scatter the black olives over all. Dress the tomato and egg wedges with a bit of the remaining dressing and serve.

Artichoke Hearts
Preparation for Cooking

Artichokes are consumed in countless forms, many of which use only the most succulent part, the heart, and that is what we are concerned with here.

Have a bowl of acidulated water ready in which to place the cleaned hearts. (They may be kept from darkening in this manner for an hour or two before cooking, but remember to drain them well.) Begin by bending back and snapping off close to the base each of the outer green leaves, allowing only the whitish, tender bottom of each leaf to remain (this is the edible portion). Keep snapping off leaves until you reach a center cone of leaves that are a pale greenish-white. Slice this off close to the base. (I find it better to work with a stainless steel paring knife because the artichoke discolors so rapidly.)

Cut the exposed base in half to make it easy to remove any inner leaves and to cut the choke (the fuzzy hairs growing out of the base); be careful not to cut away too much of the heart itself. Pare away the green outer parts of the leaves remaining on the outside and also peel the tough skin from the stem, which should always be left on. Slice as directed in the individual recipe and immediately drop into the acidulated water.

Artichoke Heart and Cauliflower Salad
serves four to six

Both vegetables are dressed while still warm with vinegar and olive oil. Look for a small, very young cauliflower with a base colored a pale shade of green for the best flavor. Try this with a rich fish dish like gravlax (this month).

2   large artichokes
1   tablespoon lemon juice
1   small young cauliflower
1   tablespoon red wine vinegar
3   tablespoons fruity olive oil
·   salt and freshly ground pepper

Cut the hearts of the artichokes into slices ½ inch thick and drop into boiling, salted water to which 1 tablespoon lemon juice has been added. Cook over moderately high heat for 8 to 10 minutes or until just tender.

While the hearts are cooking, separate the cauliflower into bite-size pieces and place in a pot of boiling, salted water; cook for 8 to 10 minutes or until just tender.

Drain both vegetables well,

place in warm serving bowl, add the vinegar, oil, salt, and pepper, and toss well. Serve immediately.

Baked Artichoke Hearts
serves four

If you have never tasted a fresh artichoke heart, you have a wonderful surprise in store for you. This is a very simple way to prepare them but the results are ambrosial. It is traditionally served with roast meat, but is just as delicious with squid and seafood stew (March).

2   large artichokes
¼   cup fruity olive oil
1 or 2 large cloves garlic, peeled
1   tablespoon parsley, minced
·   salt and freshly ground pepper

Preheat oven to 350 degrees.

Slice each heart (already cut into halves) into 6 thick pieces. Place them in a shallow, ovenproof dish and drizzle with the olive oil, turning them to coat. Shred the garlic over them, sprinkle with the parsley, and salt and pepper to taste. Cover the dish tightly with foil and bake for 35 to 40 minutes, removing the foil for the last 10 minutes of baking to lightly brown the hearts. They should be tender enough to offer no resistance to a knife when done. Serve immediately as a first or vegetable course.

Fried Artichoke Hearts
serves four

Catherine dei Medici was credited with introducing the artichoke, her favorite vegetable, to France. It is recorded that she especially doted on the hearts when fried, and on one occasion she consumed such an enormous number of the succulent morsels that she almost burst. You have been warned. This dish, too, goes best with simple roasts.

2   large artichokes
2   tablespoons lemon juice
·   flour for dredging
1   egg, lightly beaten

·   light vegetable oil such as safflower or corn oil
·   salt
·   lemon wedges

Preheat oven to 200 degrees.

Add the lemon juice to a bowl of cold water.

Cut the artichoke hearts into slices ½ inch thick and drop them immediately into the water. When you have finished slicing them all, drain well.

Have ready a skillet containing ½ inch of oil standing over moderately high heat. Flour each piece of the heart heavily, transfer it to the beaten egg to coat thoroughly, and drop into the hot oil. Let the hearts brown on one side, then turn over and brown the other side. The whole cooking process should take no longer than 2 to 3 minutes. Do not overcook or they will become mushy. Remove the fried hearts to a plate and keep warm in the oven until all are done. Sprinkle them with salt and serve with lemon wedges.

Stuffed Artichokes
serves four

These stuffed artichokes are too rich to serve as a first course; however, they make a splendid light entree for lunch or a light supper. A good-quality canned tuna or fresh crabmeat may be substituted for the shrimp as an interesting variation.

4	large artichokes
4	tablespoons olive oil
1	cup onion, finely chopped
½	cup celery, finely chopped
2	large garlic cloves, peeled and finely chopped
½	pound Pacific shrimp, cooked (do not use canned)
2	cups fresh breadcrumbs
1	cup grated Parmesan or mixture of Parmesan and Romano cheeses
·	pinch dried hot pepper flakes or dash Tabasco
·	salt
½	tablespoon finely grated lemon rind
¼	cup parsley, finely chopped
1	egg, lightly beaten

Trim off and discard the stems and any small bottom leaves of the artichokes. With kitchen shears, cut off about ¼ inch of each lower leaf; using a sharp knife cut off about 1 inch of the top. Bring a large pot of salted water to a boil; add 1 tablespoon olive oil, drop in the artichokes, and cook for about 20 minutes. Remove them, invert them in a colander to allow them to drain, and discard all but 1 cup of their cooking liquid.

When the artichokes are cool enough to handle, gently spread the leaves until you have reached the center. Remove the choke with a spoon or a grapefruit knife and discard it. Set the artichokes aside while you prepare the stuffing. Preheat the oven to 350 degrees.

Heat 3 tablespoons of olive oil in a skillet, add the onion, celery, and garlic, and saute over medium heat about 5 minutes until the vegetables are tender but not brown. Remove from the heat and stir in the shrimp meat, breadcrumbs, and grated cheese and season with the hot pepper flakes, salt, lemon rind, and parsley. Stir in the beaten egg to bind.

Divide the stuffing into 4 parts. Stuff each artichoke center with half its alloted share; use the remaining stuffing as follows: gently pull each large leaf away from the body and place about 1 teaspoon of stuffing in the pocket. When finished, press the leaves back in shape. Continue until all 4 artichokes are stuffed.

Place the artichokes in a pot (with lid) large enough to hold them in one layer. Around them pour the reserved cooking liquids, cover, and bake for about 30 minutes or until just tender. Serve at once.

Gratin of Potatoes and Artichoke Hearts
serves four

The combination of potatoes and artichoke hearts is an especially pleasing accompaniment to roast lamb, veal, or chicken. Try it also without the artichokes but richly laced with garlic.

4   cups artichoke hearts (about
     4 large artichokes)
     sliced ¼ inch thick
5   cups new potatoes, peeled
     and sliced ¼ inch thick
·   salt and freshly ground
     pepper
1   cup grated Swiss cheese (the
     imported variety has the
     best flavor)
3   tablespoons breadcrumbs
1   tablespoon butter
½   pint heavy cream

Preheat the oven to 375 degrees.

First, prepare the artichoke hearts and keep them in acidulated water while you peel and slice the potatoes; then drain and dry the hearts thoroughly. Butter a shallow gratin pan (for this recipe, I use an oval one measuring 14 by 8 inches). On the bottom put a layer of half the artichoke hearts; season them with salt and pepper and sprinkle one quarter of the cheese on them. On top of them place a layer of half the potatoes, seasoning and adding cheese as before; continue for 2 more layers. Mix the remaining cheese with the bread crumbs and coat the top heavily with this mixture. Cut the butter into small pieces and dot the top with them. Pour the cream into the dish around the edges. Place in the middle level of the oven and bake for 45 to 50 minutes, until the top is crisp and brown and the vegetables are tender. Serve immediately.

Roast Potatoes with Rosemary and Sage
serves four

These potatoes are as crisp and brown as if they were deep-fried and their flavor is ambrosial, particularly with lamb or steak. Dried herbs can replace the fresh ones if absolutely necessary; in that case reduce their quantity by half.

6   medium baking potatoes, peeled
1   tablespoon each fresh rosemary and sage, finely chopped
·   salt and freshly ground pepper
⅓   cup olive oil

Preheat the oven to 375 degrees.

Cut each of the potatoes in half, then cut each of the halves into thick wedges. Place the potato wedges in a mixing bowl, add the herbs, salt, pepper, and olive oil, and mix with your hands, making sure each wedge is coated with oil and herbs.

Place the potatoes with their oil in a lightweight, shallow ovenproof container large enough to hold them all in a single layer. Place the pan in the middle of the oven and bake for about 1 hour, turning the potatoes occasionally so they are evenly browned.

Braised Peas with Mint
serves four

There is nothing more heavenly than young sweet peas simmered in butter, chicken stock, and a little fresh mint.

2   pounds sweet peas, unshelled
4   tablespoons butter
1½   cups chicken stock, lightly seasoned
·   salt and freshly ground pepper
1   teaspoon fresh mint, finely chopped

Shell the peas only when ready to cook them. Melt the butter in a heavy saucepan; add the peas and stir to coat them with the butter. Saute over low heat for about 3 minutes, then add the chicken stock, salt, and pepper, and bring to a boil. Reduce the heat and cook the peas, at a simmer, for 10 to 15 minutes, depending on their age. During the last few minutes of cooking, stir in the mint. When the peas are done the liquid should be reduced almost to a glaze. Taste for seasoning and serve at once.

Risi e Bisi (Risotto with fresh peas)
serves four

A tasty combination of fresh peas and rice cooked together in chicken broth and seasoned with onion, garlic, and a bit of grated lemon rind. Makes a delicious accompaniment to lamb, chicken, or veal.

2½ cups chicken stock, well flavored
2½ tablespoons butter
2 tablespoons onion, finely chopped
1 garlic clove, finely chopped
1½ teaspoons lemon rind, finely grated
1¼ cups fresh peas, shelled (about 1 pound)
¾ cup short-grain Italian rice
⅓ cup dry white vermouth
1 tablespoon butter, softened
⅓ cup grated Parmesan or mixture of Parmesan and Romano cheeses

Place the chicken stock in a small saucepan and keep it at a simmer over low heat.

In a 1½-quart heavy saucepan melt the butter, add the onion and garlic, and saute over low heat for about 8 minutes until the onion turns golden. Add the lemon rind, peas, and rice and stir until all are well coated with butter. Cook for a few minutes until the rice takes on color, add the vermouth, and stir occasionally with a fork (a spoon makes the grains of rice stick together) until the liquid is absorbed.

Add 1 cup of the warm stock and allow this to be absorbed into the rice over low heat, stirring with a fork occasionally. Add the next cup of stock and repeat. Do not add any more liquid to the risotto until all of the previous liquid is absorbed. When the last half-cup of stock is absorbed, the rice and peas should be tender. Stir in the softened butter, grated cheese, and salt and pepper to taste. Serve immediately.

Gravlax
serves eight to ten

Fresh salmon marinated in salt and dill and served with a mustard sauce: a longtime favorite in the Scandinavian community in the Northwest. Gravlax is traditionally served as part of a smorgasbord accompanied by a mustard and dill sauce. With the snow pea and watercress salad (April), it could well serve as a main dish. Such fish dishes present problems in the wine department: here a soft Pinot Grigio or a Tocai d'Alsace would serve best.

3 to 3½ pounds center cut fresh salmon, cleaned and scaled
1 large bunch fresh dill
¼ cup coarse salt (Kosher or sea salt)
¼ to ½ cup sugar
2 tablespoons white peppercorns, crushed

Ask the fish dealer to cut the salmon in half lengthwise and to remove the backbone and the small bones. Put half of the fish, skin side down, in a wide, deep glass, enamel, or stainless-steel baking dish or casserole. Wash and then shake dry the bunch of dill and place it on the fish. (If the dill is of the hot-house variety and not very pungent, chop the herb coarsely to release its flavor and sprinkle it over the fish instead.)

In a separate bowl, combine the salt, sugar to taste, and the crushed peppercorns. Sprinkle this mixture evenly over the dill. Top with the other half of the fish, skin side up.

Cover the fish with aluminum foil, then set on top of it a heavy platter slightly larger than the salmon. Pile the platter with 3 or 4 cans of food; these make convenient weights that are easy to distribute evenly.

Refrigerate for 48 hours or up to 3 days; turn the fish over every 12 hours, basting with the liquid marinade that accumulates; separate the halves of fish a little to baste inside and replace the platter and weights each time.

When the gravlax is finished, remove the fish from its marinade, scrape away the dill and seasonings, and pat it dry with paper towels. Place the separated halves skin side down on a carving board and slice the salmon thinly on the diagonal, detaching each slice from the skin.

Mustard and Dill Sauce for Gravlax
makes approximately ¾ cup

4 tablespoons dark, highly seasoned prepared mustard
1 teaspoon powdered mustard
3 tablespoons sugar
2 tablespoons white vinegar
⅓ cup vegetable oil
3 tablespoons fresh dill, chopped

In a small, deep bowl, mix the two mustards, sugar, and vinegar to a paste. With a wire whisk, slowly beat in the oil until it forms a thick mayonnaiselike emulsion. Stir in the chopped dill. The sauce may be refrigerated in a tightly covered jar for several days, but it probably will need to be shaken vigorously or beaten with a whisk to remix the ingredients before serving.

Herbed Cheese

serves six to eight

This is one of my favorite summer appetizers, an herbed cream cheese much like Boursin but without the accompanying price tag. Fresh herbs are essential; even if you add only two or three of those recommended, you will be amazed by the fine flavor. I like a mixture of thyme, summer savory, chives, sage, and parsley. The addition of feta cheese takes the taste beyond the ordinary as well as giving a slight tang that you will find most appealing. With a good cracker or bread and a fragrant Gewurztraminer this dish serves well on the summer patio or more formally as a first course.

2   tablespoons fresh herbs, minced
½   pound feta cheese (Greek style)
½   pound cream cheese
1   tablespoon heavy cream (optional)
·   freshly ground black pepper
·   dash of cayenne pepper
1   large clove garlic, put through a press

Put the feta cheese, cut into chunks, in the container of a food processor and process until creamy. Add the cream cheese and blend together until well combined. Remove and place in a serving bowl, adding the cream if the mixture seems too thick (remember that it will thicken when it is chilled).

Add the black pepper and cayenne to taste, the garlic paste, and minced fresh herbs; mix in thoroughly. (Herbs minced by hand are far superior.) Chill for at least ½ hour. This mixture will keep, tightly covered in the refrigerator, for about a week.

Variation: Use 2 tablespoons coarsely chopped green peppercorns (packed in water) instead of the fresh herbs.

Seviche

serves four as first course

Seviche, a dish originating in Peru, uses a technique that appears also in other cuisines; the raw fish is "cooked" by marinating it overnight in citrus juice. Seviche incorporates a paste of fresh hot green chilies and fresh coriander, giving the fish a mellow and slightly peppery tang.

Fresh coriander has a rather musty, assertive flavor and you will either love it at once or never wish to smell or taste it again. Commonly used throughout the world, coriander leaves can be found in the markets of Morocco, China, the Middle East, India, South America, and Mexico: May is too early to find coriander at your supermarket, but it is readily available in many Asian shops.

The type of fish called for here is a firm-fleshed whitefish such as red snapper, lingcod, rock cod, sea bass, or striped bass. Shrimp and scallops are also excellent when treated in this manner and very often I like to use a mixture of fish and shellfish.

Seviche makes a grand first course to a simple roast, but today's lighter appetites may well find it perfectly satisfactory as a main course for a light lunch. Serve with a good sourdough bread and unsalted butter, with perhaps a cream of lettuce soup (April) and a simple white wine to round it out. Try an Entre-Deux-Mers from Bordeaux.

1½ pounds firm-fleshed fish, skin and bones removed
3 fresh hot green chilies, each about 3 inches long
1 small bunch fresh coriander
1 large clove garlic, peeled
· salt
· juice of 4 to 5 fresh limes
1 small red onion, peeled, cut in half, and sliced paper-thin
2 tablespoons fresh orange juice
5 tablespoons fruity olive oil
· freshly ground pepper
1 or 2 whole ears of corn, cooked
· black olives
· lettuce leaves

Cube the fish into bite-sized chunks and place them in a glass or ceramic bowl. Cut the chilies in half; remove the seeds and discard them. Cut the flesh of the chilies in half again and mince together with about a quarter of the coriander and the garlic until you have a pastelike texture. Use either a chef's knife or a mortar and pestle; quite a bit of the flavor of an herb is lost if it is minced in a blender or food processor.

Add the chili mixture to the fish, sprinkle with salt, and add the lime juice—just barely enough to cover the contents of the bowl. Cover tightly and refrigerate for 24 hours.

Pour the fish into a sieve and drain thoroughly, reserving 1 tablespoon of the marinade. Mix the fish with the sliced onion, sprinkle with the reserved marinade, and add the orange juice, vinegar, more salt, and pepper. Mix gently but thoroughly and set aside.

Using a very sharp knife, slice the corn into rounds right through the cob. Mound the seviche on lettuce leaves and garnish with the corn, olives, and the remaining coriander.

Medallions of Pork with Potatoes and Herbs
serves four

Medallions are similar to tiny fillet steaks; they should be cut from the end of the loin. Or boned loin chops may be used. There are many satisfying alternatives for accompaniments: asparagus in egg-lemon sauce (April), braised peas (this month), and dandelion salad (April) are just a few of the possibilities in this book. Nothing too fancy with this homely dish: a St. Julien from Bordeaux is just the ticket.

3   tablespoons butter
1   teaspoon vegetable oil
1½ pounds pork loin slices, ½ inch thick
2   medium onions, peeled, cut in half, and thinly sliced
8 to 10 small new potatoes, peeled and sliced ¼ inch thick
2   tablespoons each fresh thyme and sage, finely chopped with
2 to 3 cloves of garlic
·   salt and freshly ground pepper to taste
1½ to 2 cups chicken stock, lightly seasoned

Preheat the oven to 375 degrees.

Melt the butter with the oil in a large heavy skillet set over high heat, add the pork slices, and brown them quickly on both sides. Reserve. Put the onions into the remaining fat and saute them until they have reached the melting stage, about 15 minutes. Reserve. Put the potatoes in a pot of boiling, salted water and cook them for 5 minutes; remove from the water and allow to drain well.

Butter the inside of a deep ovenproof casserole with a lid. In it place a layer of potatoes, sprinkling them with a bit of the herb and garlic mixture, salt, and pepper. Over this layer put half the onions; then place the pork slices on top, sprinkling them with the herb mixture and salt and pepper. Cover with the rest of the onions and the remaining potato slices, seasoning with herbs, salt, and pepper.

Cover the layers with enough chicken stock to reach almost midway up the side of the container. Cover the container and bake in the middle of the oven for about 40 minutes or until the pork is tender. Remove from oven and serve at once.

Roast Chicken with Rosemary and Garlic

serves four

Although most roast chicken recipes call for tarragon, you will find that the combination of rosemary and garlic used here lends a delicious, subtle, and highly aromatic flavor. The chicken is roasted at a slightly higher temperature than usual, which results in a beautifully brown, crisp skin and moist, tender meat. It can be served hot from the oven, but I find it most appealing when just slightly warm.

This is one of the most flexible of dishes: try it with baked artichoke hearts (this month) for one effect, with a salad Nicoise (this month) for another, with potatoes in pesto sauce or Italian rice salad (both August) for yet others. A good Muscadet or, even better, a Pouilly Fume, is a superb complement.

2½ - to 3-pound chicken
½   lemon
3 or 4 sprigs fresh rosemary
4   cloves garlic, unpeeled and left whole
3   tablespoons butter
·   salt and freshly ground pepper
1   tablespoon dry white vermouth

Preheat the oven to 425 degrees.

Wipe the chicken inside and out with the cut side of a lemon. Dry the outside of the bird with paper toweling. Into the cavity put 1 or 2 sprigs of fresh rosemary, the garlic cloves, 1 tablespoon butter, and a light sprinkling of salt and pepper.

Truss the chicken tightly, making sure the legs and wings are tied close to the body. Sprinkle the outside of the bird with a little salt and pepper and the remainder of the rosemary, finely chopped. Place the chicken in a shallow ovenproof roasting pan.

In a small pan melt the remaining 2 tablespoons butter with the vermouth. Baste the chicken with a little of this mixture and put in the oven. The chicken will take about an hour to roast and must be basted with the butter and vermouth every 10 or 15 minutes. Remove from the oven when done, cover (not too tightly) with foil, and let stand for an hour before serving.

Kulebiaka

serves six to eight

Kulebiaka, one of the world's most elegant dishes, has its origins in the peasant kitchen. It began as a coarse mixture of salmon, rice, mushrooms, and eggs (sometimes cabbage, onions, and eggs) encased in a breadlike pastry. The French took this dish some degrees higher by adding refinements to the filling and using a brioche dough for the casing. My version uses a cream cheese pastry, which has a rich and flaky texture somewhat like puff paste. This is a tricky pastry to handle; it must be kept chilled and worked quickly or it becomes sticky.

I have suggested adding the fillings in layers, giving a more pleasing visual effect and allowing each ingredient to stand on its own while subtly blending with the others.

If there is any pastry left over, it can be frozen and used to make miniature pirozhkis, small turnovers filled with ground lamb or beef, minced onion, and minced hardboiled egg and seasoned with a bit of curry powder.

This is an ideal dish for spring or summer picnics. If you are going to go to the trouble involved in making this elaborate dish, the best wine is none too good: take along a delicate blanc des blancs champagne, the best Alsatian Riesling you can find, or a good-quality California Riesling.

PASTRY:

12	ounces cream cheese
3	sticks sweet butter (¾ pound)
3	cups unbleached white flour
½	teaspoon salt

FILLING:

Salmon mixture:

	2-pound piece of fresh salmon, poached (reserve 1 cup poaching liquid for duxelles mixture)
.	juice of 1 lemon
2	tablespoons capers, coarsely chopped

Duxelles mixture:

3	tablespoons butter
1	cup onions, peeled and finely chopped
1	garlic clove, peeled and finely chopped
.	pinch of sugar
½	pound mushrooms, cleaned and finely chopped
2	tablespoons flour
1	cup reserved poaching liquid from the salmon
1	tablespoon lemon juice
2	tablespoons fresh dill, finely chopped
.	salt and freshly ground pepper

Rice mixture:

½   cup rice, cooked
1   tablespoon fresh dill, finely
    chopped
·   salt and a dash of cayenne
    pepper to taste

Topping:

2   hardboiled eggs, shelled and
    coarsely chopped
1   tablespoon melted butter
    mixed with
¼   teaspoon mild curry powder

Egg glaze for pastry:

1   egg yolk mixed with
1   teaspoon water

The night before, make the
pastry. Mix together until
creamy the thoroughly chilled
butter and cream cheese (both
cut into chunks), using a pastry
blender or an electric mixer. Sift
in the flour and salt and work it
in with a pastry blender until a
dough is formed. Divide the
dough into 2 parts, one slightly
larger than the other, sprinkle
with a little flour, wrap in
waxed paper, and chill
overnight in the refrigerator.

The next day, poach the salmon
(see method at "Potted
Salmon"), reserving 1 cup of the
poaching liquid for later use.
Skin and carefully bone the fish

and break into large flakes. Mix
the salmon with the lemon juice
and capers and set aside.

Melt the 3 tablespoons butter in
a skillet, add the onions and
garlic, sprinkle with a pinch of
sugar, and saute over medium
heat for about 5 minutes. Add
the mushrooms, turn the heat to
high, and saute until all excess
moisture is drawn off the
mushrooms, taking care not to
burn the mixture.

Remove from heat and add the
flour, mixing it well into the
mushrooms, then add ½ cup of
the reserved poaching liquid.
Place the skillet back over
medium heat and stir until the
mixture becomes thick. (The
consistency should be a loose
paste; if it is too thick, add a bit
more broth.) Add the lemon
juice, dill, salt, and pepper and
mix well; set aside.

Allow the cooked rice to cool
slightly. Mix in the butter, dill,
salt, and cayenne and mix well.
Reserve.

While the salmon is poaching,
let the pastry sit at room
temperature for about 15
minutes. Preheat the oven to
400 degrees. Roll out the smaller
piece of dough, using a floured
pastry cloth and floured rolling
pin cover. (This pastry tends to
become extremely sticky if
handled in any other manner.)
The dough should be about ⅛
inch thick when rolled out. You
may cut it into any shape

desired: I usually make it into an 11-inch circle. Place the dough directly on a greased rimless baking sheet.

Spread the rice mixture evenly over the circle to within ½ inch of the edge. Over the rice spread half of the duxelles mixture, using a wet metal spatula to facilitate spreading. Cover this with all of the salmon, mounding it slightly in the center. Cover in turn with the remaining half of the duxelles. Top this with the chopped eggs and sprinkle with the curry butter.

Roll out the remaining pastry, using the same methods, and cut into a 13-inch circle. Moisten the exposed ½-inch rim of the base with a little water and place the 13-inch circle on top, pinching the upper and lower layers together with your fingers or a fork to seal. Trim off any excess. Using a pastry brush, paint the dough with the egg glaze. This will allow the pie to turn a lovely golden brown when baked. Cut a small circle out of the top of the pie and insert an inverted pastry tip to act as a funnel.

Bake about 25 minutes or until golden brown. Remove from oven and let cool for 45 minutes before serving. The entire pie may be assembled and baked earlier in the day and lightly warmed in a 300-degree oven for 20 minutes before serving.

June, Fresh Fruit

Menu 1
Warren's Gazpacho (June)
Chicken Majorca (June)
Saffron Rice
Green Bean and Lemon Saute (June)
Cream Cheese Mousse with Raspberry Sauce (June)

Menu 2
Quiche Orientale (August)
Cutlets Pojarski (June)
Buttered Noodles
Watercress and Snow Pea Salad (April)
Strawberry Tart (June)

Tomato Sherbet
Green Bean and Lemon Saute
Green Bean and Pepper Saute
Warren's Gazpacho
Eggplant Parmigiana
Green Bean Puree
Chicken Hunter's Style
Chicken Majorca
Chicken Curry
Cutlets Pojarski
Cream Cheese Mousse with Raspberry Sauce
Raspberry Tart
Strawberries in Orange Cups
Raspberries in Cassis
Peaches in Vouvray
Fruit Fools
Strawberry Fool
Peach Fool
Peaches with Raspberry Fool
Strawberry Tart

Fresh fruit is available almost throughout the entire year. Fruit that is shipped over hundreds and sometimes thousands of miles. Fruit that is ripened in transit, or perhaps never ripened at all. Fruit that is raised for its visual appeal and to hell with flavor.

There are many different fruit varieties that are being "phased out" of existence simply because they do not resemble the apparently perfect product the normal consumer is programmed to purchase. The lesson to be learned here is to purchase local fruit — and vegetables too — in season. In most cases, local produce can be on your table the same day it was picked, and its flavor is always unbeatable. I don't believe I have ever tasted finer strawberries than the unbelievably dark crimson, almost black variety that is grown in the Northwest. Another local specialty is the Babcock peach — the skin colored in shades of creamy, pale yellows and pinks reminding one of an Impressionist painting, the flesh delicate and unforgettable. In Seattle it is not a difficult task to patronize the local farmers. One need only visit the Pike Place Market to find the best of local produce. Or you may spend a day in the sun, picking berries at a local farm: surely a fitting way to celebrate the return of summer.

Once having found the best fresh fruit, the question is, how to serve it? Ripe fruit in its prime should be enjoyed as such and not tampered with. "Serve it simply" is the rule: fill a bowl with strawberries or raspberries and accompany them with a French triple-cream cheese. Or take the same berries and arrange them in a fruit tart. Prepare an uncooked raspberry or strawberry sauce to pour over a cream cheese mousse or concoct a fruit fool flavored with the puree of over-ripe berries. Orange shells may be hollowed out and filled with sliced strawberries mixed with a little creme Anglaise.

Peaches seem too delicate to pair with cheese; I like them served with a chilled bottle of Vouvray, or if they are very ripe, sliced and left to steep in this slightly sweet and flowery-tasting wine. If you are fond of zabaglione, that frothy cloud of egg yolks and Marsala, you will find it even more appealing when chilled and combined with sliced ripe peaches or raspberries. Pair the large black Bing cherries with a creamy Munster cheese for a simple after-dinner feast, or drizzle a little anisette liqueur over cubes of ripe melon for a refreshing combination that is much favored in Spain. When you have access to fruit that has such fine flavor, it seems a shame to do too much more to it: allow its flavor to speak for itself.

In this chapter and in those that follow, you will find many dishes that rely on pastry for their base. There is, admittedly, a knack to making good pastry. This is not difficult to learn but it does take practice.

With the proliferation of food processors now being sold, it is not unlikely that many cooks have never prepared a pastry shell by hand. This is a method that every cook should know. If you have not learned the prerequisites for a good pastry done by hand, how will you recognize one that is made in a machine? Every cook should master at least one pastry, and master that one really well. You will find that once you've learned just one aspect of pastry-making, you will feel little or no trepidation attempting another.

Of major importance when attempting pastry is correct equipment. I find a pastry blender irreplaceable; I never could (and still cannot) blend the necessary fat into the flour with a fork, a knife, or my fingers. A pastry blender, which may be purchased for a dollar or two, will assist you in producing the perfect pastry shell. Another boon to the pastry maker is the pastry cloth and rolling pin cover, often sold as a set. If you do not possess a marble slab, and few of us do, the cloth will completely discourage the pastry from sticking either to your working surface or to your rolling pin.

A few final tips: use only unbleached flour for pastries; they will be much easier to handle. Always make sure any fat (butter, lard, etc.) is thoroughly chilled: the reward will be greater flakiness. The less you handle a pastry the more tender it is likely to be, so do not over-work the dough, and allow it to rest, chilled, after preparation and after rolling out.

Tomato Sherbet
serves four

An unusual and deliciously refreshing first course. Serve mounded in scooped-out lemon halves. For an elaborate summer meal, this dish would make a superb entremet; it is really too fragile to serve with another course as a side dish.

2   tablespoons olive oil
2   tablespoons onion, finely chopped
1¼ pounds fresh ripe tomatoes, peeled, seeded, and coarsely chopped
4   leaves fresh basil, finely chopped
·   salt and freshly ground pepper
·   pinch of allspice
1   cup mayonnaise made with lemon juice instead of vinegar
1   tablespoon lemon juice

¼   cup heavy cream, lightly whipped
·   dash Tabasco
·   pinch of sugar (optional)

Heat the olive oil in a skillet, add the onion, and saute for about 5 minutes. Add the tomatoes, basil, salt, pepper, and allspice and raise the heat to reduce quickly any liquid released by the tomatoes. Reduce heat and simmer 15 to 20 minutes, until they form a thick sauce. Remove from heat and allow to cool slightly.

Place the cooked tomatoes in the container of a food processor fitted with the steel knife blade and blend to a fine puree. Mix this puree into the mayonnaise along with the lemon juice and heavy cream. Season with the Tabasco and salt and pepper to taste (a pinch of sugar may be necessary here if your tomatoes are not very ripe). Pour this mixture into ice trays (or other shallow containers) and freeze for at least 5 hours.

Green Bean and Lemon Saute
serves four

1	pound green beans, cut into 3-inch lengths
2	tablespoons butter
·	the zest of 1 lemon
·	juice of ¼ lemon
·	salt and freshly ground pepper

Put the beans into boiling, salted water and cook for 6 to 8 minutes. Pour into a colander, refresh under cold water, and drain well. Melt the butter in a skillet, add the beans, lemon zest and juice, salt, and pepper and saute over medium heat for 3 to 4 minutes, tossing well. Serve immediately.

Green Bean and Pepper Saute
serves four to six

1	pound green beans, cut into 3-inch lengths
2	medium green peppers, seeded and cut into julienne
2½	tablespoons butter
¾	cup onion, finely sliced
·	small pinch sugar

Put the beans into boiling, salted water and cook for 6 to 8 minutes, pour into a colander, refresh under cold running water, and drain well. Blanch the julienne strips of green pepper in boiling water for 1 minute, immediately plunge them into cold water, and drain well.

Melt the butter in a skillet set over medium heat, add the onions, sprinkle with a small pinch of sugar, and saute for 5 minutes. Add the beans and the peppers and cook only long enough to heat the vegetables through; they should still be crisp. Season with salt and freshly ground pepper.

Warren's Gazpacho
serves four to six

What this recipe lacks in authenticity, it more than makes up for in flavor and originality. It should be presented as a first course in a glass container (a two-quart glass souffle dish would be suitable), showing each of the vegetables in its individual layers. Use only your finest chicken stock and degrease it thoroughly.

1   teaspoon saffron
4   cups chicken stock
2   small green or red bell peppers, seeded and cut into small dice
2   medium new potatoes, peeled and cut into small dice
2   bunches scallions, thinly sliced (use only a little of the green tops)
2   large ripe tomatoes, peeled, seeded, and cut into small dice
2   small unwaxed (local) cucumbers, not peeled but seeded and cut into small dice; or substitute an English cucumber (always having an unwaxed skin)
·   salt and freshly ground pepper
6   tablespoons mild white wine vinegar
4   cloves garlic, put through a press
·   olive oil
·   lemon wedges

Heat ½ cup of the chicken stock and pour it over the saffron; allow to steep for 1 hour.

There should be about 2 cups each of the peppers, potatoes, tomatoes and cucumbers and 1½ cups of scallions. Layer the vegetables, in any order you prefer, in a 2-quart or larger glass container, seasoning each layer lightly with salt and pepper. Combine the saffron in its stock with the remaining 3½ cups of stock and stir in the vinegar and the garlic pulp. Pour the stock carefully over the vegetables so as not to disturb the layers and refrigerate overnight to marinate.

Serve the gazpacho in small, individual bowls and pass a cruet of olive oil and the lemon wedges so that guests may season their own.

Eggplant Parmigiana
serves four to six

My version of this dish, slightly unorthodox, covers the eggplant slices with a crisp breadcrumb crust, overlaps them, fills the space in between with a dense, homemade tomato sauce, and coats the top lightly with a bechamel sauce thickened with Parmesan cheese. It is baked just long enough to allow the ingredients to heat through.

This dish may be served as a main course with the addition of a good French or Italian bread, green beans in a lemon and oil dressing, and fruit and cheese for dessert. It may also be used as a vegetable course.

Tomato sauce:

1   tablespoon olive oil
2   tablespoons onion, finely chopped
1   clove garlic, finely chopped
·   pinch of sugar
3   cups tomatoes, skinned, peeled, and finely chopped
·   pinch allspice
·   pinch of mild chili powder
·   salt and freshly ground pepper

Eggplant:

1½-pound eggplant, unpeeled and cut into slices ½ inch thick
·   flour, seasoned lightly with salt and pepper
1   egg, lightly beaten
·   breadcrumbs
·   vegetable oil for frying

Parmigiana sauce:

1   tablespoon butter
1   tablespoon flour
1   cup milk
·   pinch each of grated nutmeg and cayenne pepper
·   scant ½ cup grated Parmesan cheese

First prepare the tomato sauce: heat the oil in a saucepan and saute the onion and garlic for 5 minutes, add the tomatoes, sprinkle with a pinch of sugar, allspice, chili powder, salt, and pepper, and bring to a boil. Reduce the heat and simmer the sauce over moderate heat for about 45 minutes or until it thickens. It should be of spreading consistency. Cover and set aside.

Preheat the oven to 400 degrees.

Coat the eggplant slices first with the seasoned flour, then dip into the beaten egg, and last coat heavily with the breadcrumbs. Repeat this procedure until all the eggplant slices are breaded. Place the slices in the refrigerator: the chilling will help the breadcrumbs to adhere.

Meanwhile, prepare the parmigiana sauce: heat the butter in a saucepan; when it is melted add the flour and blend it into the butter with a wire whisk. Cook over low heat for 5 minutes; do not allow the roux to brown. Add the milk, stirring all the while, and bring to a boil. Reduce the heat and cook until the sauce is thickened. Season with the nutmeg and cayenne, and add the cheese, stirring until it has melted. Taste and season with salt, if necessary. Cover with a round of waxed paper placed directly on the surface of the sauce and set aside.

Heat enough vegetable oil to just cover the bottom of a large heavy skillet. Add the eggplant and fry it a few slices at a time until golden brown (2 or 3 minutes on each side), adding more oil as needed. Drain the cooked slices on absorbent paper.

To assemble: lightly butter an ovenproof platter about 14 inches long. Place the smallest slice of eggplant at one end of the platter and spread with some of the tomato sauce; place the next largest slice overlapping on top of this and again spread with some of the tomato sauce. Continue in this manner until you have reassembled the entire eggplant.

Remove the waxed paper from the parmigiana sauce and spoon it over the center of the overlapping slices of eggplant: spoon the remainder of the sauce around the sides. Bake the eggplant for about 10 minutes, running the dish under the broiler for 2 or 3 minutes to lightly brown the top. Serve at once.

Green Bean Puree

serves four

Green beans, by themselves, tend to make a watery puree, but with the addition of separately cooked peas the puree will have more body and a better color.

2 pounds fresh green beans
5 tablespoons butter
¼ cup onion, finely minced
1 small clove garlic, finely minced

1 teaspoon lemon rind, finely grated
1 cup peas, cooked
· salt and freshly ground pepper

Cut the green beans into pieces about 2 inches long. Place them in a large pot of boiling, salted water and cook them for about 8 minutes or until barely tender.

Run the beans under cold running water and drain well.

In a large heavy skillet melt 3 tablespoons of the butter, add the onion and garlic, and saute over low heat until the onion is softened but not brown. Add the beans and lemon zest and saute for an additional 5 minutes; remove from heat and allow to cool slightly.

While the beans are sauteing, place the cup of cooked peas in the container of a food processor fitted with the steel knife blade and blend to a fine puree; remove and place in mixing bowl.

When the beans have finished cooking, place them, along with the butter they were sauteed in, in the container of the food processor (it need not be washed out) and puree them. Place the bean puree in the bowl along with the pea puree and blend well; season with salt and pepper to taste. May be made ahead to this point.

Just before serving melt the remaining 2 tablespoons butter in a small, heavy enameled saucepan, add the puree, and cook over low heat, stirring occasionally until it is heated through. Serve immediately.

Chicken Hunter's Style
serves four to six

Chicken parts sauteed in a fresh tomato sauce with fresh and dried mushrooms and Italian bacon (pancetta). This is best served over your favorite pasta cooked al dente. It will go best with a vigorous vegetable dish like the green bean and pepper saute (this month). Beaujolais was made to go with dishes like this.

½ ounce dried Italian boletus mushrooms
3- to 3½-pound whole chicken,

   cut into serving pieces
· seasoned flour for dredging
3 tablespoons olive oil
½ pound fresh mushrooms, cleaned and thickly sliced
· squeeze fresh lemon juice
⅓ cup pancetta, cut into small cubes
⅓ cup onion, finely chopped
⅓ cup carrot, finely chopped
2 cloves garlic, finely chopped
1 tablespoon lemon rind, finely grated
½ cup dry white vermouth, or dry white wine

2½ pounds fresh ripe tomatoes, peeled, seeded, and coarsely chopped
- pinch dried hot pepper flakes
- salt and freshly ground pepper

Place the dried mushrooms in a small container, pour boiling water over them to cover, and allow them to soak for 30 minutes.

Dredge the chicken with the seasoned flour and shake off any excess. Heat the olive oil in a large heavy skillet and saute the chicken until brown on all sides. Remove the chicken to a 4- or 5-quart pot and set aside. In the oil remaining in the skillet, quickly saute the mushrooms with the lemon juice until golden brown; remove from the pan with a slotted spoon and reserve.

Pour off all but 1 tablespoon oil from the skillet, add the pancetta, and cook over medium heat until it turns brown and begins to release its fat. Add the onions and carrots and saute for 5 minutes. Drain and coarsely chop the mushrooms; add them, the garlic, and the lemon zest to the onion and carrot mixture and continue to cook for another 5 minutes. Pour in the vermouth, raise the heat, and reduce the liquid slightly.

Add the vegetable mixture to the chicken with the tomato pulp, season with the dried hot pepper flakes, salt, and pepper, and just simmer over very low heat for about 45 minutes or until the chicken is tender. Taste for seasoning, adjust if necessary, and serve immediately over pasta.

Chicken Majorca
serves four

Another chicken sauteed in a fresh tomato sauce, but here the seasoning is very different: the sauce is enriched with prosciutto, grated orange rind, and red currant jelly. Serve with saffron rice and a green salad. You might want to begin with the gazpacho (this month). Serve a hearty Barbaresco or a Rubesco Riserva.

3- to 3½-pound chicken, cut into serving pieces
· salt and freshly ground pepper
3 tablespoons olive oil
¼ cup Madeira
1 tablespoon onion, finely chopped
1 tablespoon prosciutto, cut into small dice (substitute a good-quality baked ham, if unavailable)
2 cloves garlic, finely chopped
· finely grated rind of one orange
1½ tablespoons flour
1 cup fresh tomatoes, peeled, seeded, and coarsely chopped
1 teaspoon tomato paste
1½ cups chicken stock
2 teaspoons red currant jelly
1 cup fresh mushrooms, thickly sliced
· squeeze lemon juice
1 cup green pepper, cut into ¼-inch strips
· fruit of one orange, all pith removed, peeled and coarsely chopped
· imported black olives

Lightly season the chicken parts with salt and pepper. Heat the olive oil in a large heavy skillet, add the chicken, and brown well on all sides. Pour off all but 1 tablespoon of oil into a smaller skillet and set aside. Heat the Madeira in a small container, pour over the chicken, and set aflame, shaking the pan until the flames subside. Remove chicken and set aside. To the oil remaining in the larger skillet, add the onion, prosciutto or ham, garlic, and orange rind and saute over moderate heat for 3 to 4 minutes. Add the flour, stirring it in well, and cook for 1 to 2 minutes. Stir in the tomato pulp, tomato paste, stock, and jelly and season with salt and pepper. Bring this mixture to a boil, stirring until it thickens. Add the chicken and cook over low heat for about 45 minutes or until tender.

While the chicken is cooking, saute the mushrooms in the smaller skillet, sprinkling with a little lemon juice; remove with a slotted spoon and set aside. Next saute the pepper strips in the same skillet for about 5 minutes, until tender but still crisp; remove and set aside.

About 5 minutes before the chicken is done, stir in the prepared mushrooms, pepper strips, and orange pieces; cook until heated through. Pour chicken with its sauce onto a serving platter and garnish with black olives. Serve at once.

Chicken Curry
serves four

This recipe for chicken curry uses only the dark meat, more flavorful in this particular preparation than breast meat, which has a tendency to dry out quickly. Melon pieces, stirred in at the last, lend an element of surprise to the dish, their cool flavor a perfect foil for the savory sauce.

Serve the curry with steamed, buttered rice that has been lightly flavored with citrus juice and a little of its zest, either lime, lemon, or orange. Accompany with chutney, coarsely chopped unsalted cashews, ripe tomatoes cut into small dice, and a good beer.

6	large chicken thighs (about 1½ pounds)
3	cups chicken stock
3	tablespoons butter
1	large onion, cut into quarters and thickly sliced
2	tablespoons fresh ginger root, cut into short julienne strips
2	cloves garlic, finely chopped
½ to 1	tablespoon imported curry paste
2	tablespoons flour
·	juice of 1 lime
½	cup sour cream or yogurt
½	small cantaloupe or honeydew melon, cut into small, bite-size pieces

Place the chicken thighs in a saucepan, add the stock, and bring to a boil. Reduce the heat and simmer the chicken for about 15 minutes, until tender. Strain and reserve the stock; remove the meat from the bones and skin and discard them. Cut the meat into bite-size pieces and set aside.

Melt the butter in a 10- or 12-inch skillet, add the onion slices, and saute them over moderate heat for 5 minutes. Add the ginger and garlic; continue to cook for another 5 minutes. Stir in the curry paste, blending it into the vegetables, and saute for 3 minutes. Stir in the flour with a wire whisk and continue to cook over low heat for 3 minutes more.

Pour in 2 cups of the reserved chicken stock, add the lime juice, and stir until the sauce has thickened. Cook the sauce over low heat, stirring occasionally, for about 20 minutes. When the sauce has reduced a bit, stir in the chicken and simmer for 5 minutes. Add the sour cream, blending it well into the sauce, stir in the melon pieces, and continue to simmer for 1 to 2 minutes more. Serve immediately.

Cutlets Pojarski

serves four

Only three-quarters of a pound of veal is required for this dish, so you might keep it in mind when you have a handful of trimmings left over after boning a leg or a breast of veal. I have tried substituting chicken breasts but the results had little flavor (though a combination of veal and chicken can be delicious). Since the cutlets are so delicate, almost any sauce seems to overpower them; serve them simply as they are or top them with a spoonful of sour cream. The watercress and snow pea salad (April) pea and bacon salad (March) or green bean puree (this month) would all make delicious accompaniments. With a dish this delicate you must not serve too vehement a wine: a Macon blanc of a good year (not too cold), or best of all, a very good premier cru Chablis.

¾ pound young veal, trimmed of any bones or fat
5 tablespoons butter, softened and cut into small pieces
½ teaspoon salt
· freshly ground pepper
· dash of Tabasco
½ cup heavy cream
1 egg, lightly beaten with vegetable oil
· breadcrumbs

Cut the veal into 1-inch pieces. Place in the container of a food processor fitted with the steel knife blade and blend for a few seconds, turning the machine alternately on and off so the grind will be even. Add the softened butter while the machine is running and blend only long enough for the butter to be absorbed. Add the seasonings, turn the machine on, and pour the cream into the funnel, blending all together well. The mixture at this point should resemble a mousse. Pour into a bowl and chill for at least 2 hours or overnight.

Place the egg beaten with 1 teaspoon oil in a shallow bowl; put the breadcrumbs in another. Remove the veal mixture from the refrigerator and divide it into four equal parts. Working with wet hands, form each portion into a cutlet shape. Dip each cutlet into the egg, then into the breadcrumbs, pressing them gently into the surface. Place the breaded cutlets into the refrigerator for a few minutes to chill; this will help the breadcrumbs to adhere.

Heat the vegetable oil ¼-inch deep in a large heavy skillet set over moderately high heat, add the cutlets, and fry them for 4 to 5 minutes on each side, turning them over carefully with a wide spatula. They should be crisp and brown when done; serve immediately. The cutlets may be kept warm in the oven (set them on a rack over a plate to keep them crisp) for about half an hour.

Cream Cheese Mousse with Raspberry Sauce
serves four

This dessert cheese mousse is very much like the French coeur a la creme but much simpler to prepare. The recipe has been adapted from Jane Grigson's fine cookbook *Good Things*, published by Penguin Books.

1 cup ricotta cheese (put through a sieve if not using food processor)
2 egg yolks
¼ cup finely granulated sugar
1½ tablespoons maraschino liqueur (substitute 1 teaspoon vanilla extract if unavailable)
½ tablespoon gelatin dissolved in 3 tablespoons boiling water
½ cup heavy cream, whipped

Sauce:
1 pint fresh raspberries

1 tablespoon creme de cassis
· sugar (optional)

Place the ricotta in the bowl of a food processor fitted with the plastic knife blade and blend until smooth. Add the egg yolks, sugar, maraschino or vanilla, and dissolved gelatin. Blend well. Fold in whipped cream. Pour into a lightly buttered 2-cup mold and chill for at least 4 hours.

Prepare the sauce: place two-thirds of the berries in the food processor and puree them. Mix in the creme de cassis; a bit of sugar may be added here if you prefer a sweeter sauce. Mix the reserved whole berries into the sauce just before serving.

Unmold the mousse onto a serving plate, pour the sauce over, and serve.

Raspberry Tart
serves six to eight

A crisp pastry shell is filled with a layer of zesty lemon mousse, then topped with fresh raspberries and glazed with red currant jelly.

10-inch pastry shell, fully baked (using a quiche pan or flan ring)
2 large lemons
5 egg yolks
⅔ cup sugar
2 teaspoons cornstarch

5 egg whites
· pinch salt
1 cup heavy cream, whipped until stiff
2 quarts fresh raspberries, cleaned
1 cup red currant jelly
1 tablespoon water

Grate the rind from the lemons with a zester or a fine grater. Juice the lemons, remove the pips from the juice, and reserve.

Beat the egg yolks with the sugar until the mixture is thick and lemon-colored. Beat in the lemon juice and the cornstarch and pour into an enameled cast-iron saucepan. Set over moderate heat and beat constantly with a wire whisk until the mixture thickens and coats a wooden spoon lightly. Remove from heat and allow to cool.

Beat the egg whites with a pinch of sugar until they are stiff. Fold them into the yolk mixture using a rubber spatula. Sprinkle with the finely grated lemon rind and fold in the whipped cream. Allow the mousse to chill for at least an hour before assembling the tart.

Melt the currant jelly with the tablespoon of water; brush the bottom and the sides of the baked tart shell with a thin layer of the glaze. Pour in the mousse and spread it evenly over the bottom. Arrange the berries on top of the mousse stem-side down in concentric circles. Brush the berries with the remaining glaze. Chill before serving.

Strawberries in Orange Cups
serves six

The ripe strawberries are sliced, then gilded with a creme Anglaise and mounded into orange shells (oranges with pulp removed). The orange shells are hollowed out with the aid of a spoon, an extremely simple task if you purchase thick-skinned navel oranges. They can be prepared and refrigerated hours before serving and can also be used as containers for individual servings of orange sherbet or an orange souffle.

1   quart fresh ripe strawberries
6   large navel oranges
     Creme Anglaise:
1   cup milk
½   cup heavy cream
4   egg yolks
6   tablespoons sugar
2   teaspoons cornstarch
1   tablespoon Grand Marnier

Clean the berries, remove and discard the hulls, and cut each berry into quarters. Cut a thin slice from the navel end of each orange and reserve it. With the aid of a dessert spoon, scrape out the pulp (reserving it for another use), being careful not to puncture the shell. Both the orange cups and their tops may be covered with plastic wrap and refrigerated for up to 6 hours.

Prepare the creme Anglaise: Combine the milk and the cream in a saucepan, bring to a boil, remove from heat, and allow to stand.

In a mixing bowl, beat the yolks with the sugar and cornstarch until they thicken into a lemon-colored cream and form a ribbon. Slowly beat in the still-warm mixture; transfer to a heavy-bottomed (ideally an enameled cast-iron) saucepan and set over moderate heat. Using a wire whisk, stir the sauce constantly until it thickens and evenly coats a wooden spoon.

Remove from heat immediately and stir in the Grand Marnier; whisk for a few minutes to cool the mixture slightly. Allow to stand until completely cooled. Place a piece of plastic wrap directly on the surface of the custard to discourage a skin from forming; chill. The sauce may be made hours in advance.

Just before serving, pour the creme Anglaise over the berries and toss together gently. Fill each of the orange cups with the berry and custard mixture, place the reserved tops on askew, and serve immediately.

Raspberries in Cassis
serves four

There is very little one can do to improve on the flavor of the raspberry. This recipe combines them with the concentrated flavor of black currants and tops them with creme Chantilly and a sprinkling of powdered Italian amaretti cookies.

1	quart fresh raspberries
4	tablespoons creme de cassis
·	finely granulated sugar (optional)
1	cup heavy cream
½	teaspoon vanilla extract
1 to 2	tablespoons confectioners sugar
·	powdered amaretti (Italian macaroons ground to a powder in food processor or blender)

Clean the berries; place them in a shallow bowl and sprinkle over them the creme de cassis (sugar may be added to sweeten them slightly if you wish). Mix the berries gently with the liqueur and chill for at least 2 hours. Prepare the creme Chantilly: whip the cream until it begins to thicken, add the vanilla extract and the sugar to taste, and continue to whip until the cream holds its shape but is not stiff. Spoon the berries into individual serving dishes, mound the creme Chantilly on top, and sprinkle with the powdered amaretti.

Peaches in Vouvray
serves four

The best peach for this dish is the white-fleshed and delicate-tasting Babcock.

4   peaches
·   finely granulated sugar (optional)
¼ to ½ bottle of Vouvray wine

Bring a pot of water to a boil; immerse the peaches in it for 1 minute. Remove, run them under cold water, and slip off the skins. Remove the pits and slice the peaches into a bowl. (You may sweeten the fruit with just a bit or sugar if you wish; this will largely depend on the sweetness of your wine.)

Pour enough wine over the peaches to cover them by 1 to 2 inches. Chill for at least an hour. Half an hour before serving, remove the bowl from the refrigerator and let stand at room temperature to warm slightly, since it is difficult to taste the delicacy of this dish when ice-cold. Serve in deep wine glasses.

Fruit Fools

The word fool comes from the French *fouler*, to crush. Traditionally, the fruit is indeed crushed after light cooking, then mixed with a custard or whipped cream or both. This is a wonderful method in which to use the profusion of ripe fruit available in early summer. I have eliminated the custard in this dessert, using only whipped cream. The fruit itself need not be cooked; in fact, the raw fruit puree has a fresh and lively flavor that is most appealing. This dessert would be welcome at the end of almost any summer meal; it is light, cool, and creamy.

The two recipes given here are for strawberry and peach fool; you may substitute whatever fruit you fancy. The proportions are approximately 1½ cups fruit puree to ½ pint whipping cream. Some fruits are more intense in flavor so the proportions must be adjusted accordingly. You may wish to sieve a puree of raspberries or blackberries to remove the pips, although I rarely do because I find their texture pleasing.

Here is a short guide to different fruits and the flavorings that complement them:

Stawberries — creme de cassis, Grand Marnier.
Raspberries — framboise liqueur, creme de cassis.

Blueberries—pure maple syrup and cinnamon.
Cherries—kirsch, maraschino.
Peaches—brown sugar and rum or bourbon or amaretto. Honey dew or casaba melons—anisette, sweet champagne. Apricots, nectarines—apricot brandy.

Strawberry Fool
serves six

1   box very ripe strawberries
1 to 2 tablespoons finely granulated sugar
1   tablespoon creme de cassis
½   pint heavy cream
1   tablespoon confectioners sugar
1   teaspoon vanilla extract (do not use imitation vanilla)
·   a few amaretti (Italian macaroons) ground to a powder

Set aside 6 whole berries to use as garnish. Stem the rest and puree in the container of a food processor fitted with the steel knife blade. Add the cassis and 1 tablespoon sugar, blend for 1 to 2 seconds to mix, and taste for sweetness. (You should not add too much sugar; the natural flavor of the berries should be apparent.) Add the other tablespoon of sugar if necessary and set puree aside.

Whip the cream in a stainless steel or copper bowl, adding the confectioners sugar only after it has begun to thicken. Add the vanilla and whip until the cream forms stiff peaks. Measure out 1½ cups strawberry puree and fold it into the whipped cream. Pour into individual souffle dishes and chill for at least 2 hours or overnight. (The fools may be frozen, but should be placed in the refrigerator section for 30 to 45 minutes before serving to let them defrost.)

Dust the surface of the fool with the powdered amaretti and garnish each with a perfect berry just before serving.

Peach Fool
serves six

2 or 3 very ripe peaches
1 to 2 tablespoons brown sugar
1   tablespoon dark rum
½   pint heavy cream
1   tablespoon confectioners sugar
1   teaspoon vanilla extract
·   a few toasted almonds

Immerse the peaches in boiling water for 1 minute. Remove and run under cold water, slipping off the skins. Cut each peach in half; remove and discard the pits. Puree the flesh in a food processor, flavoring it with the rum and 1 tablespoon sugar; taste for sweetness and add the other tablespoon of sugar if necessary. Set this mixture aside.

Whip the cream in a stainless-steel or copper bowl, adding the confectioners sugar only after it has begun to thicken. Add the vanilla extract and whip until the cream forms stiff peaks. Measure out 1½ cups peach puree and fold it into the whipped cream. Pour into 6 individual serving dishes and chill for at least 2 hours or overnight. Before serving, garnish the top of each fool with the toasted almonds.

Peaches with Raspberry Fool
serves four

A variation of peach Melba that makes a light and refreshing dessert.

2   large peaches
1   cup sugar
1   cup water
½   inch vanilla bean
½   recipe raspberry fool (see "Fruit Fools")
·   whole raspberries and toasted almond slices

Bring a pot of water to a boil; immerse the peaches for 1 minute. Remove and run them under cold water; the skins will slip off. Cut each peach in half and remove the pit. Combine the sugar, water, and vanilla bean in a pot, bring to boil, and cook for 5 minutes. Then add the peach halves, reduce the heat, and gently poach them until just tender. When done, remove the pan from the stove and allow the peaches to cool in the liquid.

Place each peach half in a coupe glass, fill the cavity generously with some of the raspberry fool, and garnish with a few whole raspberries and the **toasted almond slices.**

Strawberry Tart
serves six to eight

The traditional filling for most fruit tarts is a creme patissiere; the one used in this recipe is a low-fat filling made with ricotta cheese. This light cheese base marries beautifully with any variety of berry and is especially good with peaches. The flavoring used here (cognac or vanilla) is a simple one but there are many variations possible: grated chocolate and orange zest with Grand Marnier, coarsely ground amaretti (Italian macaroons) with Amaretto liqueur, finely powdered and toasted hazelnuts with rum — the combinations are endless.

Pate Brisee:

1¼ cups unbleached white flour
6 tablespoons butter, cut into small cubes
2 tablespoons shortening
¼ teaspoon salt
½ tablespoon sugar
3 tablespoons ice water

Filling:

1½ cups ricotta cheese
5 tablespoons finely granulated sugar (or to taste)
1 tablespoon cognac or 1 teaspoon pure vanilla extract
· ripe strawberries (about 2 quarts), hulls removed

Glaze:

1 cup red currant jelly
1 tablespoon water

Garnish:

1 tablespoon finely ground hazelnuts (optional)

For the pastry: in a large bowl combine the flour, butter, and shortening (both well chilled); sprinkle with the salt and sugar and work together with a pastry cutter until the texture resembles coarse cornmeal. Add the ice water, tossing with a fork until all the water is incorporated into the dough.

Form the dough into a ball, kneading lightly with the palms of the hands for a few seconds to distribute the fat evenly and reform into a ball. Dust the dough with a light coating of flour, wrap in waxed paper or plastic, and refrigerate for at least 2 hours.

Preheat the oven to 400 degrees. Roll out the pastry into a 1- or 2-inch round approximately ⅛ inch thick; fit it into a 10-inch quiche pan or flan ring, and trim off any excess, saving for another use. Line the pastry with foil, fill with rice or beans to weight the pastry and keep the bottom from puffing up, and bake in the middle of the oven for about 10 minutes, until the pastry just begins to shrink away from the sides of the pan.

Remove the foil with the rice or beans, place the tart shell back in the oven, and bake until it is lighlty browned and crisp, 10 to 15 minutes. Oven temperatures vary quite a bit so be sure the pastry is fully baked before removing from oven.

Allow the pastry shell to cool in its pan and prepare the filling: place the ricotta into the container of a food processor fitted with the steel or plastic knife blade and blend for a few seconds to remove the grainy texture. Add the sugar and cognac or vanilla and blend until smooth. (If not using a food processor, put the ricotta through a sieve to remove grainy texture, then add flavorings.)

Heat the currant jelly with the water in a small saucepan until liquid. Allow the glaze to cool slightly, then paint the inside bottom and sides of the tart shell with a little of the glaze. This will ensure a crisp crust if the tart is not consumed immediately.

Pour the ricotta mixture into the prepared tart shell and spread it evenly over the bottom. Arrange the berries on top of this stem-side down, building toward the center in concentric circles. Brush the berries with a heavy layer of glaze and sprinkle lightly with the ground hazelnuts. The tart can be served immediately or chilled for an hour or two.

Menu 1	Menu 2
Pissaladiere (July)	Risi e Bisi (May)
Lamb Riblets a la Grecque (July)	Trout Grilled with Fennel Butter (July)
Red Pepper and Potato Salad (July)	Grated Zucchini Saute (April)
Green Bean Puree (June)	Roasted Pepper Salad (July)
Melon in Anisette (July)	Raspberries in Cassis (June)

Roasted Sweet (Bell) Peppers
Roasted Pepper Salad
Red Pepper and Potato Salad
Corn with Chili Butter
Pissaladiere
Terriyaki Spare Ribs
Grilled Salmon Steaks with Cucumber Butter
Trout Grilled with Fennel Butter
Morrocan Chicken
Tandoori Chicken
Chicken Saute with Peppers
Game Hens in Lemon Pepper Marinade
Grilled Rack of Lamb
Lamb Riblets a la Grecque
Lamb Shashlik
Pizza all'Amatriciana
Piperade
Watermelon Sherbet
Melon in Anisette

The smell of food grilled out of doors: this was the first method of cooking and, in many ways, it remains the best.

This is not to say that it is the most simple, as evidenced by the proliferation on summer patios of chicken pieces and steaks that are indistinguishable from the charcoal they were grilled over. One of the most common mistakes made in cooking over coals is to first char the outside of the meat, until it has a crust resembling that of burnt wood, and then to overcook it. When properly done, however, grilling over coals can produce the finest-flavored meat, fish, or poultry one has ever tasted.

There are really very few tools necessary for grilling out of doors, contrary to what most purveyors of this kind of equipment would have you believe. Owning a good grill is most important, and this is a matter of personal choice; I have achieved almost the same results on an hibachi perched on a fire escape outside my New York apartment window as I have on a deluxe Weber grill set out on my porch in the Northwest. My preference is for the latter, as it comes equipped with a domed lid that allows it to act as a small oven and eliminates the constant turning of meat to avoid excessive browning. The only utensils I have found necessary are a pair of long-handled tongs for turning the meat, and a good thermometer. Because the cooking time differs greatly—depending on its initial temperature, how thick it is, and so on—a reliable meat thermometer is absolutely a necessity for the outdoor chef; and the Taylor Bi-Therm, which is calibrated from 0 degrees to 220 degrees, is an ideal tool.

If you live in an area like ours, where fresh fish is most abundant, you may wish to invest in one other utensil, a fish grill—either the sort that is fish-shaped or the more useful rectangular hinged grill frame—that allows you to turn the fish over without losing most of the flesh that would normally stick to your grill. These fish grills are usually priced from $12.

Most of the recipes for cooking over coals in this chapter depend on a marinade. I have a prejudice against the all-purpose barbecue sauce that is often heavily napped on anything from a good steak to fruit shishkabobs. This thick, red-brown, prepared sauce made from an astounding number of ingredients is guaranteed to kill the natural flavor of anything with which it is allowed to come into contact. A good piece of beef or lamb needs no other seasoning than a light sprinkling of salt and pepper at the onset.

As for other marinades, I prefer the tangy flavor of fresh lemon juice as a base: lemon juice mixed with a little oregano is a marinade especially good on breast of lamb, an inexpensive cut of meat with a fatty flavor which is eliminated by the zesty lemon. Cornish game hens have an ill-founded reputation for having no flavor; when they are marinated in lemon juice, black and red pepper, and a little olive oil and quickly grilled, they become moist, tender, and most flavorful. There are some complicated marinades in this book such as the one for tandoori chicken, which provides the bird with an unusual and most delicious flavor. But on the whole, a marinade should complement rather than change the flavor of the meat or poultry it is paired with; it should not be thought of as a cover-up to disguise a cut of meat that is not quite up to par.

One of the few rules to keep in mind when grilling out of doors is: keep it simple. The most rewarding aspect of this method of cooking is that it allows the flavor of the food, whether it be rack of lamb or red peppers, to speak clearly. So avoid using a profusion of wood chips; a few will lend a delicate smokey flavor, but too much will overwhelm. Instead, try sprinkling a large pinch of a suitable dried herb over the coals during the last ten minutes of cooking, to impart just a fragrance of high summer.

Roasted Sweet (Bell) Peppers

Roasted peppers may be used in any recipe calling for cooked or sauteed peppers. They will add a more subtle flavor and a more interesting texture. Keep in mind that any of these recipes may be prepared with green bell peppers, although you will not find them as succulent as the red.

In the broiler: Preheat to highest temperature. Set broiler rack so that the tops of the peppers will be about 4 inches below the heat source. Spread foil over the oven rack and place the whole peppers on it. Roast, turning occasionally, until the skin is charred and almost black all over.

Remove the peppers, wrap them in a tea towel, and allow them to steam for about 5 minutes. Transfer the peppers from the towel to a colander and run cold water over them until they are cool enough to handle. The skins should slip off easily under running water. Remove the core and seeds and slice the flesh into strips.

On outdoor grill: Place the rack 4 to 6 inches above very hot coals. Set the whole peppers on the rack and proceed as in the recipe above. This method will take a bit longer than if done in the oven, but the peppers will take on a marvelous smoky flavor.

Roasted Pepper Salad
serves four

A simple, yet satisfying dish composed only of roasted peppers mixed with slices of garlic, tossed with a good red wine vinegar and olive oil, and left to marinate for an hour or two. This is a wonderful accompaniment to grilled fish or chicken.

The peppers may also be used for an hors d'oeuvre: cut small slices of French or Italian bread, top them with thin slices of feta cheese, and finally add one or two slices of roasted pepper.

4   roasted red (or green) bell
    peppers, cut into strips ½
    inch thick
1 or 2 cloves garlic, thinly sliced
1½ tablespoons red wine
    vinegar
4   tablespoons fruity olive oil
2   tablespoons parsley, finely
    chopped
·   salt and freshly ground
    pepper

Place the peppers in a serving dish, add the sliced garlic, vinegar, and oil, and season with salt and pepper. Toss together, check the seasoning (roasted peppers seem to need quite a bit of salt), and allow to stand at room temperature for an hour or two.

Red Pepper and Potato Salad
serves four to six

An interesting variation on an old standard. Cooked potatoes are sliced and, while still hot, tossed with squares of roasted red pepper and cubes of crisp bacon, seasoned with minced onion and parsley, and dressed with oil and vinegar.

6 to 8 medium new potatoes
6   rashers of bacon, thick
    sliced, cut into large dice
¼   cup onion, finely chopped
1   clove garlic, finely chopped
2 or 3 tablespoons chicken stock
    (optional)
4   roasted red peppers, cut
    into 1-inch squares
3   tablespoons parsley, finely
    chopped
1½ tablespoons red wine
    vinegar
6   tablespoons olive oil
·   salt and freshly ground
    pepper

Place the potatoes in a pot of boiling salted water and cook them until they are tender enough to offer no resistance when pierced with a knife. Drain and peel, holding them with a towel to avoid burned fingers. Slice the potatoes and place in serving bowl. Sprinkle them with chicken stock.

While the potatoes are cooking, fry the bacon until crisp and brown, remove from skillet, and drain thoroughly on paper towels. Pour out all but 2 tablespoons of fat from the skillet, add the onion and garlic, and saute for about 5 minutes or until tender but not brown.

Pour the onion and garlic mixture with its oil over the potatoes, add the red pepper squares, parsley, oil, vinegar, salt, and pepper and toss gently to avoid mashing the potatoes. Serve at once.

Corn with Chili Butter
serves four

An amusing accompaniment to most grilled meats and also much easier to eat than corn on the cob.

4   ears very fresh corn
·   large pinch sugar
6   tablespoons butter
½   teaspoon mild chili powder
·   generous squeeze lemon juice
·   salt

Husk the corn; using a very sharp knife, slice each ear into rounds 1 inch thick. Bring a large pot of water, with a pinch of sugar, to the boil. Add the corn rounds, bring to a boil again, and cook for no longer than 3 minutes.

Meanwhile melt the butter with the chili powder, add the lemon juice, salt to taste, and keep warm. Drain the corn thoroughly, place in a deep serving dish, pour the chili butter over it, and toss so that each piece of corn is coated with the butter mixture. Serve at once.

Pissaladiere
serves eight to ten

Pissaladiere is a dish served up by the bakers and street vendors of Nice in Provence. It is composed of bread dough spread with a mixture of onions that have been cooked almost to the melting point in olive oil, garnished with a latticework of anchovies, and dotted with black olives.

There are as many different versions of this dish as there are cooks who prepare it. Sometimes a few tomatoes are added to the onions, but this is a rather recent development. You will see recipes calling for a pastry foundation, and this version is served in many restaurants and private homes. I prefer the chewy texture of a thick pizza dough or a brioche dough; my favorite recipe is in James Beard's *New Recipes for the Cuisinart Food Processor*, published in 1976 by Cuisinarts Inc.

The flavor of the onion is essential to this preparation. When Walla Walla sweets are in the local markets, this lovely mild-flavored onion should be used for this dish. Serve it as a first course with a California Chardonnay or Zinfandel to taste.

After your dough has risen until double in bulk, punch it down and knead several times. Shape into a rectangular form using your hands or a rolling pin and press into a greased baking sheet with sides (17 by 11 inches), pushing the dough a bit higher on the sides to form a rim. Cover and let rise until doubled, about 1 hour.

1   recipe pizza or brioche dough
¼   cup fruity olive oil
3   pounds Walla Walla sweets, very thinly sliced
2   garlic cloves, finely chopped (optional)
3 to 4 sprigs fresh thyme, finely chopped
1   bay leaf
½   teaspoon salt
·   freshly ground pepper
·   scant ½ cup grated Parmesan cheese
2   2-ounce cans anchovy fillets, drained and separated
·   imported black olives, pitted and cut in half

While the dough is rising, heat the olive oil in a heavy 4-quart Dutch oven; add the onions, garlic, thyme, bay leaf, salt, and pepper. Cover and cook over moderate heat for 5 minutes.

Remove the cover, raise the heat to high, and cook until the juice released from the onions has evaporated, about 5 minutes. Cover once again, reduce heat, and simmer for about 1 hour until the onions have almost melted into a puree. Taste for seasoning and set aside until the dough is finished.

Preheat the oven to 350 degrees. When the dough in the baking pan has doubled in bulk, sprinkle the surface with the grated cheese and cover with the onion mixture (bay leaf and thyme sprigs removed), leaving a 1-inch border. Over this, make a lattice pattern with the anchovy fillets. (If you are not overly fond of the strong taste of anchovy, you may wish to soak them in milk for about 10 minutes; this method removes the too-salty flavor.) In each of the open spaces remaining, place half an olive.

Place in the middle of the oven and bake for about 45 minutes. Serve just slightly warm or at room temperature.

Teriyaki Spare Ribs
serves four

There is no meat that is more succulent when grilled than pork, and among the most popular cuts for grilling are spare ribs. Country-style ribs are thick and meaty; they are cut from the blade ends of the pork loin and butterflied. They are complemented beautifully by this soy-based teriyaki marinade. Serve with corn with chili butter (this month) and the orange and radish salad (September). A light, peppy red wine is required: try a California Gamay Beaujolais, or a

Beaujolais Superieure (or a real Fleurie) from France.

4 pounds country-style spare ribs
Marinade:
½ cup soy sauce
¼ teaspoon dried mustard
· juice of ½ lemon
¼ cup sugar
3 tablespoons dry sherry or gin
1 large clove garlic, put through a press
3 or 4 dashes Tabasco
1-inch piece of fresh ginger, unpeeled, cut into paper-thin slices
2 tablespoons (Oriental) sesame oil
· salt and freshly ground pepper

Prepare the marinade: in a shallow container large enough to hold all the ribs in one layer combine the soy sauce, dried mustard, lemon juice, sugar, sherry or gin, pressed garlic, Tabasco, and ginger slices; stir well. While stirring, pour in the sesame oil and 1 cup of water; blend and season with salt and pepper. Taste the marinade; if you prefer a bit more sugar, add it. Place the ribs in the teriyaki sauce and marinate them for at least 8 hours or overnight.

Grilled pork should be basted frequently. Build a moderately hot fire, place the ribs on the grill, and cook them for 20 minutes; then they may be basted and turned. Repeat this process twice more at 20-minute intervals. The ribs should be done in about 60 minutes. When done, brush them with a bit more of the marinade and serve.

Grilled Salmon Steaks with Cucumber Butter
serves four

Cooked fish is delicate and must be handled with care, so it is wise to invest in a hinged fish grill. If you do not own one, be sure to grease the grill of your barbecue liberally, so the fish can be removed from it easily. Serve a light and springy side dish like risi e bisi (May) or the watercress and sugar pea salad (April).

For salmon the wine of choice is a Saumur—or try a dry Chenin Blanc or Chardonnay.

4 salmon steaks, 1 inch thick
Cucumber butter:
1 small cucumber
1 large shallot, finely chopped
⅓ cup butter, cut into small bits
1 tablespoon lemon juice
· salt and freshly ground pepper
· dash Tabasco

First prepare the cucumber butter. Peel the cucumber, cut it in half, and remove its seeds. Grate the flesh, place it in a shallow bowl, and sprinkle lightly with salt. Allow to stand for 15 minutes, then transfer to a sieve to drain for an additional 15 minutes. Rinse the cucumber flesh under cold water, squeeze out excess moisture by hand, and dry thoroughly with paper towels.

Place the prepared cucumber in the container of a food processor fitted with the steel knife blade. Add the shallot and the butter and blend; add the seasonings, mix, taste, and adjust if necessary.

Remove the butter from the processor container and divide it in half; place half of the mixture on a sheet of waxed paper and roll into a tube shape; leave the other half of the butter out in a small bowl at room temperature.

When the coals in your grill are moderately hot, brush each side of the salmon steaks with some of the softened cucumber butter. Grease the grill and place about 4 inches above the coals. Place the salmon on the grill and cook for about 4 minutes; turn over and cook the other side for 5 to 6 minutes, or until the fish flakes easily when tested with a fork.

Remove from grill and top each piece with a slice of the chilled cucumber butter. Serve at once.

Trout Grilled with Fennel Butter
serves four

The trout is wrapped in foil to keep in the succulent juices. Fennel butter is also complementary to other fish: salmon, snapper, bass, etc. Serve with potatoes in parsley sauce (April) or the green beans sauteed with lemon or peppers (June) and a dry Riesling or Gewurztraminer.

2	teaspoons fennel seeds
1	large clove garlic, finely chopped
·	pinch salt
1	tablespoon lemon juice
·	pinch cayenne pepper or dash Tabasco
·	freshly ground pepper

4	tablespoons butter, softened
4	fresh trout
·	aluminum foil

First prepare the fennel butter: place in a mortar the fennel seeds, garlic, and salt and grind into a coarse paste. Add the seasonings and the butter and blend well.

Stuff the cavity of each fish with one quarter of the fennel butter. Tightly wrap each trout in a double layer of foil.

When the coals are red-hot, place the trout on the grill and cook for 8 or 9 minutes per side. Remove from the heat when done and serve in the foil.

Moroccan Chicken
serves four

Do not allow the number of herbs and spices in this recipe to discourage you; the resulting flavor is a mellow and almost delicate one. I prefer to make the herb paste with a mortar and pestle rather than in a machine because the herbs lose less of their flavor that way.

This dish calls for a light but flavorful accompaniment: try the roast red pepper salad from this month's recipes, or the orange and radish salad or eggplant caviar from September. For wine, try a St. Emilion or Pomerol from Bordeaux, or a Cabernet or Central Coast Zinfandel from California.

1 small bunch fresh coriander (about ½ cup, loosely packed)
1 small bunch fresh mint (about ½ cup, loosely packed)
2 cloves garlic, coarsely chopped
1 tablespoon paprika
· pinch saffron leaves or powdered saffron
· large pinch powdered cumin
1 teaspoon salt
2 tablespoons olive oil
3- to 3½-pound chicken, cut into half or quarters

Prepare the herb paste: cut off and discard the stems from the coriander and the mint, coarsely chop the leaves, and place in a mortar. Scatter the garlic and the spices on the top. Mash the herbs and spices into a paste, working in the olive oil little by little until the paste is dense enough to hold its shape.

Wash the chicken parts and dry them thoroughly. Make small, deep cuts in the flesh with the aid of a sharp paring knife. Rub the herb paste over the entire surface of the chicken, working it into the incisions. Allow the meat to stand uncovered at room temperature for at least 2 hours.

When the coals in your grill are moderately hot, place the chicken pieces, bone side down, on the grill and cook for 40 to 50 minutes, or until the chicken is tender. During the last 10 minutes of cooking, the chicken may be turned skin-side down to brown. Remove from heat when done and serve immediately.

Tandoori Chicken
serves four

The best-known of all tandoori dishes is a chicken preparation in which whole chickens are first skinned, rubbed with a mixture of salt and lime (or lemon) juice, and marinated for at least 12 hours in a masala of yogurt, onion, fresh ginger, garlic, green chilies, and various spices.

The trussed chickens are then speared on long iron spikes and placed in the tandoor, a large clay jar, usually sunk neck-deep in the ground, that holds a charcoal fire on the bottom and heats the sides to the scorching point about halfway up. An important ingredient is added by the smoke that comes from the marinade dripping on the coals; it imparts a mellow fragrance that permeates the bird.

While a tandoor may not be part of your batterie de cuisine, you can duplicate this succulent dish quite easily on your outdoor grill. The addition of hickory or cherrywood chips to the hot charcoal gives a particularly interesting and subtle smoky flavor. You may adjust the quantity of hot peppers to taste: the amount called for gives a spicy but not overwhelming heat to the final product.

Garam masala is a seasoning made from ground cardamom, black pepper, cumin, coriander, cinnamon, and cloves; it is available at the shops specializing in Eastern condiments.

As an accompaniment, serve with corn on the cob East Indian style: seasoned with salt, pepper, and lemon juice. Or make a banquet of it with cucumbers in sour cream (February), curried eggs (August) and a California Gamay or Beaujolais Villages. Other beverage possibilities are a Hermitage or a dry ale or pilsner beer.

2½- to 3-pound chicken (fryer or broiler)
1   large lime or lemon
2   teaspoons salt
1   large onion, chopped
3 or 4 cloves garlic, chopped
1-inch piece of ginger root, peeled and chopped
3   small fresh hot green chili peppers with seed pods removed and chopped (or the equivalent in canned green chiles)
1   teaspoon each ground coriander and ground cumin
¼   teaspoon each ground allspice, ground cloves, ground cinnamon
.   freshly ground black pepper
8-ounce container unflavored yogurt
1   teaspoon garam masala (optional)

Remove the skin from the chicken, ignoring the wings; truss well and make small deep cuts all over the bird with a sharp knife. Mix the lime or lemon juice with the salt and rub into the bird. Allow to stand for 1 hour.

Meanwhile, prepare the masala or marinade: put the chopped onion, garlic, ginger, and peppers into the container of a food processor fitted with the steel knife blade and blend into a smooth paste. Add the spices (with the exception of the garam masala) and the yogurt and blend to mix.

Place the chicken into a large glass or enamel bowl (do not use metal) and pour the marinade over it, coating it thoroughly. Cover the bowl with plastic wrap (do not use foil) and allow it to marinate at room temperature for at least 12 hours or overnight, turning occasionally.

Heat the coals to red-hot and sprinkle them with a handful or two of wood chips that have been soaked in water for 30 minutes and drained. Remove the chicken from the marinade and grill for 45 to 50 minutes.

Sprinkle with the garam masala and serve with lemon wedges.

Chicken Saute with Peppers
serves four

This dish calls for red peppers that have been roasted to remove their tough, bitter skins; the technique, which sounds complicated at first, is well worth mastering: see "Roasted Sweet Peppers" elsewhere in this chapter. Serve the chicken with one of the green bean sautes (June) or the watercress and sugar pea salad (April) and a light Italian wine: a Soave, Bardolino, or Valpolicella.

3- to 3½-pound chicken, cut into serving pieces
· flour
· salt and freshly ground pepper
4 tablespoons olive oil
⅓ cup pancetta (or bacon) cut into small dice
¼ cup onion, finely chopped
1½ pounds fresh ripe tomatoes, peeled, seeded, and coarsely chopped
1 large clove garlic, finely chopped
½ cup dry red wine
¼ teaspoon dried marjoram
3 red bell peppers, roasted and cut into strips
· black olives and lemon wedges

Dredge the chicken pieces in flour that has been lightly seasoned with salt and pepper; shake off any excess. Heat the olive oil in a heavy 12-inch skillet, add the chicken and brown on all sides over moderately high heat.

Remove chicken and add the pancetta (or bacon). Reduce the heat and saute, allowing it to brown lightly, for about 5 minutes. Stir in the onion and continue to cook for another 5 minutes, stirring frequently.

Add the tomatoes and garlic to the skillet along with the wine and the marjoram, season with salt and pepper, and cook over high heat for about 5 minutes. Reduce the heat, add the chicken pieces, spooning the sauce over them, and cook at a simmer for 35 to 40 minutes, basting the chicken frequently with the sauce.

Stir in the roasted pepper strips, continue to cook for another 5 minutes, then taste and correct seasoning if necessary. Arrange chicken pieces on serving platter, cover with sauce, and garnish with black olives and lemon wedges.

Game Hens in Lemon Pepper Marinade
serves two to four

Cornish game hens are often thought of as having very little flavor; usually their only fault lies in being very overcooked. This simple marinade—lemon juice, black and red peppers, salt, and olive oil—gives the birds a zesty flavor. They are grilled for no longer than 40 minutes, allowing the meat to be moist, tender, and most flavorful.

Serve with a Caesar salad (May), rice and green bean salad (August) or a roast red pepper and potato salad (this month), along with a Hermitage or Valpolicella.

2	Cornish game hens, each weighing about 1½ pounds
·	the juice of 7 to 8 lemons
1½	tablespoons black peppercorns
1	teaspoon coarse salt

| 1 | teaspoon dried hot red pepper flakes |
| ¼ | cup olive oil |

Wash the hens. Dry them and split each in two.

Prepare the marinade: grind the black peppercorns, salt, and red pepper flakes with a mortar and pestle for a minute or two; the peppers should be coarsely ground. Combine with the lemon juice and the olive oil in a shallow nonmetal dish large enough to hold the game hens in one layer.

Place the hens in the marinade skin-side down and spoon some of the marinade over them. Allow them to stand at room temperature for 4 to 6 hours, turning occasionally. If you wish to marinate them overnight, the dish should be covered tightly and refrigerated.

Heat the coals to moderately hot. Drain the game hens, reserving the marinade. Place the birds bone-side down on the grill. Cook for 30 to 40 minutes, basting every 10 to 15 minutes with the marinade. During the last 10 minutes of cooking, the hens may be turned skin-side down to brown. Remove from grill when done and baste once more with marinade. Serve at once or allow to cool to room temperature.

Grilled Rack of Lamb
serves two

One of the most delectable of meats when done on an outdoor grill. Accompany with red pepper and potato salad (this month) and baked artichoke hearts (May).

With a dish so simple and delicious, the possibilities are endless: the roast red pepper salad in this chapter would do nicely, but so would potatoes in pesto, ratatouille, caponata, or Italian Rice salad (all in August). A round, robust wine is called for: a St. Emilion, or a Fetzer Zinfandel or Burgess Cabernet from California.

1¼ pounds rack of lamb
· salt and freshly ground pepper

Score the fat side of the rack of lamb with a sharp knife. Season lightly with salt and pepper and cover the exposed ends of the bones with a piece of foil. Place the rack over very hot coals, fat side down, to sear for 2 minutes. Turn bone-side down and allow to cook for 35 to 40 minutes. Remove when a thermometer registers 140 degrees for medium rare meat. Allow to stand for 5 minutes before carving.

Lamb Riblets a la Grecque
serves four

Breast of lamb marinated in a zesty lemon and oregano base and then grilled: an inexpensive and delightful main course or appetizer. Serve with a roast pepper and potato salad (this month) or gazpacho or a tangy tomato sherbet (both June). This dish calls for a big Zinfandel or a Chateau Neuf du Pape; or try it with Greek retsina if your taste runs that way.

3 pounds breast of lamb, cut into 3- or 4-inch lengths
· juice of 4 or 5 lemons
1 tablespoon dried oregano
· salt and freshly ground black pepper
2 or 3 garlic cloves, peeled and sliced (optional)

Remove any excess fat from the

riblets; put them in the lemon juice, oregano, salt and pepper to taste, and garlic. Marinate for at least 3 hours or overnight, turning frequently.

Drain the meat, reserving the marinade, and grill over red-hot coals for 30 to 45 minutes, brushing frequently with the marinade, until the riblets are crisp and well browned.

This dish may also be done in a 400-degree oven; the cooking time remains the same, but you must place the riblets on a rack so the fat is allowed to drain off.

Lamb Shashlik
serves four

Of all the marinades for lamb, I confess a preference for those based on lemon juice: the tang of citrus complements this meat beautifully. Accompany with a fragrant vegetable dish like eggplant caviar (September), caponata, or ratatouille (both August) and a robust Zinfandel or Cotes du Rhone.

- · juice of 4 large lemons
- 1 large onion, peeled and cut into paper-thin slices
- 1 teaspoon grated fresh ginger
- 1 large garlic clove, thinly sliced
- ¼ cup olive oil
- 1 tablespoon salt
- · freshly ground pepper

2 pounds leg of lamb, trimmed of any bone and fat and cut into 1- to 1½-inch cubes

Combine the ingredients for the marinade. Place in a shallow bowl and add the lamb cubes. Allow the lamb to marinate for at least two hours, turning occasionally.

Heat the coals in your grill to red-hot. Drain the lamb cubes and thread them on four flat-bladed skewers. Place on the grill and cook for about 10 minutes for medium rare lamb, turning the skewers occasionally. Remove from heat and serve immediately.

Pizza all'Amatriciana
serves six to eight

Here is a dish that combines a classic Roman pasta sauce with a Neapolitan pizza dough. The results, I think, are very special. The sauce is deceptively simple: fresh tomatoes, onion, hot pepper, and pancetta (an Italian bacon cured in salt and spices and rolled into the shape of a sausage). My favorite dough is from Craig Claiborne's *New York Times Cookbook;* it is not difficult to make and produces a thick, chewy crust. (This same crust may be used as the base for pissaladiere.) If you haven't the time to make your own, perhaps you can find an excellent frozen pizza dough such as is available at Borracchini's Ginger Belle Bakery in Seattle. Serve with a good Zinfandel or perhaps a Cella Lambrusco.

Sauce Amatriciana:

3 pounds fresh tomatoes, peeled, seeded, and coarsely chopped

2 tablespoons olive oil

1 small onion, finely chopped

¼ pound pancetta, sliced thin and then cut into thick julienne

· large pinch dried hot red pepper flakes

· pinch each of sugar and allspice

· salt

¼ cup grated Romano cheese

¼ pound whole-milk mozzarella cheese, coarsely grated

¼ pound provolone cheese, coarsely grated

While the dough is rising, prepare the sauce: heat the oil in a 3-quart pot, add the onion, sprinkle with a pinch of sugar, and saute 5 to 7 minutes. Add the pancetta and saute about 3 minutes — do not brown. Add the tomatoes, red pepper flakes, allspice, and salt to taste. Cook over high heat for 5 minutes, stirring.

Reduce the heat to a simmer and cook uncovered for approximately 1 hour. Do not add tomato paste; the tomatoes act as their own thickening agent. When done, the sauce should be smooth and of fairly thick consistency. Allow the sauce to cool. (This sauce may also be used over spaghetti or bucatini.)

Preheat the oven to 500 degrees. Lightly grease an 11- by 17-inch rectangular baking sheet with sides. Place the dough in the pan, and press and stretch with the fingers until dough touches the sides of the pan at all points. Turn over edges on all sides to form a rim. Spread the sauce over the dough, leaving a 1-inch rim; lightly dust the sauce and edges of the dough with Romano cheese. Cover this with the mozarella and provolone cheeses and sprinkle a few drops of olive oil over all.

Bake in the middle of the oven until browned, 15 to 20 minutes. Cool for a few minutes, cut the pizza in half lengthwise, then crosswise 5 or 6 times. Serve immediately.

Piperade
serves four

A dish characteristic of the Basque country. A saute of peppers, onions, tomatoes, and ham bound together with loosely scrambled eggs, piperade makes a wonderful lunch or light summer supper. Serve with a light Spanish red wine or a similar California: a Dry Creek Rose of Cabernet, perhaps.

4   tablespoons olive oil
1   cup prosciutto (or good baked ham), cut into thick julienne
1   medium onion, cut in half and thickly sliced
2   cloves garlic, finely chopped
2   large ripe tomatoes, peeled, seeded, and coarsely chopped
·   salt and freshly ground pepper
·   pinch of sugar (optional)
·   dash Tabasco
2   roasted red peppers (see "Roasted Sweet Peppers"), cut into thin strips
5   eggs, lightly beaten
2   tablespoons parsley, finely chopped
·   croutons made from French or Italian bread, thinly sliced and fried

Heat the olive oil in a heavy 10-inch skillet, add the prosciutto (or ham) and saute until it is lightly browned around the edges. Remove with a slotted spoon and reserve.

Add the sliced onion to the skillet and saute over moderate heat until tender but not brown, about 5 minutes. Stir in the garlic and the tomatoes and season with salt, pepper, and Tabasco; use the sugar only if your tomatoes are not very ripe.

Raise the heat and allow the juices from the tomatoes to evaporate, stirring frequently. Add the reserved prosciutto and the red pepper strips to the skillet, mixing them into the tomatoes. Reduce the heat to a simmer, pour in the eggs, and stir until they begin to thicken into soft creamy curds. Sprinkle with the parsley, surround with the fried croutons, and serve immediately.

Watermelon Sherbet
makes one quart, serves six

This recipe is one of the few that can be made successfully without an ice cream machine. Other melons may be substituted for the watermelon, but they must be very ripe to allow for the fullest flavor. A good greengrocer should be able to guide you in the selection of a ripe melon. Failing that, rely on your nose, for a ripe melon gives off a faint and slightly sweet aroma. (No amount of shaking or thumping or squeezing will tell you anything about the ripeness of a particular melon.) A bit of lemon juice was used in the sherbet to cut its sweetness; with another type of melon (honey dew or Casaba), you might wish to also add two or three tablespoons of anisette.

4 to 4½ pounds ripe
    watermelon
1½ tablespoons lemon juice
1   cup sugar
1½ teaspoons unflavored gelatin
½   cup heavy cream
1   large egg

Cut the flesh of the melon from the rind and remove all seeds. Cut the flesh into cubes about 1 inch square and puree in a food processor or blender. Strain the puree through a sieve and reserve both pulp and liquid. There should be about ¾ to 1 cup of pulp.

Add the lemon juice to the pulp and the sugar. Stir until the sugar is completely dissolved. Allow the mixture to stand at room temperature for about 2 hours or until it resembles a syrup.

Soften the gelatin in 2 tablespoons of the reserved watermelon juice; stir until it is dissolved. Stir in ¼ cup of the juice, heated to the boiling point. Stir the gelatin mixture slowly into the puree, pour into a shallow metal container, and freeze for 1 hour.

Beat the heavy cream until stiff. Separate the egg; beat the white until stiff and lightly beat the yolk. Remove the watermelon mixture from the freezer, place in a chilled bowl, and beat with an electric mixer until frothy. Fold in the whipped cream, egg white, and yolk.

Pour the sherbet back into the metal container and freeze for 4 to 5 hours, stirring the mixture 2 or 3 times during this period to break up the ice crystals. (Unlike most sherbets made in the home freezer, this one needs only to be stirred a few times during the freezing process rather than to be removed from its container and beaten with a mixer).

May be served immediately or placed in a covered container and held for future use.

Melon in Anisette

serves four

At first glance, a rather unusual combination but one that is most refreshing. Use a good Spanish or Italian anisette.

1   large honey dew melon
⅓   cup imported anisette liqueur

Cut the melon in half and remove the seeds. Cut the flesh into bite-size pieces (or into balls with the aid of a melon baller) and place in a serving bowl. Sprinkle with the anisette, cover, and refrigerate for at least an hour.

August, Dining al Fresco

Menu 1
Curried Stuffed Eggs (August)
Boned Stuffed Chicken Roll (August)
Italian Rice Salad (August)
Caponata (August)
Peaches in Vouvray (June)

Menu 2
Salmon Seviche (August)
Spanish Pork Roast (August)
Potatoes in Pesto Sauce (August)
Ratatouille (August)
Raspberry Tart (June)

Soupe au Pistou
Salmon Seviche
Potted Salmon
Shellfish Salad with Tomato Mayonnaise
Fish Salad with Green Sauce
Curried Crab and Rice Salad
Italian Rice Salad
Quiche Orientale
Curried Stuffed Eggs
Caponata
Ratatouille
Potatoes in Pesto Sauce
Louisiana Crayfish Boil
Boned Stuffed Chicken Roll
Chicken Marengo
Pork Loin Tonnato
Spanish Pork Roast
Frozen Cheese Bombe
Lemon Ices (Granita de limone)

Seattle's Pike Place Market in any season is a delight for all the senses, but especially now, at the height of the growing season, when a bounty of fresh vegetables and fruits is spread out before you like a painter's palette: the royal purples of the eggplant, the subtle yellows and ambers of peaches and apricots, the verdant greens of zucchini and cucumbers, the brilliant reds of tomatoes. Walking through the crowded aisles is an inspiration, a rite of summer. Here you smell the sweet odors of fish and meat, the damp, earthy smells of fresh produce. Here, merchants are proud of their produce and eager to share with you their expertise in preparing it.

There is a rhythm to shopping the Pike Place Market (or any real market); you should not just dash in with a list, make your purchases, and leave: you must go through it rather slowly, keeping a sharp eye open for what is freshest. You must allow the Market itself to suggest to you what will be on your menu. One of the most satisfying reasons for Market shopping is the dialogue: tell the merchant that the tomatoes you need are for a sauce rather than for slicing, and he will pull out some lovely overripe (and perhaps slightly squashy) ones that will be just perfect — and at a better price.

August is usually the most pleasant of the summer months in the Northwest. Lives seem to slow down in tune with the warmth of the season and the prevailing mood is one of relaxation and contentment. Appetites tend to lag in these lazy months, so menus should be planned around dishes that will tease and awaken the palate. Light but not bland food should be your goal, prepared with a minimum of fuss, able to be served and eaten easily. Instead of taking along a roast chicken on a picnic, for instance, and having to contend with the bones, take a boned chicken roll (boned chicken stuffed with a spinach and sausage mixture and hardboiled eggs). Most of the dishes in this chapter can be prepared hours in advance, but remember that many meat and vegetable dishes taste better if served at room temperature rather than ice-cold; a little warmth gives the flavors a chance to assert themselves.

August is high season for eggplant, a vegetable that has gained in popularity here in America, but not so much as to be always prepared well. For the last thousand years or so, it has been the mainstay of the Mediterranean cuisine and its versatility is enormous: Moroccans add it to couscous, Greeks stuff it, in North Africa it is made into a jam, Lebanese pickle it, in Yugoslavia it is made into a relish, and in France it is made into the famous ratatouille.

When purchasing eggplant, look for firm and shiny globes. The stem should be fresh and green; avoid eggplants that are soft or of poor color, and those that have dark spots. Select small to medium sizes, for a large and heavy eggplant will usually contain more of the bitter seeds. If you choose wisely at the greengrocers you will find it is not always necessary to draw out the bitter juices by salting. And always use eggplant within a day or two of purchasing.

I remember walking through the Pike Place Market four or five years ago and coming across a bin of wriggling, green-black crustaceans that resembled tiny lobsters. A sign above them read, "danger, live crayfish." After questioning the fishmonger, I found that the crayfish were local. I had thought that this legendary creature was available only in the bayous and marshlands of Louisiana. Not so: there are crayfish in the lakes and rivers of Wisconsin, Minnesota, Oregon, Washington, and many other places. There isn't much meat on them, since they are usually three to six inches long; but what there is is succulent and sweeter-tasting than lobster. They are obtainable at the Market for only a short time, mid-July to September or October, depending on the vagaries of the weather or the fishermen.

These delicious morsels are almost as versatile as eggplant and can be used in many ways: in gumbos or jambalayas, mixed with other seafood in a salad, in paella, and in chioppino or other fish stews. One of the tastiest methods of preparation is simply to cook them in a spicy court bouillon, better known as a Louisiana Boil. It's a pity these wonderful crustaceans have been almost ignored by local restaurants and cooks; they are one of the chief splendors of the Northwest summer.

Soupe au Pistou
serves six to eight

This is a peasant soup popular in the south of France. It is composed of a number of the freshest seasonal vegetables, which always include at least two or three different varieties of beans (string beans, Roman or broad beans, shell beans, chickpeas, etc.). The dish is seasoned lightly with saffron and thickened at the table with a basil, garlic, cheese, and olive oil paste that is not for the faint of heart.

I have used a small amount of salt pork to give the vegetables a slightly richer flavor without imparting a definite meat taste to the soup. The fresh shell beans are important: there is a great difference in taste between these and the dried variety. Serve this dish with a Fitou or a Bardolino wine.

Soup:

2 tablespoons olive oil
½ cup diced salt pork, blanched
2 medium onions, coarsely chopped
2 medium red peppers, coarsely chopped
2 cups carrots, peeled and diced
2 cups potatoes, peeled and diced
1 pound (weight before shelling) fresh cranberry or other beans, shelled
3 large very ripe tomatoes, peeled, seeded, and coarsely chopped
⅛ teaspoon salt
· salt and freshly ground pepper to taste
· bouquet garni composed of 2 bay leaves, 2 sage leaves, sprig of thyme
3 small zucchini, diced
½ pound string beans, cut into ½-inch lengths
½ pound Roman or broad beans, cut into ½-inch lengths
3 ounces vermicelli, broken into 1-inch lengths

Pistou:

1 bunch fresh basil (about 3 cups), cleaned
4 large cloves garlic, peeled
1 teaspoon salt
½ cup fruity olive oil
1 cup freshly grated Parmesan or mixture of Parmesan and Romano cheeses

In a heavy enameled 6-quart soup pot, place the olive oil and the salt pork cubes; saute over medium heat until the pork is becoming brown and crisp at the edges. Add the onions and red peppers and saute for 5 minutes until the onions are golden; then add the carrots, potatoes, and shelled beans. Stir until all the vegetables are coated with fat, then saute them over low heat for an additional 5 minutes. Add the tomatoes, saffron, salt, pepper, and bouquet garni and cover all with water. Bring to a boil, reduce the heat, and simmer for about an hour. The soup can be made ahead to this point.

To the simmering soup add the zucchini, string and Roman beans, and vermicelli and continue to cook for 15 minutes more, until the beans and the pasta are both tender. Taste for seasoning, remove bouquet garni, and serve.

While the soup completes this last simmering, prepare the pistou: in the container of a food processor fitted with the steel knife blade place the basil, garlic cloves, and salt and blend to a coarse paste. While the machine is running, add the olive oil in a thin stream. Remove the basil paste to a small bowl, stir in the grated cheese, and mix thoroughly. If the pistou is not to be used immediately, cover it completely, placing plastic wrap directly on the surface.

Serve the pistou at the table separately in a bowl, allowing each person to add a tablespoon or more to his soup. An additional bowl of grated cheese may also be passed if desired.

Salmon Seviche
serves six

An unusual treatment for salmon. The lime juice neutralizes the oiliness of the fish and refines its flavor. The green peppercorns used in the marinade should be packed in water; avoid those packed in vinegar, as they have an undesirable tart aftertaste. Serve as a first course with a dry Riesling or a light Chardonnay (i.e., a Pouilly Fuisse).

1½ pounds salmon
2½ tablespoons green
       peppercorns (water-packed)
1   cup onion, sliced paper-thin
·   juice of 6 limes
1   teaspoon salt
·   dash Tabasco
¼ cup plus 3 tablespoons olive
   oil

Remove the skin from the salmon; carefully remove and discard any bones. Cut the fish into 1-inch cubes.

Pound the green peppercorns lightly with a mortar and pestle (about half of them should be mashed). Put them in a shallow nonmetallic bowl with the onion, lime juice, salt, Tabasco and ¼ cup olive oil; mix together well. Add the salmon and turn it in the mixture so that the fish is coated with the marinade. Cover with plastic wrap and refrigerate for 24 hours.

Before serving: drain the fish in a sieve, reserving a tablespoon or two of the marinade. Dress the salmon with a mixture of 1 tablespoon of the marinade and 3 tablespoons olive oil. Taste and add the other tablespoon marinade if desired.

Serve the seviche on lettuce with wedges of lemon and hardboiled egg.

Potted Salmon
makes about two and a half cups

May also be prepared with leftover poached salmon. A bit of tarragon or chives may be added to the salmon mixture if desired, but the latter should be used only if fresh, dried chives have little or no flavor.

1½-pound piece of salmon, center-cut
· lemon juice to taste
· dash Tabasco
6 to 8 tablespoons butter, cut into chunks

Prepare a court bouillon and bring to a boil in a large enamel casserole with lid. Reduce the heat and simmer for 45 minutes.

Wrap the salmon in cheesecloth and tie the ends tightly with string. Lower the fish into the simmering liquid. Cover, bring to a boil, and cook over high heat for 2 minutes only. Immediately remove the casserole from the heat and allow the fish to cool, covered, in the bouillon. This is an absolutely foolproof way to poach fish of any size to perfection.

Remove the salmon from the casserole when cooled; remove and discard the cheesecloth. Clean off the skin and remove all bones, flaking the fish as you go along. Place the cleaned salmon in a food processor or blender and blend until it is smooth. Add the lemon juice, Tabasco, and the butter, bit by bit, while the machine is running. Blend until the butter is totally absorbed into the salmon. Taste for seasoning, adding salt if necessary. Pack tightly into a serving container and chill 2 to 3 hours before serving. Serve with thinly sliced rye or pumpernickel. If potted salmon is to be held longer than one day, cover the top with a half-inch layer of clarified butter.

Shellfish Salad with Tomato Mayonnaise
serves four to six

This dish makes a marvelous summer first course or a light luncheon for two or three with a Saumur wine or a medium-dry Riesling, like a good German Rheingauer.

1	pound scallops (if sea scallops are used, cut each in half)
1	pound shrimp

Court bouillon:

¼	cup wine vinegar
1	quart water
1	rib celery, coarsely chopped
1	thick slice onion
1	thick slice lemon
·	few sprigs of fresh thyme or parsley
½	bay leaf
1	teaspoon salt
·	few peppercorns

Sauce:

1	tablespoon olive oil
½	tablespoon onion, finely chopped
2	large ripe tomatoes, peeled, seeded, and finely chopped
2	leaves fresh basil, finely chopped
·	salt and freshly ground pepper
1½	cups mayonnaise made with lemon juice instead of vinegar
1	tablespoon cognac

Garnish:

·	thin slices lemon
·	parsley

Combine all the ingredients for the court bouillon. Bring to a boil and cook for 15 minutes. Add the scallops, reduce heat, and simmer them for 4 to 5 minutes, until just tender. Remove them with a slotted spoon and set aside to drain.

Add the shrimp in their shells to the court bouillon and simmer them for 5 minutes; remove and allow to drain.

While the court bouillon is cooking prepare the sauce: in a small skillet heat the olive oil, add the onion, and saute until soft but not brown, about 5 minutes. Add the tomatoes, salt, pepper, and basil, turn the heat up, and quickly reduce any liquids released by the tomatoes. Simmer the tomato mixture for 20 minutes until it forms a thick sauce. Remove to a mixing bowl and allow to cool slightly. Mix in the mayonnaise and the cognac; taste and adjust seasoning if necessary.

Shell the shrimps, combine them with the scallops in a serving dish, and toss with the tomato mayonnaise. Chill for an hour or two before serving. Garnish with the lemon slices and the parsley.

Fish Salad with Green Sauce
serves six

Any firm white fish can be used for this recipe: sea bass, striped bass, cod, halibut, etc. This dish can be made to go farther by adding to it a half pound of boiled and thickly sliced potatoes. It is best, though, as a first course; serve with a fragrant Pouilly Fume.

2	pounds firm white fish fillets
	Court bouillon:
1	cup dry white vermouth or dry white wine
2	cups water
1	rib celery, coarsely chopped
1	thick slice onion
1	thick slice lemon
·	few sprigs thyme or parsley
½	bay leaf
1	teaspoon salt
·	few peppercorns
	Sauce:
1	bunch parsley, stems removed
4	shallots, peeled
1	tablespoon capers
1	teaspoon finely grated lemon rind
1-inch	squeeze anchovy paste
2	tablespoons wine vinegar
6	tablespoons olive oil
·	salt and freshly ground pepper
3	ripe tomatoes, peeled, seeded, and coarsely chopped
2	small cucumbers, peeled, seeded, cut into quarters lengthwise, and then cut crosswise into 2-inch lengths
½	cup black olives, pitted and sliced
2	hardboiled eggs, quartered

Combine all the ingredients for the court bouillon. Bring to a boil and cook for 15 minutes. Add the fish, reduce the heat, and simmer for about 5 minutes until the fish is tender. Remove the fish, drain well, and separate into large flakes, removing and discarding any bones you may come across. Set aside while you prepare the sauce.

Finely chop the parsley, shallots, capers, and lemon rind together by hand; the mixture will resemble a coarse paste when done. Place it in a small mixing bowl, stir in the anchovy paste, vinegar, and oil and season to taste with salt and pepper.

In a serving bowl, combine the cooked fish with the tomatoes, cucumbers, and black olives, pour the sauce over, toss gently, and garnish with the hardboiled eggs. Serve immediately. This dish may be made ahead and refrigerated, but it should be brought back to room temperature before serving.

Curried Crab and Rice Salad
serves four

A savory combination of rice, crabmeat, and aromatic vegetables seasoned with curry powder. The secret of a good curry flavor lies in cooking the powder rather than using it right out of the bottle.

This salad is lovely stuffed into hollowed-out tomatoes and can be served as a first course or as an accompaniment to a roast.

1   cup long-grain rice
3   tablespoons butter
½   cup onion, peeled and
     finely chopped
⅓   cup celery, cut into small
     dice
⅓   cup green bell pepper, cut
     into small dice
1   tablespoon curry powder (or
     to taste — depending on
     strength)
6   ounces crabmeat, cooked,
     carefully cleaned, and
     flaked (substitute cooked
     shrimp meat, if desired)
½   cup heavy cream
·   salt and freshly ground
     pepper
·   small handful parsley, finely
     chopped
·   lemon slices

Cook the rice; when done

remove it to a serving bowl to cool and to allow the grains to separate.

While the rice is cooking, melt the butter in a skillet, add the onion, celery, and green pepper, and saute for 3 minutes; stir in the curry powder and continue to cook for a few minutes more until the vegetables are tender but still crisp. Remove from heat and stir the vegetables into the rice; add the crab or shrimp meat and toss together.

Just before serving, season the heavy cream lightly with salt and whip gently; it must not be stiff. Season the salad with pepper and parsley, fold in the whipped cream, taste for seasoning, and serve garnished with lemon slices.

Italian Rice Salad
serves four

1   cup long-grain rice
¼   pound green beans, cut into
     1-inch lengths
3 to 4 tablespoons red or white
     onion
1   tablespoon olive oil
1   large ripe tomato
¼   cup pitted olives coarsely
     chopped (mixture of Greek
     Calamata and Spanish
     green)
3   tablespoons parsley, minced
     together with ¼ teaspoon
     dried summer savory
2 to 3 tablespoons red wine
     vinegar
¼   cup olive oil
·   salt and freshly ground
     pepper

Cook the rice, removing it to a platter when done to cool and to allow the grains to separate.

While the rice is cooking boil the green beans in salted water until they are tender but still crisp. Saute the onion in the olive oil for 2 to 3 minutes. Skin and seed the tomato and chop it into large dice.

When the rice is cool, mix in the

beans, sauteed onion, tomato, olives, parsley, and savory. Toss with the vinegar and olive oil. Season to taste with salt and pepper. Chill for about an hour before serving.

Quiche Orientale
serves six to eight

The seasoning lifts this crab quiche out of the ordinary. It is a subtle blend of saffron, mild curry powder, and a dash of Pernod. The results are an uncommonly delicious savory that is suitable for lunch or the buffet table. A Saumur or a dry Riesling or Vouvray would blend nicely.

10-inch pastry shell fitted into a quiche pan or flan ring
3 eggs
1 cup heavy cream
· salt
· pinch each of fresh grated nutmeg and cayenne pepper
1 tablespoon mild curry powder
1 tablespoon Pernod
· scant ½ pound crabmeat, cooked, carefully cleaned, and flaked
1 tablespoon sliced almonds.

Preheat oven to 400 degrees.

Line the uncooked pastry shell with a sheet of aluminum foil and fill with raw rice or beans.

Bake the shell for 10 minutes, then remove from the oven, take out the foil lining and the rice or beans, and bake the shell for another 10 minutes, until the pastry shrinks away from the sides of the pan and the bottom starts to take color. Remove from the oven and allow to cool slightly.

Turn oven down to 350 degrees. Beat together well the eggs, cream, and seasonings with a wire whisk. Check the seasonings; you may add a bit more curry powder if you wish. Blend the crabmeat and the Pernod into the egg mixture and pour into the partially baked pastry shell.

Bake for 20 to 25 minutes or until the custard is just set (insert a knife into the middle of the quiche; when it is withdrawn the blade should be clean). During the last 10 minutes of baking, sprinkle the top with the sliced almonds. Serve warm or at room temperature.

Curried Stuffed Eggs
makes forty-eight pieces

In true East Indian fashion, a melange of spices flavor these eggs rather than a curry powder out of a jar.

1½ tablespoons vegetable oil
½ teaspoon black mustard
    seeds
½ teaspoon cumin seeds
2 tablespoons fresh ginger,
    finely chopped
2 tablespoons onion, finely
    chopped
1 teaspoon salt
1 teaspoon tumeric
· pinch of cayenne pepper
2 dozen hardboiled eggs
2 tablespoons finely chopped
    Major Gray's chutney
2 to 3 tablespoons mayonnaise

In a small skillet heat the oil over moderate heat till a light haze forms over it. Stir in the mustard seeds and cumin seeds and immediately add the ginger and onion; saute for 2 minutes.

Add the salt, turmeric, and cayenne and continue to saute until the onions are soft and lightly colored.

Remove the yolks from the eggs and place them in a mixing bowl; cut the whites in half lengthwise and reserve. Combine the yolks with the onion and ginger mixture. Put them in the container of a blender or food processor fitted with a steel knife blade and blend to a paste.

Remove to a bowl and add the chutney and enough mayonnaise to lighten the texture; blend thoroughly. Place the stuffing mixture in a pastry bag fitted with a number 2 star tip and pipe it into the reserved egg halves.

Caponata
serves six

Caponata is a cooked "salad" of Italian origin, composed of eggplant, sweet peppers, onions, and celery and seasoned with a slightly sweet-sour sauce made of capers, olives, tomato paste, and a robust red wine vinegar. Each element in the salad is cooked and seasoned separately, then combined and quickly sauteed for a brief but fruitful marriage of flavors. The artichoke hearts are an unusual touch. While I don't often advise the use of frozen vegetables, the time spent on preparing as many fresh artichokes as are called for in this dish is prohibitive. This recipe developed from Paula Wolfert's caponata in her inspiring book, *Mediterranean Cooking*.

·	olive oil
2	packages frozen artichoke hearts (do not substitute canned)
1	clove garlic, peeled
·	lemon juice
·	salt and freshly ground pepper
1	cup celery cut into julienne strips
·	pinch of sugar
2	medium eggplants, cut into large cubes but not peeled
2	tablespoons parsley
½	teaspoon garlic, finely chopped
18	small white onions, peeled and boiled for 10 minutes
2	tablespoons red wine vinegar
3	medium red or green bell peppers, roasted and cut into strips about ¼-inch wide (see "Roasted Sweet Peppers")
4	ounces tomato paste
1	cup water
1	tablespoon capers, chopped
½	cup each pitted black and green olives, blanched in boiling water for 5 minutes
1	teaspoon herbes de Provence (a combination of thyme, savory, basil, fennel seed, and lavender flowers, available in specialty shops)
2	tablespoons pine nuts, toasted in a small skillet over medium high heat for 3 to 5 minutes

Heat olive oil in a heavy 10-inch skillet. While still half frozen, saute the artichoke hearts with a garlic clove for about a minute on each side. Remove with a slotted spoon to a 12-inch skillet and season with salt, pepper, and a squeeze of lemon juice. Remove the garlic and discard.

In the same pan saute the celery strips over moderately high heat for 4 or 5 minutes, adding more oil if necessary. Sprinkle the celery with salt, pepper, and a pinch of sugar and remove with slotted spoon to the larger skillet.

Add more oil to the small skillet and fry the eggplant cubes at high heat for about 5 minutes or until barely tender and lightly browned. Season with salt and pepper and toss with the parsley and chopped garlic. Transfer this in its turn to the larger skillet.

Lightly brown the onions in the oil remaining in the smaller skillet, sprinkling them with salt, pepper, and a pinch of sugar. Add the vinegar and reduce to a glaze over high heat, shaking the skillet to avoid scorching. Transfer the glazed onions to the larger skillet. Add the roasted red or green pepper strips to larger skillet.

Mix the tomato paste with 1 cup water and add to the 10-inch skillet with the capers and the blanched olives and simmer for a few minutes more. Correct the seasoning, adding salt if necessary, pepper, and a dash more vinegar if desired.

Pour this mixture over the vegetables in the 12-inch skillet, sprinkle with the herbes de Provence, and gently mix all the ingredients. Cook over low heat for about 5 minutes, or just long enough for the flavors to meld without allowing the vegetables to lose their shape. Garnish with the toasted pine nuts and serve at room temperature.

This dish tastes better when prepared a day or two in advance. Before serving, remove from refrigerator and allow to come to room temperature.

Ratatouille
serves six to eight

This delicious melange of vegetables, a specialty of Provence, has hundreds of variations, but its basic ingredients always remain the same: eggplant, onion, bell pepper, zucchini, and tomato.

One of the commonest mistakes with this dish is overcooking the vegetables into a "stew" of shapeless and unrecognizable ingredients. This recipe calls for each vegetable to be individually and briefly cooked; they are then combined and allowed to simmer gently together with the seasonings. Ratatouille can be served hot, cold, or at room temperature.

7 to 8 tablespoons olive oil
2 medium eggplants, unpeeled and cut into 1½-inch cubes
3 medium onions, peeled and cut in half and then into slices ½-inch thick
2 medium red or green bell peppers, seeded and cut into strips ½ inch wide

3 to 4 small zucchini, cut into 1-inch cubes
4 large very ripe tomatoes, peeled, seeded, and coarsely chopped
2 or 3 cloves garlic, peeled and thinly sliced
· salt and freshly ground pepper
1 teaspoon herbes de Provence (dried herb mixture) chopped together with 1 tablespoon fresh basil
1 teaspoon finely grated lemon peel
½ cup beef stock
· imported black olives and lemon slices

Heat 2 tablespoons olive oil in a heavy 12-inch skillet. Cook half the eggplant cubes over moderately high heat till tender and lightly browned. Remove and repeat with remaining eggplant, adding 2 tablespoons more olive oil. Remove and set aside.

Add another tablespoon of oil to the same skillet and saute the

170

onions and red or green peppers over medium heat until they are tender but still crisp. Remove and set aside.

Add another tablespoon of oil to the skillet (if necessary) and saute the zucchini cubes over moderately high heat until they are tender; remove and reserve.

Add another tablespoon of oil to the 12-inch skillet and cook the tomatoes and garlic over high heat till all moisture is evaporated. Season with salt, pepper, the dried and fresh herbs, and lemon peel, lower heat, and continue to cook for 10 minutes more. (A small pinch of sugar may be added to the tomatoes, if they are not very ripe.)

Put all the cooked vegetables in a heavy 3- or 4-quart pot, add the tomato sauce and the beef stock, and simmer gently for 15 to 20 minutes. Serve garnished with imported black olives and lemon slices.

Potatoes in Pesto Sauce
serves four

The blandness of the potatoes makes a perfect background for this herb paste composed of fresh basil, garlic, Parmesan, olive oil, and pine nuts. Pesto may also be used to sauce pasta, poached white fish, and rice.

1   bunch fresh basil, about 3 cups
1   teaspoon salt
3 to 4 garlic cloves, peeled and cut in half
3   tablespoons pine nuts, toasted lightly over high heat in a small skillet
½   cup fruity olive oil
½   cup freshly grated Parmesan (or combination of Parmesan and Romano)
8   medium new potatoes, peeled and cut into thick slices

Prepare the pesto: wash the basil, removing the stems, and dry well. Place in the container of a blender or food processor with the salt, garlic and pine nuts and puree. While the machine is running, add the olive oil in a thin stream; remove the paste, put in a bowl, and mix in the grated cheese. Place a piece of plastic wrap directly on the surface of the pesto until serving time, or cover top with ¼-inch olive oil and refrigerate. It will keep this way for 2 or 3 days.

Add the potato slices to boiling, salted water and cook until they are just tender. Drain the potatoes, reserving 1 tablespoon of the cooking liquid. Mix the pesto with the liquid, pour mixture over potato slices, and toss together. Serve immediately.

Louisiana Crayfish Boil
serves four

It is difficult to ascertain just exactly how many crayfish constitute one serving; a good rule of thumb is to serve a dozen for each person, and if your guests are true crayfish fanciers, to add another dozen or two "for the pot." Serve with Caesar salad with mint (May) and a robust California Sauvignon Blanc or Frascati.

4   lemons, cut in quarters
2   large onions, peeled but left whole, each stuck with 3 cloves
2   stalks celery, coarsely chopped
4   dried red hot chilies, left whole
6   garlic cloves, left whole with skins intact
6   bay leaves, crumbled
2   tablespoons whole allspice
¼   cup mustard seeds
1   small handful fresh thyme (substitute parsley if unavailable)
¼   cup sea salt
48   live crayfish

In a 12- to 14-quart stockpot, combine all ingredients except the crayfish and cover with 8 quarts of water. Bring to a boil over high heat, cover tightly, reduce heat to a simmer, and cook for 45 minutes.

While this is cooking, rinse the crayfish in plenty of cold water —this may be done in batches your kitchen sink. When the court bouillon is ready, add the crayfish—about 2 dozen at a time—and boil them uncovered for about 5 minutes. Remove with a large skimmer and repeat the procedure with the remaining crayfish.

Place all the crayfish in a large colander to drain. When they are cool enough to handle, arrange them on your largest platter, claws facing out, and allow to cool a bit longer. Garnish the platter with slices of lemon and parsley sprigs.

Boned Stuffed Chicken Roll
serves six

A delightful presentation: boned chicken rolled around a sausage and spinach stuffing. The roll must be allowed to stand for 3 to 4 hours after roasting so that the filling holds together when it is sliced.

Serve with a first course of curried eggs and Italian rice salad or potatoes in pesto (all this month); or with roasted peppers with or without potatoes (July). For wine try a Soave or Frascati.

3- to 3½-pound whole plump
chicken
2 or 3 Italian sweet sausages,
skinned and chopped
5 tablespoons olive oil
¾ cup onion, finely chopped
1 large garlic clove, finely
minced
10-ounce package frozen
chopped spinach, cooked
and drained
· salt and freshly ground
pepper to taste
¼ teaspoon marjoram
¼ cup freshly grated Parmesan
or Romano cheese
1 egg, lightly beaten
6 ounces pancetta (Italian-
style bacon), thinly sliced
2 hardboiled eggs, peeled

Preheat the oven to 400 degrees. Cut the chicken down the back and remove all the bones, including the leg bones and the large bone in the wings; reserve the outer two joints of the wings and the carcass for making a stock. Do not remove the skin. Saute the sausage meat in 1 tablespoon olive oil until browned. Add the onion and garlic and cook for about 5 minutes. Add the cooked spinach and saute over moderately high heat until all excess moisture is absorbed; season with salt, pepper, and marjoram. Remove from heat and mix in the grated cheese and the beaten egg.

Put the boned chicken on your working space, skin-side down. Arrange pieces of leg and wing meat over any holes or thin spots; cover the carcass with waxed paper and pound the meat lightly to produce a more uniform thickness.

Cover the exposed meat with the pancetta. Over this, spread the sausage and spinach mixture, leaving a 1-inch margin on all sides. Place the two eggs, end to end, on the short side nearest to you. Roll up the chicken, tucking in tne sides as you roll. Tie the roll with kitchen string every 2 inches along its length, and season the chicken lightly with salt and pepper.

In a shallow, ovenproof dish, pour the remaining 4 tablespoons olive oil, add the chicken, and roll it around in oil until its surface is lightly covered. Put in the oven and roast for about 1 hour, basting every 10 or 15 minutes. Allow the chicken to stand for 3 to 4 hours before serving. Remove strings and slice into ½-inch thicknesses.

Chicken Marengo
serves four

This historic dish is said to have been invented hurriedly by Napoleon's chef on the eve of the battle of Marengo. The chicken is first browned, then flamed in cognac, and finally simmered in a fresh tomato sauce. The dish is served surrounded by fried croutons and cooked crayfish, a delightful presentation. Serve with the green bean and pepper saute gazpacho (both June) or the orange and radish salad (September). Try a Soave, a Chardonnay, or California Sauvignon Blanc with this.

1   large chicken (about 3½ pounds), cut into serving pieces
·   salt and freshly ground pepper
4   tablespoons olive oil
⅓   cup cognac or good brandy
1   tablespoon onion, finely chopped
1   large garlic clove, minced or put through a press
6   large, very ripe tomatoes, peeled, seeded, and coarsely chopped
·   small pinch of sugar
¼   cup dry white vermouth or dry white wine
3   slices of bread sauteed till golden brown in olive oil or butter
6   cooked crayfish

Season the chicken pieces with salt and pepper. Heat the olive oil in a skillet over moderately high heat, add the chicken, and brown evenly on all sides. Heat the cognac or brandy in a large ladle held over high heat. Pour it over the chicken pieces and ignite, shaking the skillet until the flames subside. Remove the chicken with a slotted spoon and set aside.

Into the remaining fat in the skillet put the onion and garlic; saute over medium heat for a few minutes until the onion is golden. Add the tomatoes, season with salt, pepper, and a pinch of sugar, turn the heat up, and reduce any juices from the tomatoes over high heat. Add the vermouth, reduce the heat, add the chicken pieces, and spoon the sauce over them. Cover and cook gently over low heat until the chicken is tender, about 40 minutes.

When the chicken is done, place it with the sauce on a serving platter. Garnish with triangles of sauteed bread and cooked crayfish for a traditional presentation.

Pork Loin Tonnato
serves six to eight

Since fine veal is so difficult to obtain, I have adapted this Italian classic using very lean pork in its place. The sauce, a mixture of mayonnaise, lemon, tuna, and anchovy, is equally delicious with poached chicken.

Serve with the raw mushroom salad (April) or with potatoes in pesto, Italian rice salad, or shellfish salad (all this month). Try a Frascati or a Soave as the wine.

4-pound pork loin roast, boneless and trimmed of excess fat, tied well
· salt and freshly ground pepper
2 small shallots, peeled
8 sprigs Italian (flat-leaved) parsley
6½-ounce can tuna packed in olive oil, drained
4 anchovy fillets, drained and cut in half
1½ tablespoons capers, drained, washed, and dried
1½ cups mayonnaise
· lemon juice
· sprigs of Italian parsley, black olives, lemon slices

The night before serving, prepare the pork.

Preheat the oven to 350 degrees. Rub the meat with salt and freshly ground pepper and place it in a shallow roasting pan. Put it in the preheated oven and roast for 2 to 2½ hours or until a thermometer reads 170 degrees, basting the meat with its own juices occasionally. Remove from oven, allow to cool, and wrap tightly in foil.

The next day prepare the sauce: in the container of a food processor fitted with the steel knife blade, place the shallots, parsley, tuna, anchovy, and capers; blend to a paste. Remove and pour it over mayonnaise and blend well. Add a little lemon juice to taste, taste for seasoning, and chill.

Just before serving, slice the pork into slices ¼ inch thick; arrange them on a large serving platter, pour sauce over all, and garnish with the parsley, olives, and lemon slices.

Spanish Pork Roast
serves six to eight

The pork loin is marinated for 24 hours in a mixture of orange juice, thinly sliced onion, bay leaves, and a bit of allspice. The meat is then roasted and allowed to cool, the marinade leaving behind a suggestion of citrus. Serve curried eggs as first course, caponata, salmon seviche, or potatoes in pesto as accompaniment (all this month). You'll need a full white wine with this: a Chardonnay, Meursault, or white Cotes du Rhone.

2 cups freshly squeezed orange juice
1 teaspoon salt
2 tablespoons sugar
½ cup onion, thinly sliced
3 bay leaves, broken up into pieces
4-pound pork loin roast, boneless
4 cloves garlic, peeled and cut into slices
· salt and freshly ground pepper to taste
· orange slices and flat-leaved parsley

Marinate the meat 24 hours before it is to be served. Combine the orange juice, salt, sugar, onions, bay leaves, and allspice and mix well. Cut small, deep slits in the roast with a sharp knife and insert in each of them a slice of garlic. Place the roast in a deep dish and pour the marinade over it. Refrigerate for 24 hours, turning occasionally.

Preheat oven to 350 degrees.

Remove the pork from the marinade, dry well with paper towels, and season it with salt and pepper. Place it in a shallow open roasting pan with the fat side up and roast for about 2½ hours or until meat thermometer registers 170 degrees.

After the first 15 minutes, baste the meat with fat accumulated in the pan. After the first half hour, add the strained marinade and continue to baste with pan juices every 15 minutes. Remove the meat when done and allow to cool at room temperature. Slice thinly and garnish with orange slices and flat-leaved parsley.

Frozen Cheese Bombe
serves eight to ten

This recipe calls for an ice cream mold such as a melon mold; do not use one with a tube center, or one with a very elaborate design on the sides: the simpler the mold, the easier it will be to remove the bombe in one recognizable piece.

Most books call for the mold to be dipped in warm water prior to unmolding, which usually does a beautiful job of melting the mixture inside and causing the partial or complete loss of design. *Cold* water is the answer; it is warmer than whatever you have just taken out of the refrigerator or freezer, but not warm enough to turn your dish to mush.

¼ pound Roquefort
¼ pound cream cheese
¼ pound Gorgonzola
¼ pound Cheshire
¼ pound ricotta
½ cup heavy cream
· salt and freshly ground pepper
· dash Worcestershire sauce
1½ tablespoons cognac

Cut all of the solid cheeses into 1-inch chunks. Put them with the ricotta in the container of a food processor fitted with the steel knife blade. Blend for a few seconds while adding the heavy cream until the texture resembles that of a thick mousse.

Season to taste with salt, pepper, and Worcestershire; add the cognac and blend well.

Pour into a 1-quart ice-cream mold that has been rinsed with cold water and freeze for at least 2 hours. Remove the mold ½ hour before serving, dip it briefly into cold water, run a thin knife around the edges to loosen the bombe, and unmold it onto a serving plate. Surround the bombe with green grapes and some good biscuits such as the Scandinavian oatmeal or British whole wheat or water biscuits.

Lemon Ices (Granita de limone)
serves four to six

A true ice or granita should have the texture of lightly packed snow, so that the grains of flavored ice melt on your tongue in a delicious and seductive manner.

⅔   cup sugar
2   cups water
2   large lemons

Combine the sugar and water in a small saucepan, place over heat, and bring to a boil; cook only long enough for sugar to melt. Remove from heat and allow to cool.

Finely grate the rind from the 2 lemons and set aside. Juice the lemons and strain to remove the pips.

Add the lemon rind and juice to the sugar syrup and mix. Pour into an ice tray or other shallow container and freeze for about 2 hours without stirring, until the ice has crystallized.

The ice may then be put quickly through a food processor or blender to break it up, or it may be spooned directly out of the container and into serving dishes.

September, Buffet Food

Menu 1
Italian Buffet:
Antipasto
Stuffed Mussels (March)
Chickpea and Salami Salad (September)
Roasted Pepper Salad (July)
Cold Vegetable Frittata (September)
Stuffed Breast of Veal (September)
Cannoli (December)

Menu 2
Charcuterie Buffet:
Rillettes de Porc (December)
Terrine of Rabbit (October)
Chicken Liver Mousse (December)
Potted Salmon (August)
Raw Mushroom Salad (April)
Carrottes Rapees (February)
Celery Root Remoulade (November)
Leeks in Vinaigrette (November)
Onion Soup (January)
Assorted Cheeses and Fruit

Tsutakawa

Moroccan Orange and Radish Salad
Cucumber and Octopus Salad
Chickpea and Salami Salad
Late Summer Bean Soup
Eggplant Caviar
Stuffed Grape Leaves
Cold Vegetable Frittata
Cheese and Onion Tart
Leek and Sausage Tart
Moussaka
Moroccan Lamb Tajin
Veal Nicoise
Stuffed Breast of Veal
Baked Corned Beef
Lemon Blueberry Souffle Glace
Blueberry Clafoutis
Blueberry Sourcream Tart

Entertaining in the home has taken on a new and more relaxed form. It is rare, these days, to be invited to an eight course sitdown dinner, and for a number of very good reasons. People today do not want to consume the rich food that was popular in the past, nor can many of us afford these gastronomic luxuries (or the elaborate table settings that usually accompany them). Very few of us are willing to spend the required number of hours on preparation even if we did have the time to do so.

The emphasis now is on unstudied and relaxed evenings, and that means relaxed for all concerned, including host and hostess. Elsa Maxwell once said, "The joy of a host or hostess at their own party must be the first element encountered by the guest." One cannot appear to be joyous if one has spent most of the last twelve hours whisking sauces and is now fraught with anxiety about whether the souffle will rise.

Because many of us are living in smaller spaces, the buffet has become an increasingly popular form of entertaining. Buffet food should ideally be easy to eat *and* to serve; it should consist of dishes that can be prepared in advance. There are other considerations: the casual presentation makes it more important that the food served be a source of surprise and delight to the guests; it should always be appealing visually. Enough of those ubiquitous raw vegetables and dips or soggy-bottomed canapes, rubbery aspics, heavily mayonnaised salads, and leather-edged cold cuts! With a little imagination you could provide a buffet in the style of a French charcuterie: terrine of rabbit, potted salmon or shrimp, rillettes, country pate, a good sausage or two, and an assortment of breads. Accompany this with a grated carrot salad, a French potato salad (dressed with oil and vinegar), and green beans vinaigrette (or substitute any green vegetable in season: asparagus, leeks, fennel, roasted bell peppers), plus a selection of cheeses and fruit for dessert. For those who hate to leave a good party: onion soup served in large mugs.

Buffets planned around ethnic themes give the inventive cook an amazing variety of dishes to draw on. Even better, dishes from divergent cuisines can be combined for an unusual eclectic menu. For example, you may wish to serve a menu based on Middle Eastern food, with moussaka as the main course; since this dish is a rather rich one it might be accompanied by a light side dish, such as a cucumber and octopus salad adapted from the Japanese.

There are many dishes scattered throughout this book that are delightful on the buffet table: paella, chou farci, poor man's pate en croute, Spanish pork roast, crab and oyster jambalaya, kulebiaka, and abbaccio alla cacciatoria. Try to plan your menus around food that needs little or no cutting after it is served: use boneless meats and slice them into individual portions. If it is feasible, present dishes already arranged in individual servings: cup a serving of vegetable salad in a leaf of Bibb lettuce; this also makes for cleaner appearance when the platter is emptied and provides a tacit "portion control," so every guest gets a fair share.

If much of your entertaining is done en buffet, you should consider purchasing large dinner plates, eleven to twelve inches in diameter, which are much easier to balance on one's lap. Also, large cloth napkins, twenty to twenty-two inches square, help to protect your guests' clothing.

Moroccan Orange and Radish Salad

serves four

An intriguing Moroccan creation: peeled, chopped orange sections and grated raw radish dressed with a mixture of lemon, sugar, salt, and cinnamon. This is a fresh and lively side dish, especially good with roast lamb or duck; it is also most delicious served with couscous.

4   medium seedless oranges
8 to 10 radishes, coarsely grated
6   tablespoons lemon juice
2   tablespoons sugar
⅛   teaspoon salt
·   powdered cinnamon

Peel the oranges with a serrated knife and cut the flesh into bite-size chunks. Mix the orange pieces with the grated radish.

Combine the lemon juice, sugar, and salt, pour the dressing over the orange mixture, and toss. Sprinkle the salad with a light dusting of the powdered cinnamon, cover tightly, and chill. The salad will keep, refrigerated, for 4 to 6 hours. Toss together well just before serving.

Cucumber and Octopus Salad

serves four

This salad was adapted from the Japanese sunomono — a mixture of sliced cucumber and octopus with rice wine vinegar, sugar, and soy sauce — but it is dressed differently. You can purchase cooked octopus at many fish markets and it is usually quite tender. If it is not, it may be simmered for a while in boiling water to which has been added a dash of vinegar. Those of you who are completely unadventurous may substitute cooked crab meat for the chewy, nutty-flavored octopus.

2   medium cucumbers
·   coarse salt
½   pound cooked octopus, cut into thin slices
1½ tablespoons lemon juice or mild wine vinegar
5   tablespoons olive oil
·   dash Oriental sesame oil (available at Oriental specialty stores and some supermarkets)
·   salt and freshly ground pepper

Peel the cucumbers; slice off the ends, cut them in half, and remove the seeds. Put the pieces in a bowl, sprinkle them liberally with coarse salt, and allow to stand at room temperature for at least ½ hour. Rinse the cucumbers under cold running water, dry thoroughly, and cut into fine slices.

Combine the octopus with the cucumber slices, dress with the lemon juice or vinegar, olive oil, sesame oil, and salt and pepper to taste. Toss mixture together well, marinate for 1 hour or longer, and serve.

Chickpea and Salami Salad
serves six to eight

Canned chickpeas (garbanzo beans) should not be substituted for the freshly cooked ones in this recipe because they tend to be rather mushy and flavorless. The salami may be replaced with any cooked garlic sausage. As a main-dish salad, serve with a Soave or Frascati.

2 cups dried chickpeas
1 medium onion
· salt
1 pound salami, thickly sliced and cut into julienne strips
1 small red onion, finely chopped
2 cloves garlic, finely chopped
8 to 10 imported black olives, pitted and coarsely chopped
1 cup flat-leaved parsley, finely chopped
2 tablespoons red wine vinegar
½ cup olive oil
· freshly ground pepper
· large pinch dried summer savory
· dash Tabasco

Soak the chickpeas overnight in water to cover.

Drain the beans, place them in a heavy 4-quart pot, and add enough cold water to cover them by 2 inches. Quarter the onion and add it, along with salt to taste, to the peas. Bring the pot to a boil, reduce the heat, and simmer for about 2 hours or until tender. Discard the onion and drain the peas thoroughly.

Place the peas in a large mixing bowl while still warm; add the salami, chopped onion, olives, parsley, and garlic. Toss well. Season the salad with the vinegar, oil, a liberal grinding of pepper, savory, and Tabasco and toss once again so that all ingredients are coated with the dressing. Serve at once, or allow to stand at room temperature for an hour or two.

Late Summer Bean Soup

serves four to six

A delicious combination of shell and green beans flavored with bits of ham.

2	pounds shell beans
1	small ham shank, about 1½ pounds
1	large onion, peeled and stuck with 4 cloves
·	small bunch of celery leaves
2	bay leaves
·	salt
3	tablespoons butter
1	cup carrots, peeled and coarsely chopped
1	cup celery, coarsely chopped
2	leeks, cleaned and coarsely chopped
2	cups green beans, cut into 1-inch lengths
·	a few sprigs of fresh thyme, minced, or ¼ teaspoon dried thyme or summer savory

Remove the beans from their shells and put them into a 5-quart soup pot with the ham shank, onion, celery leaves, bay leaves, and salt. Cover all with water, bring to a boil, reduce heat, and simmer for 1 to 1½ hours, until the beans are tender. Remove the ham and reserve; discard the onion, celery, and bay leaves.

Pour the beans into a sieve over a mixing bowl to catch the cooking liquid; reserve it.

Remove the ham from its bone and chop it into small dice; saute the meat in the butter for 2 or 3 minutes until it is lightly brown. Add the carrots, celery, leeks, and half of the cooked beans; season with salt and freshly ground pepper and saute over medium heat for 5 minutes. Add the reserved cooking liquid from the beans (saving about ½ cup) to the vegetables. Cook the soup for about 45 minutes. Puree the remaining reserved beans with the half cup of cooking liquid in a blender or food processor fitted with the steel knife blade. Stir the puree into the soup and add the thyme or summer savory and the green beans. Cook over medium heat for another 10 minutes or until the green beans are just tender. Taste for seasoning and serve.

Eggplant Caviar

This is actually a sort of relish; there are many different versions. It is served as an hors d'oeuvre or part of a buffet; accompany it with toasted rounds of French bread or strips of toasted pita bread.

1½-pound eggplant
¼ cup olive oil
1 cup onion, finely chopped
2 cloves garlic, finely chopped
1 large ripe tomato, peeled, seeded, and finely chopped
2 green bell peppers, roasted and finely chopped
· salt and freshly ground pepper
· dash Tabasco
¼ cup parsley, finely chopped
· juice of ½ lemon
· dash red wine vinegar

Preheat the oven to 425 degrees. Cut off and discard the green cap from the eggplant. Put the plant in a shallow pan and roast it for 30 to 35 minutes, until soft. Remove the eggplant from the oven and allow it to cool long enough so that it can be handled.

Heat 2 tablespoons of the olive oil in a 10-inch skillet. Add the onion and garlic and saute over moderate heat for about 10 minutes; do not brown.

Cut the eggplant in half and scoop out the pulp. Chop it finely and add the mince to the onions. Also add the tomato and the roasted peppers at this point; season lightly with salt and pepper and saute for an additional 10 minutes, until most of the excess moisture is evaporated.

Remove from heat and stir in the remaining 2 tablespoons olive oil, lemon juice, vinegar and parsley. Taste for seasoning, correct if necessary, and chill for 1 hour before serving.

Stuffed Grape Leaves
makes approximately fifty

1½ pounds preserved grape leaves
Filling:
¼ cup golden raisins
¼ cup Madeira
3 tablespoons olive oil
1 large onion, finely chopped
2 or 3 garlic cloves, finely chopped
· salt and freshly ground pepper
1½ pounds lean ground lamb
· grated rind of 1 lemon
2 tablespoons fresh mint, finely chopped

2 tablespoons parsley, finely chopped
2 tablespoons tomato paste
· pinch of allspice
2 tablespoons pine nuts (you may substitute coarsely chopped walnuts)

Put the raisins in the Madeira to soak for 30 minutes. Rinse the grape leaves under cold running water to remove the taste of the brine; dry them well.

Heat the olive oil in a skillet; add the onion and garlic, season lightly with salt and pepper, and saute over medium heat for 10 minutes. Take care not to brown them.

In a large mixing bowl, combine the ground lamb with the raisins and their liquid, the onion and garlic mixture, and all other ingredients except the grape leaves; blend the mixture with your hands. Add salt and pepper to taste.

To assemble the dish: put a grape leaf, glossy side down, on your workspace. Shape some of the filling into a small roll (2 to 3 inches long) and put it in the center of the leaf. Turn the stem end of the leaf up to cover the filling, fold each of the sides in tightly, and continue to roll up. Repeat this process until all the filling has been used up.

Arrange the grape leaves in a compact layer in a heavy 12-inch skillet. Add enough water to cover the little cylinders to the halfway level; scatter thin lemon slices over them, and weigh them down with a plate or lid slightly smaller than the skillet. Cook the grape leaves over moderate heat for 60 to 80 minutes, adding more water if necessary.

The grape leaves may be served hot or chilled.

Cold Vegetable Frittata
serves six to eight

A frittata is the Italian version of the omelette. While it is most delicious when served hot, it becomes a delightful appetizer when cooled and cut into wedges. Make a meal of it with good French bread and a Chardonnay, a Sancerre, or a light Chianti.

½   cup olive oil
1   small unpeeled eggplant, cut into small cubes
2   fresh artichoke hearts, cut into cubes
1   medium onion, cut in half and sliced thin
1   large ripe tomato, peeled, seeded, and cut into cubes
2   green or red bell peppers, roasted (see "Roasted Sweet Peppers") and cut into thin strips
9   large eggs
·   salt and freshly ground pepper
·   dash Tabasco
⅓   cup grated Romano or Parmesan cheese

Preheat the broiler.

Heat half the olive oil in a heavy skillet and quickly saute the eggplant cubes over moderate heat until tender. Remove and put in a mixing bowl. Add the artichoke heart cubes to the skillet and saute them in the same oil until just tender. Remove them and put with the eggplant.

Add the onion to the oil remaining in the skillet and saute it for about 5 minutes; then raise the heat and add the tomato cubes and cook until all the moisture released by the tomato is evaporated. Put in the bowl with artichoke and eggplant and add the roasted pepper slices. Season the vegetables lightly with salt and pepper and toss them all together. Add the eggs, Tabasco, and grated cheese and mix together well.

Heat the remaining oil in a heavy 12-inch skillet and pour in the egg and vegetable mixture, stirring briskly until it begins to set. Cook over moderate heat until the bottom is browned, then give the skillet a shake to loosen it. Run the frittata briefly under the broiler until the top turns a golden brown. Turn it out onto a platter and allow to cool at room temperature. Cut into small wedges and serve.

Cheese and Onion Tart
serves ten to twelve

This savory tart may be prepared and baked in advance and gently reheated just before serving. As a variation, you may wish to add six ounces of baked ham, cut into julienne. In this case, you should reduce the amount of grated cheese to half a pound. Serve as a first course with ratatouille or the fish salad with green sauce (both August). For wine, an Alsatian Riesling or a Vouvray.

½ recipe cream cheese pastry (see "Kulebiaka") or your own pastry
6   tablespoons butter
4   cups Walla Walla sweet onions, thinly sliced
    salt and freshly ground pepper

6   large eggs
2½ cups half and half
1   teaspoon Dijon mustard
·   pinch freshly ground nutmeg
·   dash Tabasco
½   teaspoon salt
¾   pound grated Emmentaler cheese
3   tablespoons grated Parmesan cheese
2   tablespoons breadcrumbs

Preheat the oven to 400 degrees. Roll out the pastry and fit into a well-greased rectangular pan with high sides (10 by 14 by 2½ inches). Spread a sheet of foil over the pastry, pressing it against the sides, and fill with rice or beans. Place in the center of the oven and bake for 10 to 12 minutes.

Remove from oven, remove foil and rice or beans, prick the pastry with a fork, and return to oven to bake for another 10 to 15 minutes. The pastry should be just starting to brown lightly and will have begun to shrink just slightly away from the sides of the pan when you take it out. Allow the pastry to cool.

Lower the oven temperature to 350 degrees. Melt the butter in a heavy pot, add the onions, and season them lightly with salt and pepper. Saute the onions over moderate heat for 15 minutes, stirring frequently. Combine the eggs, half and half, mustard, nutmeg, Tabasco, and salt in a mixing bowl. Beat well. Add the grated Parmesan cheese and the bread crumbs and mix.

Put the onions in the bottom of the cooled pastry shell and spread them over the surface. Sprinkle the grated Emmentaler cheese over them and pour the egg mixture over all. Combine the grated Parmesan with the breadcrumbs and mix. Sprinkle the top of the tart with this and dot with butter.

Bake the tart in the upper third of the oven for 15 minutes; then increase the heat to 425 degrees and continue to bake for another 15 to 20 minutes, until the custard has puffed and browned and a knife inserted in the center comes out clean. Allow to stand 20 minutes before serving.

Leek and Sausage Tart
serves six

A savory combination of leeks and sausage baked in a crust: a good choice for lunch or supper. It is superb with a really good California Beaujolais; Parducci's is a good choice.

¾   pound link pork sausage, lightly seasoned
2   tablespoons butter
4   cups leeks, cleaned and cut into ¼-inch thick slices
·   salt and freshly ground pepper
4   ounces cream cheese
2   eggs
¼   cup milk
¼   teaspoon salt
·   dash each of cayenne pepper and freshly grated nutmeg
10-inch unbaked pastry shell (quiche or flan)
1 to 2 tablespoons breadcrumbs

Preheat the oven to 375 degrees.

Blanch the sausages in boiling water for 5 minutes to stiffen them; drain, slash the skins, and remove and discard them. Cut the sausage meat into bite-sized pieces; put them in a skillet with the butter and saute over medium heat until the sausage is cooked; remove and reserve.

Put the leeks in the remaining oil, season them with salt and pepper, and saute them over medium heat for about 10 minutes, until tender.

While the leeks are cooking, combine the cream cheese with the eggs, milk, salt, and spices and blend well.

Mix the leeks and the sausage bits and fill the pastry shell with the mixture. Pour the cheese and egg mixture over this, top with the breadcrumbs, and bake in the middle of the oven for about 1 hour or until the pastry is lightly browned. Remove and allow to cool for 10 minutes before serving.

Moussaka
serves ten to twelve

This dish has been claimed by the Greeks, the Turks, the Armenians, and a score of other nations. It is hard to imagine a handful of widely scattered cooks simultaneously devising an idea so unique; what is probably closer to the truth is that the dish arose out of a subtle intermingling of all these cultures.

A good moussaka is free from excess oil; I have suggested broiling the eggplant slices rather than frying them, since they absorb much less oil that way. Be sure also to use a very lean ground lamb; ideally, grind it yourself. Serve with the octopus and cucumber salad (this month) or the fish salad with green sauce (August) and a Chianti Classico or a California Grignolino.

3   large unpeeled eggplants, cut into slices ½ inch thick

·   olive oil

Lamb mixture:

2   tablespoons each butter and olive oil
2½ cups onion, finely chopped
2   cloves garlic, finely chopped
3   pounds lean ground lamb
1-pound tin Italian plum tomatoes, drained and coarsely chopped
2   tablespoons tomato paste
2   bay leaves
·   pinch of oregano
¼   cup golden raisins, soaked in dry red wine to cover (optional)
·   salt and freshly ground pepper
2   cups dry red wine
·   pinch each allspice and cinnamon
2   tablespoons parsley, finely chopped
3   tablespoons walnuts, coarsely chopped

Bechamel sauce:

8   tablespoons butter
6   tablespoons flour
5   cups hot milk
½   cup ricotta cheese
·   salt and freshly ground
    pepper
·   dash freshly ground nutmeg
1   cup grated Kefalotiri or
    Romano cheese

Preheat broiler to 450 degrees.

Brush both sides of the sliced eggplant with a little olive oil and put them on foil-lined baking sheets. Broil the slices 5 to 6 inches from the heat source until lightly browned; turn over and repeat the process. They should be cooked no longer than 5 minutes per side. Set the broiled eggplant aside and lower temperature to 350 degrees.

Heat the butter and olive oil in a large skillet and cook the onion and garlic in it until golden. Add the ground lamb and cook, breaking the lumps apart with a fork, for 6 to 8 minutes. Add the tomatoes, tomato paste, bay leaves, oregano, raisins (drained), salt, pepper, wine, allspice, cinnamon, and parsley and mix well. Cook over moderately high heat until all moisture has evaporated. Remove the excess oil with a bulb baster. Mix in the walnuts and set aside.

Prepare the bechamel: melt the butter in a saucepan and add the flour, stirring constantly with a wire whisk. Cook the roux over moderate heat for 5 minutes, taking care that it does not brown. Stir in the hot milk, a little at a time, and whisk well after each addition.

When the sauce thickens, remove it from the heat and season with salt, pepper, and nutmeg. Put the ricotta cheese through a sieve, stir in, and set aside.

Oil or butter an ovenproof baking dish (10 by 14 by 2½ inches) and arrange half the eggplant slices on the bottom, sprinkling them with one-third of the grated cheese; add the lamb mixture, sprinkling again with one-third of the grated cheese; cover with the remaining eggplant slices. Pour the bechamel sauce over all and use the remaining grated cheese to dust the top.

Bake for approximately 1 hour or until the top is a golden brown. Remove from the oven and allow to stand 40 minutes before serving.

This dish should be made a day in advance in order to allow the flavors to mingle and soften. Traditionally it is served slightly warmer than room temperature, which makes it ideal fare for entertaining.

Moroccan Lamb Tajin

serves six

A tajin is a shallow, domed-shaped ceramic pot; it is also the name for the dish cooked inside it. This savory lamb stew is flavored with saffron, cinnamon, allspice, ground ginger, and honey and laced with whole almonds and raisins. Serve it with steamed couscous and the eggplant caviar and orange and radish salad (this month). A Cotes du Rhone or Fitou from the subtropical south of France would go well with tajin.

1   teaspoon saffron
3½   cups chicken stock
3   pounds (boned weight) lamb, cut from the leg and cut into 1-inch cubes
·   flour, seasoned with salt and pepper
4   tablespoons olive oil
1½   pounds small onions, peeled and cut in half
2   cloves garlic, finely chopped
½   cup raisins
½   cup whole blanched almonds
½   teaspoon cinnamon
½   teaspoon ground ginger
¼   teaspoon ground allspice
·   large pinch paprika
4   dashes Tabasco
¼   cup honey

Preheat the oven to 350 degrees. Put the saffron into a small bowl or cup; heat the chicken stock, pour it over the saffron, and allow to steep.

Flour the lamb cubes lightly and shake off any excess. Heat the olive oil in a large heavy skillet, add the lamb cubes, and brown them on all sides over high heat. **Remove the lamb and put in a 3- or 4-quart Dutch oven.**

Brown the onion lightly in the oil remaining in the skillet. Remove it from the skillet and reserve. Put the garlic in the skillet and saute it, stirring for 1 to 2 minutes.

Add the remaining 3 cups of chicken stock, raise the heat, and reduce the liquid for about 5 minutes, scraping up the brown particles from the bottom of the pan.

Pour the saffron in its stock over the lamb cubes. Season with the spices listed and add the raisins, almonds, and honey. Stir the mixture so that the spices coat the meat. Pour in the stock with the garlic. Cover the pot and place in the oven to bake for 40 minutes. Remove the pot from the oven, stir in the onions, cover again, and continue to bake for another 20 to 30 minutes, until the meat is tender. Serve the tajin over steamed couscous.

Veal Nicoise

serves eight

A dish typical of the region around Nice; the veal is simmered in a fresh tomato sauce seasoned with anchovy, orange peel, onion, garlic, herbs, and black olives. The olives must be the imported kind, either from Southern France or Greece, and they must be quickly blanched to remove excess salt. Serve with saffron rice and a spinach salad. For wine choose a Fitou, a Cotes du Rhone, or the like.

5	pounds boneless veal, cut from the leg
·	flour, seasoned with salt and freshly ground pepper
6	tablespoons olive oil
32	small white onions, skinned
·	pinch sugar
1¼	cups onion, finely chopped
4 or 5	cloves garlic, finely chopped
4	anchovy fillets, finely chopped
3	pounds fresh ripe tomatoes, peeled, seeded, and chopped
½	teaspoon dried rosemary
½	teaspoon dried thyme
¼	teaspoon dried fennel seeds
1	cup dry white vermouth or dry white wine
1½	cups chicken stock
	3-inch piece of dried orange peel (optional)
1	bay leaf
6	ounces imported black olives, blanched, pitted, and halved

Remove any excess fat from the veal and cut it into 1½-inch cubes; dust them lightly with the seasoned flour.

Heat the olive oil in a heavy 12-inch skillet. Add only enough veal cubes to the pan as will fit comfortably in one layer; brown them thoroughly. Remove and put in a heavy 5- or 6-quart Dutch oven; continue until all veal is browned.

Add the whole, peeled onions to the oil remaining in the skillet and sprinkle with a pinch of sugar. Saute them for about 5 minutes, shaking the pan frequently, until they have browned. Remove and set aside.

Pour off all but about 1 tablespoon oil from the skillet and add the minced onions. Saute them over moderate heat for 5 minutes, then add the garlic and anchovy. Stir well and continue to saute the mixture for another 5 minutes. Stir in the tomato pulp, raise the heat, and allow all moisture released by the tomatoes to evaporate. Meanwhile, briefly grind the rosemary, thyme, and fennel seed with a mortar and pestle and add them to the tomatoes, along with the vermouth, chicken stock, orange peel, and bay leaf. Bring the sauce to a boil and pour it over the veal. Place the Dutch oven on low heat and simmer the stew for 30 to 40 minutes. (Do not add any salt at this point.)

When the veal is almost tender, add the onions and continue to cook for another 15 minutes. When the onions are tender, add the olives and stir them in well; continue to cook for only another 2 to 3 minutes. Taste for seasoning, adding salt and pepper if necessary. Remove the orange peel and bay leaf and serve at once.

Stuffed Breast of Veal
serves ten

There are many recipes in the Italian cuisine for stuffed breast of veal. The ingredients in the stuffing vary widely from town to town but may all have one thing in common: you will not find these delectable dishes on the menu of any of the grand hotels or restaurants, for the preparation is considered "a dish of the people." It may be found on the Sunday dinner table from Milan to Rome, it may be purchased by the pound in a rosticceria, and it is sometimes even seen in the humble trattorie.

This recipe was given to me by a friend whose expertise in these matters is truly wonderful. I have added a fresh artichoke heart to the stuffing; its green color makes a delicate contrast to the cream color of the meat and it also lends an indescribable flavor to the finished dish. The stuffing also includes whole sausages, julienne of carrot, and pitted black olives; when the veal is sliced you will have a lovely mosaic-like effect.

Preparation for this dish should begin at least six hours before you plan to serve it: the veal must be allowed to cool for four hours if the meat and stuffing are to hold together. Since this is a rather rich main course you should serve it with foods that are light and cool. I like to surround the veal with tomatoes stuffed with a creamy rice salad and garnish the platter with sprigs of Italian parsley or watercress. Accompany with a simple green salad vinaigrette and fruit in season for dessert. For more elaborate meals, add the Italian rice salad, the caponata, the ratatouille, or potatoes in pesto (all August). You should serve a really good but not expensive wine with this: a Chianti Classico or a St. Emilion.

1   boned breast of veal, about
    5 pounds
1   tablespoon olive oil
1   small onion, finely chopped
1   rib of celery, finely chopped
1   large fresh artichoke heart,
    cut into small cubes
5   sweet Italian sausages
¼   cup grated Parmesan or
    Romano cheese
1   egg, lightly beaten
6   ounces each of thinly sliced
    mortadella and pancetta
    (both available at good
    Italian markets)
6 to 8 pitted black olives
4   thin strips of carrot, cut into
    lengths of 4 to 6 inches and
    cooked

Preheat oven to 450 degrees.

Heat the olive oil in a 10-inch skillet, add the onion and celery and saute over moderate heat for about 3 minutes; then add the artichoke heart and cook for another 5 minutes. Remove two of the sausages from their casings, crumble the meat, and add it to the skillet. Saute the sausage meat until all traces of pink in the meat are gone.

Remove the mixture from the heat, add the grated cheese and the egg and mix well. Season the breast of veal lightly with salt and pepper and spread the filling on it, leaving a 1-inch border all around the edges. On top place a layer of mortadella slices, then cover with a layer of the pancetta slices, making the sure all of the sausage mixture is covered. In the middle, place the three remaining whole sausages end to end and surround them with the carrot strips and the olives in any way that suits your fancy. Starting with the shortest end nearest to you, roll up the veal tightly and tie together with heavy kitchen string every 2 inches along the length of the meat. Season lightly with salt and pepper.

Pour enough olive oil into a heavy ovenproof casserole just to cover the bottom. Add the stuffed veal, rolling it around in the oil so that the surface is lightly coated. Put in the oven uncovered and roast for 15 to 20 minutes to brown. Reduce heat to 325 degrees, cover and roast for 2 hours. Remove from oven, place meat on a serving platter, and cover loosely with foil. Allow the stuffed veal to rest for at least 4 hours before serving. Remove string and slice into half-inch thickness with a very sharp knife.

Baked Corned Beef

serves six to eight

Purchase your corned beef from a good source; Market House Corned Beef at 1124 Howell sells some of the best in Seattle. Although unorthodox, this method of baking corned beef slowly at a low temperature results in extremely flavorful and tender meat with very little shrinkage. If you prefer a slightly spicier meat, do not wash off the spices.

Cabbage and potatoes are traditional with corned beef. Still harmonious but less literal would be Brussels sprouts in vinegar (November) and potatoes in parsley sauce (April). You'll need a crisp and robust wine; try a dry Rose, Valpolicella, Beaujolais, or Hermitage.

Place a 4½-pound corned beef brisket into a heavy 5- or 6-quart Dutch oven, add enough water to cover the meat by half, cover, and bake at 300 degrees for 4 or 4½ hours, until tender. Remove the meat, brush off excess spices, slice thin, and serve.

Lemon Blueberry Souffle Glace

serves eight

Souffles are a festive ending to almost any meal, but one is not always ready to sacrifice the time away from guests to the last-minute preparations required. If you have had any trepidation about attempting souffles before now, you will be overjoyed to learn that there is a species of souffle that is foolproof: the cold souffle. They can be prepared hours in advance or even the night before; they will rise majestically out of their molds, resisting any attempt to deflate them.

A souffle glace may be flavored with almost anything you fancy, including numerous spirits and liqueurs such as Benedictine, creme de cassis, kahlua, and anisette. Toasted almonds, hazelnuts, or pistachios are delicious when the basic mixture is simply flavored wtih vanilla or melted chocolate.

1	tablespoon unflavored gelatin
·	juice of 1½ lemons
6	egg whites, chilled
¼	teaspoon cream of tartar
¼	cup granulated sugar
2	cups heavy cream
½	cup confectioner's sugar
1	box fresh blueberries (1 dry pint), pureed
	grated rind of 1½ lemons

Combine the gelatin with the lemon juice in a small pot and

set over low heat until the gelatin has melted, 2 to 3 minutes. Remove from heat and allow to cool.

In a stainless-steel or copper bowl (neither egg whites nor cream will build properly when beaten in ceramic or glass), beat the whites until they start to froth. Add the cream of tartar and continue beating, adding the granulated sugar gradually, until the whites form stiff peaks. Fold in the gelatin mixture and set aside.

In a stainless-steel or copper bowl, beat the heavy cream, adding the confectioner's sugar little by little until the cream is stiff. Sprinkle the lemon zest over the top of the cream, pour in the pureed blueberries, and fold in gently with a rubber spatula. Add the beaten egg whites to this mixture and carefully fold them in.

Pour the souffle mixture into a 1½-quart souffle dish to which you have affixed a 3-inch collar made of aluminum foil or waxed paper. Cover with plastic wrap and freeze for at least 4 hours or overnight. Remove the collar carefully and serve.

Blueberry Clafoutis
serves six to eight

This custardlike cake is usually baked in a shallow pan; I prefer to use a souffle dish, which gives the clafoutis an even creamier texture.

6   large eggs
2   cups milk
¾   cup flour
½   cup finely granulated sugar
1   teaspoon vanilla extract
1   tablespoon cognac or good brandy
3   cups fresh blueberries
·   confectioner's sugar

Preheat the oven to 375 degrees.

Prepare the batter: beat together the eggs and milk; with the aid of an electric mixer, slowly add the flour and then the sugar. Flavor with the vanilla extract and the cognac and blend well.

Pour enough of the batter to just coat the bottom of a 2-quart souffle dish, sprinkle the blueberries over, and cover with the remainder of the batter. Bake in the middle of the oven for about 1 hour or until the top of the clafoutis is a golden brown. Dust the top lightly with confectioner's sugar and serve while still warm.

Blueberry Sourcream Tart
serves six to eight

A luscious combination of blueberries and sour cream.

10-inch pastry shell (fitted into a quiche or flan ring)
3   large eggs
1   cup sour cream
½   cup sugar
2   cups blueberries
·   large pinch cinnamon
·   small pinch freshly grated nutmeg

Preheat the oven to 400 degrees. Place a layer of foil over the surface of the pastry and fill it with rice or beans to keep from puffing while baking. Put in the center of the oven and bake for 15 minutes. Remove the pastry from the oven and take out the foil and the rice or bean filling. Put the pastry shell back in the oven to bake for an additional 10 minutes. Allow the shell to cool slightly before filling.

Reduce oven heat to 325 degrees.

Combine the eggs, sour cream, and ¼ cup of the sugar; beat well. Toss the blueberries in a mixing bowl with the remaining sugar and the spices. Place the blueberries in the bottom of the prebaked shell, cover with the egg and sour cream mixture bake in the center of the oven for about 45 minutes, until the crust is browned and the custard is done. Allow to cool slightly before serving.

October, Flavors of Autumn

Menu 1
Chanterelle Soupe Grand'mere (October)
Rabbit a l'Alsacienne (October)
Potato Pancakes (October)
Watercress and Walnut Salad (October)
Poached Pears with Ginger Cream (October)

Menu 2
Terrine of Rabbit (October)
Roast Pheasant with Dirty Rice (October)
Brussels Sprouts with Cheese and Breadcrumbs (November)
Roquefort Cheese Strudel with Ripe Pears (October)

Watercress and Walnut Salad
Terrine of Rabbit
Potato Pancakes
Potatoes Sauteed with Juniper Berries
Chanterelle Soupe Grand'mere
Roast Quail with Bread Sauce
Roast Pheasant with Dirty Rice
Roast Chicken Stuffed with Chanterelles
Rabbit with Paprika Sauce
Rabbit a l'Alsacienne
Pork Loin Braised in Cider
Poached Pears with Ginger Cream
Apples Baked in Meringue
Apple and Custard Tart
Apple, Pear, and Hazelnut Tart
Bread Pudding with Apples
Roquefort Cheese Strudel

Autumn: brilliant sun-warmed days, with just a hint of the cold that will follow. The season's produce takes its cue from the brightly colored foliage, and the market place is filled with pungent and heady aromas: apples, cider, pears, pumpkins, squash, hazelnuts, and juniper. Senses are reawakened to the traditional specialties of the season: game and wild mushrooms.

Roy Andries de Groot once remarked, "One of the saddest things about cooking in America is that we as a nation are so afraid of being poisoned by wild mushrooms that we restrict our entire supply to a single mass-produced type, which is one of the blandest of all the species. How different is this from France where the skilled gathering of wild woodland mushrooms is still a thriving business, so that the corner grocery in even a small town can usually offer five or six different types."

The Pacific Northwest is blessed with a wealth of wild mushrooms.

There are even a few eminently edible varieties in many back yards. And there are good books on the subject: *The Savory Wild Mushroom,* by Margaret McKenny and Daniel Stuntz (University of Washington Press, 1971); Orson Miller's *Mushrooms of North America* (Dutton). A few places in Seattle sell fresh wild fungi. Joe Schwab, usually to be found at the foot of Stewart Street in the Pike Place Market, sells fresh chanterelles and morels in season, at very fair prices. Uwajimaya, at South Sixth and South King, in the International District, has a small selection of wild fungi in season; the most notable is the matsutake, a pine mushroom much revered by the Japanese and having a superb aroma and flavor quite unlike any other mushroom.

Game birds, once available only to those who hunt, are now raised on game farms and forest preserves throughout the country. The advantages of these partly or wholly domesticated game birds are obvious: their age is certain, therefore cooking times may be more accurately gauged; also, one need not be on the lookout for buckshot in every bite.

Both quail and pheasant have a mild and pleasantly gamey flavor, but the flesh of both has a distinct tendency to dry out if not properly treated. The cooking technique to be used for wild fowl is determined by their age; young birds may be successfully roasted but older ones must be braised or even stewed for maximum tenderness. As with any game, the cooking time depends largely on the age and condition of the bird. While a few people prefer their game on the rare side, generally speaking the tests for doneness are the same as those for domestic fowl. The leg is pierced with a fork and the juices that run out must be clear, not tinged with pink; also, the leg should move rather freely at the joint. Do not expect the same amount of tenderness found in chicken: game birds have sinewy flesh.

Rabbit is now commercially grown and available fresh almost everywhere. In spite of being raised today industrially, much like chicken, rabbit still stubbornly retains most of its fine flavor, a taste like a cross between chicken and veal. Domestic rabbit is killed young, and because its flesh is delicately flavored, it needs no marination. It may be used in any recipe calling for chicken, but (depending on age), it may need longer cooking by thirty minutes or so.

Watercress and Walnut Salad

serves four to six

The peppery flavor of the watercress is accented by grated lemon peel, chopped walnuts, and a tangy lemon dressing.

2	bunches fresh watercress, trimmed and washed
·	the juice of ½ lemon
·	pinch dry mustard powder
·	pinch salt
1-inch squeeze anchovy paste	
1	shallot, finely chopped
·	dash Tabasco
6	tablespoons olive oil
·	freshly ground pepper
⅓	cup walnuts, coarsely chopped
·	finely grated rind of 1 lemon

Place the drained watercress in a salad bowl and chill until serving time. Prepare the dressing: combine the lemon juice, mustard powder, salt, anchovy paste, shallot, and Tabasco and mix well. Slowly add the olive oil, stirring constantly, and season with a liberal grinding of black pepper. Taste and adjust seasoning if necessary.

Scatter the walnuts and lemon rind over the top of the watercress. Add only enough dressing to just moisten the leaves and toss gently. Serve at once.

Terrine of Rabbit

for a one-and-a-half-quart terrine

A terrine, strictly speaking, is an earthenware or porcelain container with straight sides that is found in both oval and rectangular shapes. It is used for baking pates of meat or game. The name of the utensil has also come to describe its contents, indicating that the pate has been cooked and served in a terrine rather than in a crust. The ground meats are very often marinated in cognac; I find this gives the pate an undesirably strong flavor, so I have eliminated this step. Serve with crisp French bread and cornichons. A dry Riesling or a Beaujolais Villages would make a suitable accompaniment.

1   pound pork fatback, cut
    into thinnest possible slices
1½ pounds rabbit, boned and
    coarsely ground
½   pound lean pork, coarsely
    ground
½   pound veal, coarsely ground
½   pound pork fatback, cut
    into small dice, not ground
2   tablespoons butter
½   cup onion, finely chopped
1   large clove garlic, finely
    chopped
½   teaspoon dried thyme
3   teaspoons salt
·   freshly ground pepper
2 to 3 juniper berries, crushed
·   pinch allspice
¼   cup toasted hazelnuts,
    coarsely chopped
¼   cup cognac or good brandy
½   cup heavy cream
2   egg yolks
2   bay leaves

Preheat the oven to 350 degrees.

Line a 1½-quart terrine or loaf pan with fatback slices, reserving a few of them for the top.

Place the rabbit, pork, veal, and fatback dice in a large mixing bowl.

Heat the butter in a small skillet; add the onions and saute them over moderate heat for about 10 minutes, stirring occasionally. Do not allow them to brown. Pour the onions with their fat into the meat mixture.

Add the salt, pepper, crushed juniper berries, allspice, and hazelnuts.

Combine the cognac with the heavy cream and the egg yolks and blend well. Pour this mixture over the meats and mix well, using your hands. To test the seasoning: bring a small skillet of water to a boil, add a teaspoon of the meat mixture, and simmer it for a few minutes. Chill it quickly in the freezer and taste; then adjust seasoning if necessary.

Pour the meat mixture into the prepared terrine; cover the top with the reserved fatback slices and place the 2 bay leaves on top. Cover the terrine with its lid (substitute a double layer of foil if you are using a loaf pan) and place it in a pan with water that reaches halfway up the sides of the terrine.

Bake in the center of the oven for about 1½ hours. The terrine is done when its juices run clear. Remove the lid, place a weight on top, and allow to cool. Then refrigerate, with the weight still in place, for 2 or 3 days. Before serving, remove the terrine from the refrigerator and allow to stand at room temperature for at least 1 hour.

Variation: Substitute blanched, sliced green olives in the same amount for the hazelnuts.

Potato Pancakes
serves four

These crisp and delicious pancakes must be made just before serving; they cannot be reheated successfully. Top each with a small dollop of sour cream.

4   medium baking potatoes, peeled
1   medium onion, peeled
1   large egg
·   flour
1   teaspoon salt
·   freshly ground pepper
½   teaspoon baking powder
·   enough vegetable oil to cover bottom of skillet by ½ inch

Grate the potatoes on a fine grater into a large sieve set over a mixing bowl. Discard any liquid that has accumulated in the bowl; add the grated potatoes from the sieve and grate the onion directly on top of them. Add the salt, pepper, baking powder, and egg and beat the mixture together. Stir in just enough flour to make a batter thick enough to hold its shape; this will depend largely on the quantity and character of the potatoes used.

Heat the vegetable oil in a large heavy skillet set over moderately high heat. Drop in a spoonful of the batter and flatten it to make a cake about 3 inches in diameter. (Fry only enough of the cakes at one time to just fill the skillet.) Fry each of the cakes 2 to 3 minutes per side, long enough for them to turn a golden brown; then turn carefully with a spatula and fry the other side. Continue in this fashion until all batter is used. Drain the pancakes on paper towels and serve.

Potatoes Sauteed with Juniper Berries
serves four

An unusual and most delicious accompaniment for any game birds. The addition of juniper berries gives the potatoes a savory and rather piquant flavor.

6 to 8 medium new potatoes
6   tablespoons butter
2   large shallots, finely chopped
1   large clove garlic, finely chopped
8 to 10 whole juniper berries, lightly bruised with a mortar and pestle
·   salt and freshly ground pepper
¼   cup parsley, finely chopped

Peel the potatoes and cut into slices. Melt the butter in a large heavy skillet; add the shallots, garlic, and juniper berries. Saute for 1 to 2 minutes, stirring. Add the potato slices, toss to coat with the butter and spices, and saute over moderate heat, stirring frequently, for 15 to 20 minutes. Sprinkle with the parsley, toss, and continue to cook for a few minutes more. Serve at once.

Chanterelle Soupe Grand'mere
serves six to eight as first course

Chanterelles are among the most delicious of all wild mushrooms; like the rest they tend to absorb liquid rather easily, so they must be washed quickly under cold running water and thoroughly dried. One of the best utensils for this purpose is a lettuce drier or spinner, available in most kitchen or hardware shops. Serve with Vouvray or Riesling wine.

1	pound fresh chanterelle mushrooms
5	tablespoons butter
·	squeeze of lemon juice
·	salt and freshly ground pepper to taste
2	leeks, thoroughly washed and finely chopped
1	large clove garlic, peeled and minced
1½	cups potato, peeled and diced
6½	cups chicken stock, lightly seasoned
1	tablespoon fresh thyme or parsley, finely chopped
1	cup sour cream
1	tablespoon red wine vinegar

Clean and dry the mushrooms as described above. Reserve 2 or 3 of the best-shaped ones; chop the remainder coarsely. Saute them in a large heavy skillet with 2 tablespoons butter and season them with lemon juice, salt, and pepper. The heat must be high to allow the mushrooms to release their juices, but take care not to brown them; do not cook them longer than 3 or 4 minutes. Remove the mushrooms with a slotted spoon and reserve the liquid.

Heat 3 tablespoons of the butter in a heavy enameled soup pot (about a 4-quart size); add the leeks, garlic, and potatoes, and saute over medium heat for 10 minutes. Add the reserved mushroom juices, chicken stock, and thyme or parsley, bring to a boil, reduce the heat, and simmer for 15 to 20 minutes or until the potatoes are soft. Add the chopped and cooked mushrooms at this point and simmer gently for about 30 minutes.

Pour the soup through a fine sieve into a large mixing bowl, reserving all liquid. Let the mushrooms and vegetables cool slightly, then puree them in a blender or food processor fitted with the steel knife blade. Rinse out the soup pot with hot water and pour the reserved liquid into it. Add the mushroom puree and mix with a wire whisk. Set the pot over low heat and add the sour cream and vinegar, allowing the soup to simmer gently. Meanwhile, slice the reserved mushrooms and add them to the soup to warm. Taste for seasoning and serve.

If you wish, the soup may be thickened slightly with a bit of beure manie (equal parts of softened butter mixed with flour) added at the end. If the soup is to be reheated, do not bring it to a boil or it will curdle. This soup can be prepared a day or two in advance.

Roast Quail with Bread Sauce
serves four

Game birds should never be washed; this takes away the flavor unique to these fowl. Quail meat is especially delicate so it is important to avoid over-seasoning it or using strongly flavored sauces. Serve with an autumnal vegetable dish such as potatoes with juniper berries and watercress and walnut salad (this month) or leeks vinaigrette or fennel and cucumber saute (November). A Graves, Chardonnay, or light Barbaresco would serve as beverage.

4	fresh quail
·	salt and freshly ground pepper
4	tablespoons clarified butter
1	tablespoon vegetable oil

Bread sauce:

3	tablespoons butter
2	shallots, finely chopped
2	tablespoons celery, finely chopped
1½	cups soft fresh breadcrumbs
2½	cups chicken stock
1	cup heavy cream
·	small pinch each cayenne pepper and freshly grated nutmeg
·	salt

Preheat oven to 375 degrees.

Wipe the game birds inside and out with the cut side of a lemon. Truss each tightly (it will be much easier to brown it). Heat the clarified butter with the oil in a large heavy skillet; add the game birds and carefully brown them over moderately high heat. Remove them and place in a shallow ovenproof dish. Brush them with some of the remaining fat and place in the oven to roast for 25 to 30 minutes, until tender. Baste frequently with the remaining fat.

Meanwhile, prepare the sauce: melt the butter in a small saucepan; add the shallots and celery and saute for about 5 minutes, until soft but not brown. Stir in the breadcrumbs and saute them until they are lightly browned. Add the chicken stock and stir until the sauce thickens. Pour in the heavy cream and season lightly with the cayenne pepper, nutmeg, and salt. Cook the sauce for another 5 minutes or so. It should be of a medium thickness; if it is too thick you may add a bit more cream or stock. Taste and adjust the seasoning if necessary.

Remove the quail from the oven, cut off the trussing string, and serve, spooning a little sauce over each; pass the remaining sauce separately.

Roast Pheasant with Dirty Rice
serves two to three

Dirty rice is a mixture of finely chopped chicken livers sauteed with onion, green pepper, and celery and tossed with cooked rice. This gives the rice a brownish and slightly "dirty" color; hence its name. Serve with chanterelle soup (this month) and braised celery root (November). A light Barbaresco, a Graves, or a good Chardonnay will all go with this dish.

2½-pound pheasant
  Dirty rice stuffing:
·   the phesant liver plus
5   chicken livers
6   tablespoons butter
1   teaspoon vegetable oil

½   cup onion, finely chopped
¼   cup each celery and green pepper, finely chopped
1   large clove garlic, finely chopped
·   salt and freshly ground pepper
½   cup short-grain rice, cooked to make 1½ cups
3   tablespoons parsley, finely chopped
·   pinch allspice
·   dash Tabasco
¼   cup dry Madeira

Preheat the oven to 375 degrees.

First, prepare the stuffing: clean and cut the livers in half. Heat 2 tablespoons of butter with the oil in a skillet; saute the livers until firm and lightly brown, about 8 minutes. Remove with a slotted spoon, set aside, and allow to cool slightly.

Add the onion, celery, green pepper, and garlic to the skillet and saute over moderate heat for 5 minutes. Chop the livers into very fine pieces and add them to the skillet with the onion mixture and continue to cook for another 5 minutes, browning the mixture slightly. Put the cooked rice in a mixing bowl, add the liver mixture, salt, pepper, parsley, allspice, and Tabasco, and mix well.

Clean the pheasant and stuff its cavity with the dirty rice. Truss the bird tightly and season the outside lightly with salt and pepper. Melt the remaining 4 tablespoons butter with the Madeira and brush the bird lightly with this mixture. Place in a roasting pan and put in the middle of the oven to roast for 1½ hours or until tender. The pheasant must be basted with the butter-Madeira mixture every 10 or 15 minutes so the meat does not become dry. Remove from oven when done and allow to stand for 10 minutes before carving.

Roast Chicken Stuffed with Chanterelles
serves four

Do not substitute canned imported chanterelles for the fresh ones; they are overpriced and have a distinct metallic taste. Serve with a watercress and walnut salad (this month), with leeks vinaigrette, or with a fennel and cucumber saute (both November). For wine try a California Sauvignon Blanc or Beaujolais, or a Bardolino.

4   tablespoons butter
1   tablespoon oil
1   cup French bread cut into 1-inch cubes
1   pound fresh chanterelle mushrooms, cleaned and coarsely chopped
·   squeeze of lemon juice
·   salt and freshly ground black pepper

2   tablespoons dry white vermouth
½   cup onion, finely minced
3 to 4 sprigs fresh thyme or parsley, finely minced
1   whole chicken (2½ to 3 pounds)

Preheat oven to 450 degrees.

Heat 1 tablespoon butter with 1 tablespoon oil in a heavy skillet; add the bread cubes and saute them over medium heat on all sides until they have turned crisp and golden. Remove from pan and allow to drain on paper towels.

Heat 2 tablespoons butter in a large skillet; add the chanterelles, lemon juice, salt, and pepper and saute over high heat until the mushrooms have released their juice and have softened, 3 to 4 minutes. Remove the mushrooms with a slotted spoon and set them aside. Add the vermouth to the liquid left in the pan and reduce over high heat to ½ cup. Reserve. Heat 1 tablespoon butter in a small skillet and saute the minced onion in it until soft and golden, 5 minutes.

Put the reserved croutons, mushrooms, onions, and thyme in a mixing bowl and mix gently; add 1 tablespoon of the reserved pan juices and check the seasoning. Use this mixture to stuff the cavity of the chicken, sewing the opening closed with a tying needle.

Truss the chicken tightly, place it in a shallow roasting pan, and paint it lightly with the pan juices. Roast the chicken for about 1 hour, basting every 15 minutes with the remaining pan juices. Remove from oven when bird has acquired a crisp, golden brown skin; remove the trussing and allow to stand for 5 minutes before carving.

Variation: Substitute fresh morels in season (early spring) for the chanterelles.

Rabbit with Paprika Sauce
serves four

Although rabbit can be treated almost like chicken in any dish, it will usually need a bit more cooking time. Use only the best imported Hungarian paprika for this dish. Serve with Brussels sprouts in cheese and breadcrumbs (November) and follow with a Roquefort cheese strudel and ripe pears (this month).

3- to 3½-pound rabbit, cut into pieces
· salt and freshly ground pepper
4 tablespoons butter
1 tablespoon vegetable oil
½ cup vermouth or dry white wine
1 cup chicken stock
2 green bell peppers, seeded and cut into julienne
1 large onion, thinly sliced
2 fresh tomatoes, peeled, seeded, and cut into julienne
1 tablespoon imported paprika
¾ cup sour cream
½ cup heavy cream, whipped

Preheat the oven to 350 degrees. Dredge the rabbit pieces with flour seasoned lightly with salt and pepper. Heat 2 tablespoons of the butter with 1 tablespoon oil in a large heavy skillet. Add the rabbit and saute over moderately high heat until golden brown.

Remove the rabbit and place it in a shallow ovenproof container large enough to hold it in one layer. Pour off all but 1 tablespoon of the fat, add the vermouth or wine and the chicken stock, and reduce the liquids over high heat, scraping up any brown particles from the bottom of the pan, for about 5 minutes. Pour this over the rabbit and place the baking dish in the middle of the oven. Bake the rabbit uncovered for about 1½ hours, basting it frequently with the pan juices.

About 10 minutes before the rabbit is done, begin the sauce. Heat the remaining 2 tablespoons butter in a skillet, add the pepper and onion, and saute them over moderate heat for about 5 minutes; do not brown. Stir in the tomato, season lightly with salt and pepper, and continue to cook for another 3 minutes. Add the paprika, reduce the heat, and cook the vegetables, stirring frequently, for 5 minutes more.

Remove the rabbit from its baking dish to a serving platter and put it in the warm oven. Degrease the pan juices and pour them into the pepper and onion mixture. Stir in the sour cream, using a wire whisk, and cook the sauce over low heat for about 10 minutes.

Slowly beat in the whipped cream and allow the sauce to cook for another 1 to 2 minutes. Pour the sauce over the rabbit and brown the dish lightly under the broiler to finish. Serve with buttered noodles.

Rabbit a l'Alsacienne
serves four

This is a casserole of richly browned rabbit and sauteed cabbage in a mustard sauce. It is an uncomplicated, lusty dish and one that I'm extremely fond of, for it seems to typify the feeling of autumn months.

I've recommended using Moutarde a l'ancienne here, a grainy French mustard from Alsace found in specialty food shops; you may substitute Pommery or Dijon if you desire. Serve with a first course of Hood Canal shrimp with homemade mayonnaise, potato pancakes, watercress and walnut salad (recipes this month) and mousse aux mandarines (December). Wine: a good Cotes du Rhone or a dry Alsatian Riesling.

1   medium Savoy cabbage, about 3 pounds, cut into 1-inch shreds
5   tablespoons butter
½   cup salt pork, rind removed and cut into small dice
2½ - to 3-pound fresh rabbit, cut into serving pieces
·   flour, seasoned with salt, pepper, and paprika
1½ medium onions, coarsely chopped
2   tablespoons flour
1   cup dry white wine or dry white vermouth
1½ cups milk
·   pinch of freshly grated nutmeg
·   salt
·   pinch cayenne pepper
1   tablespoon Moutarde a l'ancienne

Preheat the oven to 350 degrees.

Bring to a boil a 10- or 12-quart stockpot filled three-quarters full of salted water; add the cabbage and allow to boil for 5 minutes. (This removes much of the overly strong taste and smell of the vegetable.) Decant the blanched cabbage into a large colander and refresh it under cold running water. Allow it to drain well and set aside.

In a heavy 12-inch skillet melt 3 tablespoons butter; add the salt pork cubes, allowing them to brown and render their fat completely. Remove the solids with a slotted spoon and reserve both them and their fat.

Wash the rabbit quickly with cold water and dry it well. Dust the meat heavily with the seasoned flour, shaking off any excess. Set the large skillet containing rendered pork fat over high heat and put in only enough pieces of rabbit to just cover the bottom. Brown the meat well, turning only once to brown the other side; continue until all the meat is browned.

To the remaining fat add half the onion and half the cabbage, sprinkling with salt and pepper. Saute the vegetables over moderate heat for about 10 minutes. Remove to a bowl and repeat the process with the rest of the onions and cabbage. Add the salt pork cubes to the cooked cabbage and set aside.

In the same skillet, prepare a roux: melt 2 tablespoons of the butter, add the flour, stirring well with a wire whisk, and cook over low heat for 5 minutes; do not brown. Add the wine or vermouth and mix in with the whisk until there are no lumps; then add the milk and blend together. Season this with the nutmeg, salt, cayenne, and mustard. (This should be a highly seasoned sauce and the taste of the mustard should be evident; add more mustard if you wish.)

In a 4- or 6-quart Dutch oven, place half the cabbage mixture, mixing it with one-third of the mustard sauce. Put the rabbit on this, spooning half the remaining sauce over it. Finally, add the remaining cabbage and sauce. The casserole should be tightly packed. Cover and bake the dish for 1½ to 1¾ hours, then serve directly from the pot.

Pork Loin Braised in Cider
serves six to eight

This succulent roast is accompanied by onions, potatoes, and apples that have also been cooked in the cider. Do not use American cider for this recipe; it is too sweet. Use a dry cider from Normandy or England.

Serve with a tangy watercress and walnut salad (this month) and a good French cider (like Cidre Bouche) or a Meursault.

4-pound pork loin roast, boned and tied
- ·   salt and freshly ground pepper
- 6   tablespoons butter
- 1   teaspoon vegetable oil
- ½   cup carrot, finely chopped
- ½   cup celery, finely chopped
- ½   cup leeks, finely chopped
- 1   large clove garlic, finely chopped
- 1   bay leaf
- ·   pinch ground cloves

3 to 4 cups cider
- 6   large onions, cut into quarters
- 14 to 16 very small new potatoes, unpeeled
- 6   large baking apples, peeled, cored, and cut into quarters

Preheat the oven to 350 degrees. Season the pork loin with the salt and pepper. Heat 3 tablespoons of the butter with the oil in a heavy 10-inch skillet; put in the pork and brown it on all sides. Remove it and set aside.

In the oil remaining in the skillet, saute the carrot, celery, leeks, and garlic over moderate heat for about 10 minutes; do not brown. Put them in the bottom of a 5- or 6-quart Dutch oven along with the bay leaf and ground cloves; put the pork on top and add enough cider to cover the meat by half.

Put the covered pot in the center of the oven and allow the meat to braise for 1 hour and 45 minutes, basting frequently. Add the onion wedges and the potatoes to the pot, adding a bit more cider if necessary to cover them. Cover and return the pot to the oven for 35 minutes.

Melt the remaining 3 tablespoons butter in a skillet and brown the apple wedges lightly. Add them to the pot and bake for another 10 minutes.

Remove the pork from the pot, place it in the center of a platter, and surround it with the apples, potatoes, and onions; keep warm. Completely degrease the sauce and put it through a sieve. Pour a little of the sauce over the meat and vegetables and serve the rest on the side. Serve at once.

Poached Pears with Ginger Cream
serves six

Fresh poached pears served with whipped cream flavored with preserved ginger and dry sherry.

6   firm pears
2   cups finely granulated sugar
1   tablespoon lemon juice
·   peel of ½ lemon
1   cinnamon stick
3   cloves
1   cup heavy cream
1½ tablespoons dry sherry
3   tablespoons confectioner's sugar
¼   cup finely minced candied ginger

Combine the sugar with the lemon juice, lemon peel, and 1 quart water in a pot large enough to hold the pears without crowding; bring to a boil. Peel the pears and add them to the sugar syrup along with the cinnamon stick and the cloves. Cook the pears at a rolling boil, frequently spooning the syrup over them, for about 25 minutes, until tender. Allow them to cool in their cooking liquid.

Beat the heavy cream until foamy; add the sherry and the confectioner's sugar and continue to beat until stiff. Fold in the candied ginger.

Place the pears on a serving platter, spoon some of the ginger cream over them, and serve immediately.

Apples Baked in Meringue
serves six

A delightfully light dessert idea: the apples are first poached in a sugar syrup flavored with lemon peel and cinnamon, then covered with meringue and quickly baked. Choose MacIntosh, Winesap, or Rome Beauty apples.

6   apples
2½ cups finely granulated sugar
1   tablespoon lemon juice
·   peel of ½ lemon
1   cinnamon stick
3   cloves
3   egg whites

Peel and core the apples. In a pot large enough to hold the apples without crowding, put 2 cups sugar, 1 quart water, the lemon juice, and the lemon peel. Bring this to a boil; then add the cinnamon stick, the cloves, and the apples. Cook the apples at a rolling boil, frequently spooning the syrup over them, for about 25 minutes, until tender.

While the apples are cooking, beat the egg whites with a pinch of sugar in a stainless-steel or copper bowl. When they are firm, add the remaining ½ cup of sugar and continue to beat until stiff.

Preheat the oven to 500 degrees.

Drain the apples thoroughly. Place the meringue in a pastry bag fitted with a star tip. Place the apples in a shallow ovenproof container and cover each one entirely with the meringue. Place in the oven for about 5 minutes, just long enough to turn the meringue a golden brown. Serve at once.

Apple and Custard Tart
serves six to eight

The flavor of the apples in this tart is enhanced by only a small amount of sugar and a bit of vanilla bean. A deep tart pan with 2-inch sides and removable bottom is used for the shell.

2   pounds baking apples
5   tablespoons butter
1-inch piece of vanilla bean,
        split in half
4   tablespoons sugar
9-inch tart pan with deep
        (2-inch) fluted sides lined
        with pate brisee (see
        "Strawberry Tart")
2   large eggs
1   cup heavy cream
1   teaspoon pure vanilla
        extract

Preheat the oven to 400 degrees.

Peel, core, and slice the apples. Melt the butter in a 10- or 12-inch skillet, add the apple slices and vanilla bean, and sprinkle with 1 tablespoon sugar. Saute the apple slices over moderate heat for 5 minutes, stirring frequently. Raise the heat and reduce the liquids released by the apples for about 5 minutes more.

Allow the apple slices to cool slightly. Then pour the apples into the prepared pastry shell and place in the middle of the oven. Bake the tart for 30 minutes. Combine the eggs, cream, the remaining 3 tablespoons sugar, and the vanilla extract in a small bowl; beat together. Pour this custard over the apples, return to oven, and continue to bake for an additional 20 to 30 minutes, until the custard has puffed and browned lightly. Allow to cool for about 30 minutes before serving.

Apple, Pear, and Hazelnut Tart
serves six to eight

The tart could be finished with latticework of pastry strips, but I decided on a meringue topping. This allows you to use all the egg whites that are left over from the filling rather than storing them in the freezer (a sound idea, but who ever remembers to use them?). The inside of the unbaked pastry shell is glazed with a bit of red currant jelly; this trick helps to keep the bottom of the tart crisp if it is not consumed immediately. Do not grate the fruit much in advance of assembling the dish or it will turn brown.

10-inch pastry shell fitted into a quiche pan or flan ring
1 tablespoon red currant jelly, melted with 1 teaspoon water
½ cup hazelnuts, toasted and coarsely chopped
3 egg yolks
¼ cup sugar
1 tablespoon rum or cognac
3 small baking apples, peeled, cored, and coarsely grated
3 small firm pears, peeled, cored, and coarsely grated
3 egg whites
· pinch of salt or ¼ teaspoon cream of tartar
3 to 4 tablespoons sugar

Preheat the oven to 350 degrees.

Paint the inside of the unbaked pastry shell with the jelly mixture, covering well both the bottom and the sides. Refrigerate the shell while preparing the filling.

Mix the nuts with the egg yolks, sugar, and rum and beat well. Squeeze all the moisture out of the grated apple and pear and stir it into the egg yolk mixture; blend well. Pour this into the prepared pastry shell and put in the oven to bake for about 1 hour, or until the pastry is a light brown.

About 10 minutes before the tart is done, prepare the topping: whip the egg whites with a pinch of salt or the cream of tartar until they are foamy and add the 3 to 4 tablespoons sugar gradually until a stiff meringue is formed. Place this into a 10- or 12-inch pastry bag fitted with a star tip.

Remove the pastry from the oven and raise the heat to 500 degrees. Pipe the meringue in a decorative fashion over the entire top surface of the tart. Return the tart to the oven for 3 to 4 minutes, only long enough to lightly brown the meringue. Remove the tart from the oven, unmold, and allow to cool. Serve at room temperature or chill slightly.

Bread Pudding with Apples
serves six to eight

There are some who profess not to like bread pudding; you may be able to change their minds with this recipe.

1½ pounds baking apples
½ cup (8 tablespoons) butter
1 cup and 2 tablespoons sugar
¼ teaspoon powdered cinnamon
1-pound loaf French or Italian bread, one day old
¼ cup seedless raisins
4 large eggs
4 cups milk
2 teaspoons pure vanilla extract
· freshly grated nutmeg

Preheat the oven to 325 degrees.

Peel, core, and cut the apples into large dice. Melt 4 tablespoons butter in a heavy 10-inch skillet, add the apples, and sprinkle with 2 tablespoons sugar and the cinnamon. Saute the apples over moderate heat for about 10 minutes, stirring frequently.

Trim off the crust of the bread and discard; cut the rest into small cubes. Using remaining butter, grease a deep ovenproof dish, add the bread cubes, the apples with their juice, and the raisins, and toss together.

Combine the eggs, milk, vanilla, and a liberal grinding of nutmeg; beat lightly. Pour this mixture over the bread and apples. Set the dish in a pan filled with 1 inch of water and place in the oven. The custard must not be cooked too quickly or it may separate: bake the pudding for 1½ hours or until it is set. Serve hot with lightly whipped cream.

Roquefort Cheese Strudel

serves twelve to fourteen as an hors d'oeuvre

Filo dough is a paper-thin pastry available at any shop specializing in Middle Eastern foods. Because of its extreme thinness it should be handled with care. Small tears in the sheets are not a problem because usually many layers of them are used; most tears can be avoided simply by remembering to remove the dough from the refrigerator an hour before using. Also, leaves that are out but not in use should be rolled in a slightly dampened towel so that they do not dry out and become brittle.

Do not confine Roquefort strudel to the hors d'oeuvres tray; serve it with fresh, very ripe pears for a savory dessert. Those of your guests who are not overly fond of sweets will find it delightful. As a first course, it goes divinely well with a light Bordeaux wine.

½   pound cream cheese
3   tablespoons unsalted butter, softened
¼   pound Roquefort cheese
2   egg yolks
·   dash cayenne pepper or Tabasco
·   few grindings black pepper
8   sheets filo dough
½   cup (1 stick) unsalted butter, melted
½   cup breadcrumbs

Cream together the cream cheese and the butter; beat in the crumbled Roquefort and the egg yolks until the mixture resembles a smooth and very thick batter. Season with the cayenne and black pepper. Chill for 1 hour. Remove filo dough from the refrigerator and allow to stand for 1 hour.

Preheat the oven to 375 degrees.

Spread a towel over your working space. Place a sheet of filo in the center of it. Brush the sheet with a light coating of butter and sprinkle it lightly with breadcrumbs. Place another sheet of dough over the first and repeat this procedure until 4 sheets have been used.

Spread half the cheese mixture in an even mound along the longest side of the pastry nearest you. Fold in the flaps of dough at the sides of the filling. Lift up the end of the towel and roll the pastry over the filling and continue to roll until the filling is completely enclosed.

Transfer the strudel to a lightly greased baking sheet and brush the top with butter. Repeat this with the ingredients remaining to form a second strudel.

Bake the strudels for 35 to 40 minutes, until golden brown. Allow to cool slightly, cut into 2-inch slices with a serrated knife, and serve warm.

November, Green Winter Vegetables

Menu 1
Potted Shrimp with Black Bread (December)
Chou Farci with Sauce Moutarde (November)
Roasted Pepper Salad (July)
Omelette Souffle with Apples and Rum (February)

Menu 2
Fennel Soup (November)
Poor Man's Pate en Croute (November)
Saute of Potatoes and Hazelnuts (April)
Green Salad Vinaigrette
Banana Rum Souffle Glace (January)

Fennel Soup
Brussels Sprouts in Vinegar
Brussels Sprouts in Cream Sauce
Brussels Sprouts with Cheese and Breadcrumbs
Braised Celery Root
Celery Root Remoulade
Celery Root in Mustard Vinaigrette
Swiss Chard Tart
Gratin of Leeks
Leeks in Vinaigrette
Fennel and Cucumber Saute
Fennel and Shrimp Vinaigrette
Fennel Saute with Prosciutto
Poor Man's Pate en Croute
Chou Farci with Sauce Moutarde
Fennel Butter Sauce
Chestnuts Flavored with Fennel Seed

The choice of produce in the winter months may seem limited to some, who see nothing on the greengrocer's tables except the most obvious root vegetables: potatoes, carrots, turnips, and onions. If they were to take a closer look at the produce stands, they would find a rather exciting display of Savoy cabbage, leeks, fennel bulb, celery root, and Brussels sprouts. This chapter is a tribute to these neglected vegetables.

Cabbage, often treated like a poor cousin of the vegetable family, can become a delicacy. True, it emits a rather strong odor when cooked, but this can easily be avoided by blanching the vegetable first in a good deal of boiling water. I prefer Savoy cabbage whenever it is available because its flavor and texture are both much more delicate than the smooth-leaved head cabbage: You will recognize the Savoy by its lacelike, curly leaves of a deep green color.

It has a shorter season in our area than any of the others but it is well worth searching out during its peak months of October and November.

Brussels sprouts are a diminutive member of the cabbage family. They are perhaps the most commonly abused winter vegetable. As with many green vegetables, overcooking is often the culprit, leaving the sprouts limp, mushy, and devoid of flavor. But when cooked until they are just tender and the leaves are still a bright green, their flavor is most pleasing. Look for small, firm heads of a bright color, avoiding those with yellowed leaves and obvious insect damage. If they are old, they will have an obvious odor even when raw. Sprouts are highly perishable and should be consumed within a day or two of purchase. They have a marvelous affinity for pork, or when treated with a bit of sugar and vinegar, they will become an unusual and flavorful accompaniment to corned beef.

Leeks, one of the world's most ancient cultivated vegetables, have been grown in Egypt and the lands bordering the Mediterranean since biblical times. They are known as "poor man's asparagus" in France. While the rest of the world is content to throw this mild-mannered cousin of the onion into the soup pot, the French serve them in savory tarts, simmered in red wine, baked in gratins. The last few years have seen a mild rise in popularity for this vegetable in our own country, so they are now widely available.

Leeks, which take no more than fifteen minutes to cook, are in season from October to March, and the price stays very much the same throughout this time: from fifty to eighty cents a bunch. When purchasing leeks, choose the smallest ones you can find, for the large ones often have a tough, woody center. This should be removed, if these are the only ones available.

Fennel, or finnochio, is a vegetable dear to the hearts of the Italian community. Classically, finocchio is paired with pork by the Italians: slivers of the bulb are "larded" into a roast. A paste is made of the bulb and leaves and spread on chops which are then grilled; even the seeds become a major seasoning in one particular type of sausage. A few years ago in Seattle, it was only to be found at the Pike Place Market, but it is now stocked in most supermarkets on a regular basis. It has a bulb-shaped base and long stems covered with lacy, dark green leaves, resembling dill. The flavor is similar to that of celery with a refreshing anise tang; the texture, too, is similar, being slightly more dense and having no "strings." It can be served either raw or cooked, although the flavor softens when cooked, becoming slightly sweeter.

The southern French have found that the flavor of fennel marries beautifully with seafood. Usually only the stalks and leaves are used: grillade au fenouil is a dish in which red mullet or sea bass is grilled over dried fennel branches. It is, indeed, an extremely versatile vegetable.

One of the more neglected root vegetables is celeriac, or celery root, a delicious winter offering usually available from November to April. Its round, knoblike shape is covered with a rough brown skin, and it is topped with an abundant mass of greenery somewhat resembling the flat-leaved Italian parsley. It has a mild celery flavor, and its texture resembles the potato; it is used as often raw as cooked. Celeriac can be added to any soup or stew that calls for celery stalks (it's marvelous, for example, in a pot au feu or a chicken fricassee), it can be made into a puree along with potatoes to create an interesting varition, or it can be made in a suave cream of celery root soup.

Fennel Soup
serves eight as a first course

This is a delicate soup using both bulb and leaves of the fennel. The anise flavor of fennel is further accentuated by the addition of Pernod. A dry Vouvray will make the beginning of the meal even more memorable.

2½ tablespoons butter
1   cup onion, finely chopped
2   cups potato, peeled and diced
2   garlic cloves, peeled and finely chopped
·   salt and freshly ground pepper

2   fennel bulbs with leaves
1½ cups dry white vermouth or dry white wine
2   quarts chicken stock, mildly seasoned
2   tablespoons Pernod

Melt the butter in a 4-quart heavy soup pot; add the onion, potato, and garlic, season lightly with salt and pepper, and saute for about 10 minutes, until the vegetables are soft but not brown.

While they are cooking, prepare the fennel: cut off the stems and leaves close to the base of the bulb and reserve. Peel away and discard any discolored outer sections of the bulb; cut it in half and wash under running water to remove all grit. Chop the fennel bulb into coarse pieces and add to the soup pot with the vegetables. Pour over this the vermouth or wine and the chicken stock, bring to a boil, reduce heat, and simmer for about 45 mintues or until the fennel is tender. Pour the soup through a sieve into a bowl; reserve vegetables. Rinse the soup pot with hot water and pour the liquid back into it. Place the vegetables in the container of a food processor fitted with the steel knife blade, reduce them to a fine paste, and add the puree to the soup pot.

Take the reserved stems and strip from them about 2 tightly packed cups of leaves; chop them finely and add them to the soup. Place the pot back on the heat, simmer for 5 or 10 minutes to warm, add the Pernod, correct the seasoning, and serve.

Brussels Sprouts in Vinegar

serves four

The Brussels sprouts are first blanched, then cooked in a light vinegar sauce. The vinegar specified is rice-wine vinegar, one of the most delicate; it is available in shops selling Oriental foods. This recipe complements corned beef especially well.

1   pound Brussels sprouts
⅓   cup rice wine vinegar
½   cup water
1½ teaspoons sugar
·   dash salt

Trim the stems off the sprouts and discard. Cut each sprout in half unless they are very small. Place in a pot of boiling, salted water and cook for 5 minutes. Remove to a colander and refresh under cold running water.

Combine the rice-wine vinegar, water, sugar, and salt in a pot large enough to hold all the sprouts and bring to a boil; add the sprouts and cook for about 8 minutes or until they are just tender. (Most of the vinegar mixture will be absorbed by the vegetable.) Serve at once.

Brussels Sprouts in Cream Sauce
serves four to six

The water chestnuts in this recipe add an interesting texture, and I find their flavor more suitable to the dish than the French chestnuts that are usually added.

1   pound Brussels sprouts
1   cup water chestnuts, cut into thick slices
2   tablespoons butter
1½ tablespoons flour
1½ cups heavy cream
·   freshly grated nutmeg
·   pinch of cayenne pepper
·   salt

Cut off and discard the stems of the sprouts. Cut a cross in the bottom of each. Drop in boiling, salted water and cook for about 12 minutes, or until the sprouts are tender. Remove them, place in a shallow serving dish, and mix in the water chestnuts. Keep warm while preparing sauce.

Melt the butter in a small saucepan, stir in the flour with a wire whisk, and cook over low heat for 5 minutes; do not allow to brown. Add the heavy cream and the seasonings and cook over low heat until the sauce thickens. Adjust the seasoning if necessary.

Pour the sauce over the sprout and water chestnut mixture and serve.

Brussels Sprouts with Cheese and Breadcrumbs
serves four

1   pound Brussels sprouts
3   tablespoons butter
¼   cup freshly grated Parmesan cheese
¼   cup dry breadcrumbs
·   salt and freshly ground pepper

Cut off and discard the stems of the sprouts. Place in a pot of boiling salted water and cook for about 8 minutes, or until the sprouts are almost tender. Remove from heat, drain thoroughly, and chop them coarsely.

In a 10-inch skillet melt the butter; when the foam subsides, add the chopped sprouts and saute them over moderate heat until they begin to brown. Sprinkle with the grated cheese, the breadcrumbs, and salt and pepper; toss the mixture together well for 1 to 2 minutes (only long enough to allow the cheese to melt) and serve immediately.

Braised Celery Root
serves four

A delicate-tasting vegetable dish that complements pork or chicken especially well.

1   celery root, about 1 pound
3   cups chicken broth
·   small pinch of dried thyme
·   salt and freshly ground
     pepper
⅓   cup freshly grated Parmesan
     cheese

Peel the celery root with a sharp paring knife. Working quickly, cut into ½-inch cubes and drop immediately into a bowl of water containing a dash of vinegar to prevent discoloration. Bring the chicken stock to a boil. Add the thyme and the celery root; reduce heat and simmer until you can pierce the vegetable easily with a knife (about 10 minutes). Drain, reserving the stock for future use, and place in a serving plate. Sprinkle with salt, pepper, and grated cheese. Toss well and serve immediately.

Celery Root Remoulade
serves four to six

This recipe is in the New Orleans style rather than the French. The addition of tiny Pacific shrimp gives it a unique Northwest flavor. Serve as an hors d'oeuvre with a dry Muscat from Oregon or an Alsatian Muscat.

Sauce:

1   egg yolk, at room
    temperature
1   tablespoon Creole mustard
    (or a good, grainy French
    mustard)
½   tablespoon red wine vinegar
2 or 3 drops of Tabasco
·   large pinch of salt
¾   cup of oil (half and half
    corn and olive oils)
·   squeeze of lemon juice
1   tablespoon capers, finely
    chopped
2   tablespoons parsley, finely
    chopped
1   teaspoon finely grated
    lemon rind
1   celery root, about 1 pound
3   ounces Pacific shrimp,
    cooked (do not use canned)

First prepare the sauce. Place the egg yolk in a mixing bowl; add the mustard, vinegar, Tabasco, and salt and beat thoroughly with a wire whisk or an electric mixer. Then add a few drops of the oil, mixing well to allow the yolks to absorb the oil completely before adding any more. Continue beating until all the oil is absorbed; add lemon juice to taste and blend. Add the capers, parsley, and lemon rind, mix well, taste for seasoning, and adjust if necessary. Set aside.

Peel the celery root and, working quickly, cut into julienne strips or grate coarsely. Mix immediately into the sauce; add the shrimp (reserving a few for garnish), mix well, and chill until serving time.

Celery Root in Mustard Vinaigrette
serves four

This has a taste similar to a remoulade but is much simpler to prepare.

1   celery root, about 1 pound
1   egg yolk
·   salt
1½ tablespoons mild red wine
    vinegar
1 to 1½ teaspoons Pommery
    mustard (or other good
    grainy French mustard)
4 to 5 tablespoons olive oil
·   freshly ground pepper

Peel the celery root and cut it into julienne strips or grate coarsely. Place in mixing bowl and reserve.

Put the egg yolk in a small bowl, add the salt, vinegar, and mustard, and mix together. Add the olive oil and pepper, blending with a small whisk or fork, and pour immediately over the celery root. Toss well and chill for 1 to 2 hours before serving.

Swiss Chard Tarte

serves six

This tart is composed of blanched, shredded chard, sauteed quickly with a bit of onion, prosciutto, and garlic, then mixed into ricotta, Parmesan, and eggs and baked in a pastry shell. It has a light and zesty flavor and—for those concerned with keeping waistlines intact—this tart can be made without the pastry: simply pour the filling into a well-greased nine-inch pie dish and bake. It can be cut intoo wedges and served in the same manner. Either way a Valpolicella or Chardonnay is the right sort of wine.

1 bunch of Swiss chard (about 1 pound)
· squeeze of lemon juice
2 tablespoons olive oil or butter
½ cup onion, finely chopped
½ cup prosciutto, cut into julienne (substitute baked ham, if desired)
2 cloves garlic, finely chopped
· freshly grated nutmeg
· salt and freshly ground pepper
1½ cups ricotta cheese
½ cup freshly grated Parmesan cheese
½ cup milk
3 eggs
10-inch partially baked pastry shell

Preheat the oven to 400 degrees.

Cut the stems from the Swiss chard and discard them. Wash the greens well and reserve. Bring a large pot of salted water to a boil and add a squeeze of lemon juice and the greens. Cook for 2 to 3 minutes until tender but still green. Remove the chard to a colander and run it under cold water to arrest the cooking process. Dry thoroughly (a lettuce dryer or spinner is good for this job) and chop it into shreds.

Heat the oil or butter in a skillet. Add the onion and saute a few minutes until it is soft but not brown; add the prosciutto and saute for a minute more. To the skillet add the chard and the garlic; saute over moderately high heat for 5 minutes, stirring, until all the moisture is absorbed. Sprinkle this mixture with the nutmeg, salt, and pepper and reserve.

Put the ricotta through a sieve (or blend in a food processor for a few seconds) to remove the grainy texture. Place it in a mixing bowl along with all but a tablespoon of the grated cheese, milk, and eggs and blend well. Add to this the chard and prosciutto mixture; blend again and check the seasoning. Pour into the prepared pastry shell, sprinkle the top with the remaining cheese, and bake in the middle of the oven for 35 to 45 minutes or until the tart is browned and puffy. Remove from oven, let stand 15 minutes, and serve.

Gratin of Leeks
serves four

Almost any vegetable is at home in a gratin. Here the leeks are wrapped in slices of ham or prosciutto, bathed in heavy cream, and drizzled with a mixture of grated cheese and breadcrumbs. This may be served as an unusual first course or as the vegetable course.

8   leeks
·   dash of vinegar
4   slices of baked ham or prosciutto
·   enough heavy cream to cover bottom of gratin dish (about ½ cup)
3   tablespoons grated Parmesan or Gruyere cheese
3   tablespoons breadcrumbs
½   tablespoon butter

Preheat the oven to 375 degrees.

Trim and clean the leeks as in "Leeks in Vinaigrette." Tie them together in a bunch with kitchen string and place them in a pot of boiling, salted water to which a dash of vinegar has been added; simmer them for 8 minutes.

Remove leeks from the water, untie them, and drain thoroughly. Wrap each slice of ham or prosciutto around 2 leeks and place in a buttered ovenproof gratin dish large enough to hold them in a single layer. Pour the heavy cream over the rolls and sprinkle the top with the cheese and breadcrumbs; dot the top with the butter cut into small bits. Bake for 20 to 30 minutes or until the top is a golden brown. Serve immediately.

Leeks in Vinaigrette
serves four

This is an extremely simple recipe. The poached leeks are dressed while they are still hot —and this is very important— with sherry wine vinegar and a good olive oil. Something wonderful happens when the vinegar and oil come into contact with the hot vegetable; the flavors of all are intensified and the aroma emitted is sheer heaven. This dish is delicious with roast beef, lamb, or chicken.

6 or eight leeks
·   dash of vinegar
2   tablespoons sherry wine vinegar (available in wine shops and specialty stores)
½   cup fruity olive oil
·   salt and freshly ground pepper

Cut off and save for the soup pot all but 2 inches of the green tops of the leeks. Slice the leeks lengthwise almost to the root end. Wash them thoroughly under cold running water to remove all the sand and grit. Cut off and discard the root end, slice each leek into 2-inch lengths, and put in a pot of boiling, salted water to which a dash of vinegar has been added. This will allow the leeks to remain white and keep their flavor. Cook over medium heat for 10 to 15 minutes or until tender. Remove, run under cold water to arrest the cooking process, and drain thoroughly.

Place the leeks in a shallow serving dish, pour the vinegar and oil over them, season with salt and pepper to taste, toss together gently, and serve immediately.

Fennel and Cucumber Saute

serves four

An unusual vegetable combination, delicious as an accompaniment to seafood.

2 medium cucumbers
1 small fennel bulb
2½ tablespoons butter
· salt and freshly ground pepper
· pinch of freshly ground nutmeg

Peel the cucumbers, cut them in half, and seed them. Cut each half in two, chop into 1-inch pieces, and put into boiling, salted water for 5 minutes. Remove, refresh under cold water, and drain well.
Cut the stems from the fennel bulb and reserve for another use. Cut the bulb into 1-inch pieces and put them into boiling, salted water; cook for about 5 minutes. Remove and refresh under cold water. Drain well.

In a small skillet melt the butter, add the cucumber and fennel, and season with the salt, pepper, and nutmeg. Cook over medium heat for 5 to 8 minutes — just long enough to warm through — and serve.

Fennel and Shrimp Vinaigrette

serves four

This combination of raw strips of fennel bulb and tiny Pacific shrimp dressed with lemon juice and olive oil makes a delightful first course.

1   small fennel bulb
3   ounces Pacific shrimp, cooked
·   salt and freshly ground pepper
1½ to 2 tablespoons lemon juice
4   tablespoons fruity olive oil

Cut the stems from the fennel bulb and reserve them for another use. Remove any outside sections of the bulb that are discolored and discard. Cut the remaining fennel into julienne.

Put in a mixing bowl with the shrimp meat, season with the salt and pepper, add the lemon juice and the olive oil, and toss well. Chill for about 1 hour before serving.

Fennel Saute with Prosciutto

serves four

1   small fennel bulb (about 1 pound)
2   tablespoons butter
3   ounces prosciutto or baked ham cut into julienne
·   salt and freshly ground pepper

Cut the stems and leaves from the fennel bulb and reserve for another use. Remove and discard any discolored outer sections of the bulb; cut the

remainder into bite-size pieces and place in boiling, salted water for 5 minutes. Remove, refresh under cold running water, and drain well.

Melt the butter in a skillet. Add the prosciutto or ham and saute over high heat for 2 minutes. Add the fennel and continue to cook for another 5 minutes, stirring frequently. Season to taste with salt and pepper and serve.

Poor Man's Pate en Croute

serves six

This savory creation of curried ground beef mixed with a puree of leeks is wrapped in filo (or phyllo) pastry. Filo resembles strudel dough: paper-thin sheets that are almost transparent in their lightness and are usually brushed with butter and layered. The end result is a pastry that explodes into crisp, golden flakes when bitten into, very much like a good croissant. Filo can be purchased at any shop that carries Middle Eastern foods. Serve with a first course of fennel and shrimp vinaigrette or fennel soup (both November) or potted shrimp (December). A Gewurztraminer from California would mesh nicely with any or all of these.

4	small leeks
·	dash of vinegar
1	tablespoon butter
½	tablespoon vegetable oil
2	tablespoons onion, finely chopped
3	cloves garlic, finely chopped
2	pounds lean ground beef
·	salt
·	dash of cayenne pepper
¼ to ½	teaspoon curry powder or paste (depending on strength of brand used)
2	eggs
4	ounces sour cream
12	sheets filo pastry
6	tablespoons melted butter

Preheat the oven to 375 degrees.

One hour before preparation, remove the filo from the refrigerator and wrap it in a damp towel. (Filo dries out rather quickly, and it should be left in the towel throughout preparation.)

Cut the tops off the leeks, leaving 2 to 3 inches of green. Slice them in half almost to the root and wash thoroughly under cold running water, spreading the leaves to rinse out all grit. Cut off and discard the root end. Slice the leeks into 1-inch lengths and drop them into a pot of boiling, salted water to which a dash of vinegar has been added. Cook for about 10 minutes, drain well, and puree in a food processor fitted with the steel knife blade. Remove puree, place in a mixing bowl, and set aside.

While the leeks are cooking, prepare the meat: saute the onion in the butter and oil until it has softened but not browned; add the beef and garlic and saute until the meat has separated and browned lightly. Season to taste with salt, cayenne, and curry, drain off any excess fat, and place in mixing bowl along with the leek puree.

Combine the eggs with the sour cream and add to the meat, blending well. Taste for seasoning. You may wish to add more curry powder to bring out the flavors of the filling, but curry should *not* be the dominant flavor.

Spread a large towel over your working space. Place a sheet of filo pastry in the middle of the towel with the long side nearest you; brush it with a light coating of melted butter. Directly on top of this, place the next sheet, brush with butter, and continue until all 12 sheets have been used. Mound the filling along the side nearest you, leaving a 1-inch border along each of the short sides. Using the towel as an aid, roll the pastry once over the filling, fold the sides over, and roll to close.

Paint the bottom of the roll with a light coating of butter; place a large pastry sheet on top of the roll, grasp the ends of the towel firmly, and invert. Baste the top of the roll with more butter and place in the oven. Bake for 30 to 40 minutes or until the top of the roll is browned and crisp. Serve immediately, using a serrated knife to slice into crosswise pieces.

Chou Farci with Sauce Moutarde

serves six to eight

There are many versions of stuffed cabbage, most of them uninspired and rather pedestrian. This recipe, which makes use of Savoy cabbage and fennel, two of the finest winter vegetables, is exceptional. Savoy cabbage is more delicately flavored than the smooth-leaved head cabbage, and its lacy dark green to yellow leaves are most attractive.

The presentation of this dish is rather unusual, since the cabbage is served whole, with the filling replacing its core. Wedges are cut from it and the mustard sauce spooned over them. Serve with an hors d'oeuvre of potted salmon (August) or potted shrimp (December) and roast pepper salad (July) or leeks vinaigrette (this month). A rose is about your best bet for wine: a true Tavel or Rose d'Anjou from France or a Dry Creek Rose of Cabernet from California.

1 large Savoy cabbage (about the size of a basketball)

Filling:
1 small fennel bulb, leaves and stems removed, finely chopped (about 1 cup) (substitute celery, if fennel is unavailable)
1 medium onion, peeled and finely chopped
2 cloves garlic, finely chopped
1 baking apple, peeled, cored, and coarsely chopped
1½ pounds pork loin, ground
2 tablespoons fresh thyme, minced, or 1 teaspoon dried thyme
¼ teaspoon ground cumin plus additional cumin to sprinkle on leaves
· pinch powdered saffron (optional)
· salt and freshly ground pepper
½ cup homemade breadcrumbs
2 tablespoons heavy cream
1 egg, lightly beaten

2   cups chicken stock
     Sauce:
2   tablespoons butter
1½   tablespoons flour
½   cup heavy cream
·   freshly grated nutmeg
·   salt and freshly ground
     pepper
1   teaspoon French Pommery
     mustard (or other grainy
     French mustard)

Preheat the oven to 375 degrees.

Bring a large kettle of salted water to a boil. Put the cabbage in whole and simmer it for 10 to 15 minutes, turning it occasionally. (This procedure removes the strong aroma from the cabbage.)

While the cabbage is blanching, place the filling ingredients in a bowl and mix together by hand. Combine the heavy cream with the egg and add to filling, again blending by hand.

Remove the cabbage to a deep pan in the sink and run it under cold water to arrest the cooking process. As soon as it is cool enough to handle easily, trim away and discard most of the stem. Place the cabbage in the center of a large piece of cheesecloth or other clean, light cloth. Pull each leaf away from the head (but do not break them off) and press gently down until you reach the tight central core of leaves; cut the core out,

mince it, and add to filling mixture, or reserve it for another use.

Season the uppermost leaves with a little salt and a sprinkling of ground cumin. Mound the filling in the center and, leaf by leaf, reform the entire cabbage, seasoning lightly between all the leaves. Bring the cheesecloth up over the cabbage, twist it tightly, tie with string, and cut off; discard any excess cheesecloth.

Place the stuffed cabbage in an ovenproof casserole, add the chicken stock, and bake for about 2 hours, basting occasionally so the cabbage will not dry out. Remove from casserole, reserving 1 cup of the stock. Keep cabbage warm while making the sauce.

Melt the butter in a small saucepan, stir in the flour with a wire whisk, and cook over low heat for 5 minutes; do not brown. Stir in the reserved chicken stock and cook until the mixture thickens. Add the heavy cream, the seasonings, and the mustard and cook over low heat for an additional 5 minutes to allow the flavors to blend.

Place the stuffed cabbage on a serving dish; cut and carefully remove cheesecloth. Slice into wedges, spoon sauce over, and serve immediately, or serve and pass the sauce separately.

Fennel Butter Sauce

serves four

A butter sauce to which has been added chopped fennel leaves and a dash of Pernod. It is wonderful on poached or grilled fish.

6 tablespoons butter
¼ cup fennel leaves, chopped finely and tightly packed
1 to 2 teaspoons Pernod

Melt the butter slowly in a small saucepan or skillet, add the fennel leaves and the Pernod, stir, and serve immediately.

Chestnuts Flavored with Fennel Seed

serves four to six

A favorite in the Appenine mountain district of Italy: the fennel seed imparts a delightful aroma to the chestnuts. Serve them with a light red wine.

40 to 50 imported Italian
    chestnuts
·   small pinch of salt
2   tablespoons fennel seeds

Cut a cross into the skins of the chestnuts at the pointed end. Bring a large pot of water to a boil, add the salt and the fennel seeds, and continue to boil for 5 minutes. Add the chestnuts and boil for about 20 minutes more or until they are tender. Drain, let cool to room temperature, and serve.

December, Foods for Entertaining and Giving

Menu 1
Oyster Stew (January)
Roast Turkey with Stuffing (December)
Whipped Yams with Cognac (December)
Brussels Sprouts in Cream Sauce (November)
Zuccotto (December)

Menu 2
Aioli Monstre, Northwest Style (December)
Chocolate Truffles Seville (December)
Espresso

Rillettes de Porc
Potted Shrimp
Whipped Yams with Cognac
Country Pate
Chicken Liver Mousse
Roast Capon with Noodle Dressing
Roast Turkey with Stuffing
Roast Ham with Marmalade Glaze
Aioli Monstre, Northwest Style
Cannoli
Tarte aux Pruneaux
Mousse aux Mandarines
Chocolate Truffles Seville
Chocolate Truffles Italienne
Zuccotto

The elaborate holiday dinner composed of many courses is today an endangered species. Such feasts are time consuming; the traditional foodstuffs are daily becoming more expensive, and the feast itself is guaranteed to add too many extra pounds to your frame. Nonetheless, we Americans are sentimental creatures at heart, most of us, and we get a great deal of satisfaction from participating in and reenacting a tradition. Because we are a land of many different peoples, moveover, methods and menus are often intermingled when it comes to celebration. One of the most delicious turkey dinners I can remember was consumed with chopsticks, and although this lent an element of the exotic to the meal, it was traditionally American in every sense.

This chapter opens with two menus, one traditional and the other offbeat. The former, a "turkey dinner with all the trimmings," needs no explanation, and in spite of my penchant for the unusual, it remains one of my favorites. The second menu is based on the Aioli Monstre, a classic dish served in Provence, the southernmost district of France. The heart of this feast is a robust garlic mayonnaise, so I would not suggest serving a meal like this to anyone who has not an abiding passion for garlic, "the truffle of the poor" as it is called in Provence. Aioli is classically served with salted cod, but to give this recipe a Northwest twist, I have substituted fresh salmon. You may, if you wish, also use any firm-fleshed white fish.

The rest of this chapter offers recipes that may be used for holiday gift giving: not a novel idea by any means, but giving gifts of food prepared with your own hands lends a most personal feeling to a holiday. With the exception of two recipes of chocolate truffles, these dishes are all some form of charcuterie: pates, rillettes, terrines, and such. The advantage of charcuterie as a gift (besides the obvious one of wonderful taste) is that the recipient may enjoy the gift at leisure; it will not become stale like the usual offerings of baked goods. Also, these gifts may be made far in advance of the season, giving the cook a flexibility uncommon at this time of year. One cannot conclude a discussion of charcuterie without mentioning the definitive book on the subject: Jane Grigson's *The Art of Making Sausages, Pates and Other Charcuterie*, published in paperback by Knopf for $4.95. Elizabeth David also has some marvelous recipes in her *French Provencial Cooking*, a Penguin paperback.

Rillettes de Porc

Rillettes originated in the Touraine region of France, an area renowned for its charcuterie—a name that, strictly speaking, is applied only to pork products but that also covers all sorts of meat preparations: sausages, galantines, cured meats, and pates.

Rillettes, more of a "potted pork" than a pate, is quite simple to make at home, albeit more time consuming than the latter; but you have the added advantage that this mixture, when properly made (the meat is sterilized by the long cooking process) and sealed, will keep for six months to a year.

Very often, the pork in rillettes will be combined with other meats; rabbit is sometimes used, although its flavor is rather overpowered by the pork. Goose or duck gives the mixture a suave and interesting flavor and this is a good way to use any leftovers from your holiday roast.

I have departed from tradition in the preparation of this dish. First, the fatback is ground rather than cubed. This enables the fat to melt entirely, leaving behind no solids, which normally would be mixed in with the meat and would give it a slightly heavier and sometimes greasy flavor.

Second, I've chosen to use very lean meat, pork loin instead of the classic pork neck, shoulder, or belly. This too allows for a lighter texture and, I believe, a better flavor.

The final step of shredding the cooked meat by hand with two forks is absolutely necessary to obtain the correct texture. If the meat is put through a grinder or blender the result is rather puddinglike and not the even mass of fibers it should be. This final process is not as arduous as it sounds; the meat has been cooked for such a long time that it almost falls apart of its own accord. Dry, robust white wines go well with rillettes: Chardonnays, Rieslings, Gewurztraminers.

1	pound fatback
2½	pounds pork loin roast with bone
.	bouquet garni composed of:
5	peppercorns
½	teaspoon dried thyme
2	bay leaves
6	garlic cloves, unpeeled
.	all enclosed in a cheesecloth bag
¼	teaspoon allspice
.	salt to taste

Grind the fatback into small pieces. Bone the pork loin (reserve the bone) and cut the meat into small cubes. Do *not* put the meat through a grinder; the entire texture of the dish will be changed.

Put the ground fatback, the cubed meat, and the bones in a heavy 4- to 6-quart Dutch oven with the bouquet garni buried in the center. Add the allspice and the salt and enough water to cover all. Place the lid on the pot and set it over low heat to simmer for about 4 hours; by this time the meat should be very tender and swimming in its own fat. The liquid should have been reduced to half its original amount.

Pour the contents of the pot through a fine sieve standing over a large mixing bowl, so that the solids collect in the sieve and the fat drips through. Reserve the fat. When all the fat is drained off, empty the meat onto your chopping board, discarding the bones and the bouquet garni. Using two forks, pull the meat into small, thin shreds. Taste the meat for seasoning; more salt is usually needed. If you like, a bit of the liquid fat can be added to the meat at this point to make the paste creamy.

Pack the rillettes lightly into small pots and seal the top of the pots with ½ inch of the reserved fat. (If the mixture is to be eaten in a day or two, no layer of fat is necessary). Place in the refrigerator overnight to firm.

The next day, remove the rillettes and on each pot put a layer of foil *directly* on top of the fat layer and another layer over the top of the pot itself. This will preserve the rillettes for 6 months to a year. Remove the rillettes from the refrigerator several hours before serving to allow the mixture to soften. Serve with French bread.

Potted Shrimp
serves six to eight

Purchase tiny cooked Pacific shrimp from your fishmonger for this dish. If they are unavailable, use raw shrimp; remove the shells and saute them briefly.

½ pound cooked shrimp meat

· squeeze of lemon juice
· dash of cayenne pepper or Tabasco
· dash of cognac (optional)
6 tablespoons butter, cut into small pieces
salt to taste

Put the shrimp (cut into pieces, if they are large) in the container of a blender or food processor fitted with the steel knife blade and blend just until the shrimp is shredded. Add the lemon juice, the cayenne or Tabasco, and the cognac.

Turn on the machine and add the butter bit by bit until it has been incorporated. Taste and add salt if necessary. Put the mixture in a small serving container, cover with foil or plastic, and refrigerate for at least 3 hours.

Whipped Yams with Cognac
serves six

A yam has orange-colored flesh and a more pronounced flavor than the yellow-fleshed sweet potato. The latter may be used for this recipe, but it may require more butter as it is dryer.

6   medium yams
·   salt
6   tablespoons butter
3   tablespoons cognac or good brandy
·   freshly ground pepper
·   dash fresh grated nutmeg

Wash the yams; do not peel them. Cut them in quarters. Bring a pot of lightly salted water to a boil; add the yams and cover. Cook the yams until just tender, about 10 minutes.

Drain the yams and, holding each piece in a kitchen towel, peel off the skins. Cut each piece in half again and put in the bowl of a food processor fitted with the steel blade. Puree the potatoes for a few seconds, adding the butter cut into small pieces through the funnel while the machine is still running. Season with the cognac, salt, pepper, and nutmeg and blend for 1 to 2 seconds. Pour the whipped yams into a serving bowl and serve at once.

Country Pate
for a two-quart terrine or pate mold

Country pates are usually identified by their coarse texture and robust seasoning. The small amount of breadcrumbs and the egg help to counteract crumbling. Bacon should never be substituted for the fatback; it will lend the pate a defined smoky flavor that is undesirable. If you cannot find pancetta in your area, substitute a good-flavored baked ham instead. Serve with French bread and cornichons. A grand cru Beaujolais or a good Beaujolais Villages completes the impression a fine country pate makes.

1½ pounds lean pork, coarsely ground
1 pound veal, coarsely ground
½ pound pancetta, coarsely ground
¼ pound pork fatback, cut into small dice, not ground
2 tablespoons butter
1 cup onion, finely chopped
4 large cloves garlic, peeled
½ teaspoon thyme
¼ teaspoon allspice
· pinch ground cloves
· salt and freshly ground pepper
¼ cup cognac or good brandy
2 eggs
¼ cup soft breadcrumbs
1½ pounds pork fatback, cut into thinnest possible slices
2 bay leaves

Preheat the oven to 350 degrees. Combine the ground pork, veal, pancetta, and diced fatback in a large mixing bowl.

Heat the butter in a skillet; add the onions and saute them over moderate heat for about 10 minutes; do not brown. Pour into the mixing bowl with the meat. Put the garlic cloves through a press and into the bowl; add the thyme, allspice, cloves, and salt and pepper to taste.

Combine and blend the cognac, eggs, and breadcrumbs; add this mixture to the meats and work the meats and seasonings together with your hands. To test for seasoning: bring a small skillet of water to a boil, add a teaspoon of the meat mixture, and simmer it for just a few minutes. Chill the bit of pate quickly in the freezer and taste; adjust the seasoning if necessary.

Line a 2-quart pate mold or terrine or loaf pan with the slices of fatback, reserving a few of them for the top. Pour in the meat mixture, cover the top with the reserved fatback slices, and top with the bay leaves. Cover the mold with its lid or use a double thickness of foil) and place it in a pan containing water, enough to reach halfway up the sides of the terrine. Bake in the center of the oven for about 1½ hours; the pate is done when its juices run clear.

Remove the lid, place a weight on top, and allow to cool. Refrigerate with the weight still in place for 2 to 3 days. Before serving, remove the pate from the refrigerator and allow to stand at room temperature for at least 1 hour.

Chicken Liver Mousse
makes approximately two cups

An extremely simple recipe that may be prepared a day or two in advance. If you wish to keep it longer, cover the top with half an inch of clarified butter. Serve it with a French, Italian, or sourdough bread and cornichons.

1   pound chicken livers
8   tablespoons butter
6   medium shallots, coarsely chopped
1   large garlic clove, coarsely chopped
·   few sprigs each of fresh parsley and thyme (if no fresh thyme is available, substitute ¼ teaspoon dried)
1   small bay leaf
⅓   cup Madeira
¼   teaspoon each powdered ginger and allspice
½   teaspoon salt
·   freshly ground pepper

Clean the chicken livers and cut each in half. Melt 2 tablespoons butter in a 10-inch skillet; when sizzling, add the shallots and saute over moderate heat for 1 minute. Add the livers, garlic, parsley, thyme, and bay leaf and season the mixture lightly with salt and pepper. Cook the livers until they are firm but still pink in the center, 6 to 8 minutes. Pour the Madeira over the livers, raise the heat to high, and reduce the pan juices to a glaze.

Remove the mixture from the heat and allow to cool for a few minutes. Remove the bay leaf, place the contents of the skillet in the container of a food processor (if using a blender, puree the mixture in 2 batches), and blend into a smooth puree. Add a bit more Madeira to taste, the ginger and allspice, salt, and the remaining 6 tablespoons butter, cut into chunks. Blend the mousse until completely smooth. Taste and adjust seasoning if necessary. Chill the mousse for 2 to 3 hours before serving.

Roast Capon with Noodle Dressing
serves 6

A superb dish for the holidays: roast capon stuffed with egg noodles and bits of chicken liver and served with a sour cream and tarragon sauce. Accompany with braised celery root (November) or broccoli puree (February). A St. Emilion, Graves, Pouilly Fume, or Sauvignon Blanc — any would serve.

5- to 6-pound fresh capon

3 cups egg noodles, ½-inch wide

7 tablespoons butter

4 large shallots, finely chopped

1 clove garlic, finely chopped

¼ pound chicken livers, cleaned and cut in half

2 tablespoons fresh parsley chopped together with

½ teaspoon dried thyme

⅓ cup Madeira

2 tablespoons heavy cream

· salt and freshly ground pepper

¼ cup dry white vermouth or dry white wine

Sauce:

¼ cup fat from roasting pan

3 tablespoons flour

1 cup stock (see preparation below)

¾ cup sour cream

· salt

· dash cayenne pepper

½ teaspoon dried tarragon

Prepare a stock using the wing tips, giblets, and neck of the capon. You will need about 1 cup.

Preheat the oven to 350 degrees.

Prepare the dressing: Bring a large pot of salted water to a boil, add the noodles, and cook them for just 5 minutes. Drain them well and toss them with 1 tablespoon butter; reserve. Melt 2 tablespoons butter in a 10-inch skillet, add the shallots and garlic, and saute them for 3 minutes over moderate heat.

Add the chicken livers and saute for about 5 minutes. Remove them with a slotted spoon and chop finely. Return them to the pan, raise the heat, and add the Madeira; reduce the liquid in the pan to half. Sprinkle the mixture with the herbs, stir in the heavy cream, and pour it over the noodles. Toss this together until it is thoroughly combined and season lightly with salt and pepper.

Stuff the capon with this dressing and truss it well. Melt the remaining 4 tablespoons of butter with the vermouth or wine and baste the bird with a little of it. Place the capon in a shallow baking pan and season the outside lightly with salt and pepper. Roast for 1 hour and 45 minutes or until tender, basting with the butter and vermouth mixture every 15 minutes.

When the capon is tender, remove from its roasting pan and keep warm. Pour off ¼ cup fat from the roasting pan into a saucepan and set over moderate heat. When it is hot, stir in the flour with a wire whisk and cook the roux for 5 minutes, taking care not to brown it. Stir in the reserved cup of stock, whisking until the sauce thickens.

Reduce the heat to low, add the sour cream, and season with salt, cayenne pepper, and tarragon. Cook this for another 5 minutes, taste, and adjust seasoning if necessary. Place in a heated sauce boat and serve with the roast capon and its dressing.

Roast Turkey with Stuffing
serves ten to twelve

The recipe given here for roast turkey with stuffing is based partly on one that has been used by my family for years. It begins with a *fresh* turkey, and those are not as difficult to get as you might think. Almost any supermarket or poultry shop can supply you with one if given enough advance notice.

The merits of a plump, juicy, untampered-with bird are obvious, as opposed to the frozen variety, shot full of oil because all the natural oil sacs on the skin have been removed, and complete with a built-in thermometer — the very idea is demoralizing.

The stuffing is a savory preparation of toasted egg-bread cubes, minced chicken livers, onion and celery sauteed to a golden tenderness, ground pork tenderloin, toasted hazelnuts, and herbs, all bound together with eggs, Madeira, and sour cream.

The stuffed bird is roasted at a low heat of 325 degrees; I find this is the only way to achieve a crisp and meltingly brown skin and still having both the dark and light meat done to a turn. The turkey must be basted often when done in this way, but the results will be more than satisfactory. For wine a Chardonnay, a Gewurztraminer, or a full-bodied Bordeaux such as a St. Julien will serve.

Stuffing:

1	loaf challah or other egg-bread
6	tablespoons butter
½	pound chicken livers, cleaned and cut in half
2	cups onion, finely chopped
½	cup celery, finely chopped
2	garlic cloves, finely chopped
1	pound pork tenderloin, ground
½	cup parsley, finely chopped
·	few sprigs fresh thyme, finely chopped, or ½ teaspoon dried thyme
¾	cup toasted hazelnuts, coarsely chopped
2	eggs
1	cup sour cream
¼	cup Madeira
·	salt and freshly ground pepper

246

12-pound fresh turkey
1   lemon
·   salt and freshly ground
    pepper
6   tablespoons butter melted
    with
3   tablespoons dry white
    vermouth or dry white wine

Preheat the oven to 200 degrees.
Prepare the stuffing: cut the
bread into ½-inch cubes, place
on pastry sheets, and toast in the
oven until the croutons are
completely dried; there should
be enough to measure 8 cups.

Heat 2 tablespoons butter in a
skillet, add the chicken livers,
season lightly with salt and
pepper, and saute for 5 to 8
minutes; the livers should be
firm but still pink in the middle.
Remove the livers with a slotted
spoon, chop them finely, and
place into a large mixing bowl.

In the same skillet, put the
remaining 4 tablespoons butter
and heat. When the butter is
hot, add the onions, celery, and
garlic and saute for about 5
minutes over moderate heat.
Add the ground pork to the
skillet and cook it just until
there are no traces of pink in the
meat. Place this in the mixing
bowl and add the parsley,
thyme, hazelnuts, and croutons.

In a small bowl, combine the
eggs, sour cream, and Madeira
and beat lightly. Pour this over
the stuffing and mix together
with your hands. Season the

stuffing to taste with salt and
pepper. This may be made a
day in advance but the bird
should not be stuffed until it is
ready for roasting.

Preheat the oven to 325 degrees.
Rub the turkey inside and out
with the cut side of a lemon.
Stuff both cavities lightly with
the dressing (it will expand
during cooking) and sew closed
with a trussing needle and heavy
kitchen string. Truss the bird
well, rub it with a bit of the
butter and vermouth mixture,
and place in the oven.

Baste the bird every half hour
with the basting mixture until
the skin is a deep golden brown,
then cover the turkey and its
pan completely with foil and
continue roasting. At 325
degrees, the bird should be
allowed 25 minutes to the
pound; a 12-pound turkey
should be done in 5 hours. The
dark meat should still have a
slightly pink color near the
bones and the white meat will
be moist and succulent.

I refuse to involve myself in any
discussions regarding the uses of
leftover turkey. Too many
abominable recipes are in
existence already. For my taste
there is nothing better than
cold, thinly sliced turkey on rye
bread with a bit of homemade
mayonnaise.

There is, however, something
wonderful that can be done with
the turkey carcass. Cut it into

manageable pieces and set it aside; coarsely chop some celery, carrot, and onion; saute them in a large stock pot until soft but not brown; add a cup or two of dry white wine, some parsley, thyme, and bay leaf, and the turkey carcass; add enough water to cover.

Cook this as you would any stock. The result should be a rich broth, redolent of turkey. After straining off all bones and vegetables, degrease the broth and bring it to a boil. Into the boiling broth, stir a mixture of 2 or 3 eggs that have been beaten with about ¼ cup of freshly grated Parmesan cheese and a dash of freshly grated nutmeg. Cook only until the egg mixture forms tiny flakes in the soup. This is called Stracciatella, roughly translated to mean "little rags," and is an old Roman favorite.

Roast Ham with Marmalade Glaze
for twelve (with ham left over)

It has become increasingly difficult to locate a good-flavored ham. Most of them are pulpy, oversmoked, and horribly oversalted, with a good deal of water added to boot. A reputable butcher should be able to supply you with a good "country-style," that is, mildly smoked, ham with no water added.

If a whole ham is impractical, the butcher will often be able to cut it in half. This will give you a piece of ham weighing 6 to 8 pounds. The butt end of the ham has more meat on it and is easier to carve; the shank end has more bone but is usually less expensive. A ham with the bone in allows the meat to stay moister and will add additional flavor. Also, after the meat is consumed, the bone may be used to flavor a number of different soups or bean dishes. Allow about ½ pound of ham per person when purchasing ham with the bone in. A precooked ham should be roasted for about 16 minutes per pound.

Serve with leeks vinaigrette or the watercress and walnut salad (both November) or whipped yams with cognac (this month). A Dry Creek Rose from California or a Hermitage would go well with ham.

6- to 8-pound, precooked ham with bone in
1   jar imported orange marmalade
¼   cup cognac or bourbon

Preheat the oven to 300 degrees. Place the ham under cold running water and scrub the rind with a stiff brush; dry thoroughly. Put the ham in a shallow pan with the skin side up and roast without basting for 1½ to 2 hours, until tender.

Put the marmalade into a small saucepan, add the cognac or bourbon, and melt over low heat.

Remove the ham from the oven and raise the heat to 400

degrees. With a sharp knife or kitchen shears, remove the rind from the ham. Score the fat in a diamond pattern and spread the surface of the meat with the glaze. Return the ham to the oven and roast only long enough for the marmalade to glaze and the fat to turn crisp.

Remove from the oven and allow to stand 20 minutes before carving.

Aioli Monstre, Northwest Style

serves ten

A scene typical in the south of France on Christmas Eve is a table laden with an immense platter: in the center a poached salt cod, surrounded by tender rings of squid or octopus, wedges of hardboiled egg and tomato, and a large variety of steamed or boiled vegetables. There may also be, on another platter, the beef from a pot au feu or a few poached or roasted chickens, and always a shallow dish of snails poached in a court bouillon of white wine and fragrant herbs. And in the center of all, the supreme complement for all this bounty, is a deep bowl piled high with the golden "butter of Provence": aioli.

This is a repast for those who have a deep and abiding passion for that "truffle of the poor," garlic. Aioli is, in essence, a garlic mayonnaise. It is prepared classically with two cloves of

garlic for each serving (this quantity may be cut in half as the garlic in France is much milder than our own), egg yolks, and a good, fruity olive oil.

A lighter version of the same sauce can be made by substituting a boiled and rather mealy potato for the egg yolks. The aioli may be prepared in a food processor or blender, but I find it tastes best when done by hand with a mortar and pestle in the traditional manner.

Our version of this legendary banquet substitutes a whole poached salmon for the salt cod and Hood Canal shrimp for the squid or octopus, although you may include either or both if you wish. The snails, albeit costly, lend a definite note of festivity to the dish and those who are fond of them already know their marvelous affinity for garlic.

As for the vegetables, the selection listed here includes ones most often used in this dish but you may substitute whatever you think suitable. At the end of this feast, you may wish to serve fresh sprigs of mint or parsley or squares of dark chocolate to those guests who fear dragon-breath. Those who want wine with this banquet might try a California Chardonnay, a Graves, or a Meursault, with the understanding that few wines can stand up to the amount of raw garlic involved.

Aioli sauce:
8 to 10 cloves of garlic, peeled
3 egg yolks at room temperature
· pinch salt
2¼ cups fruity olive oil (or a mixture of half olive oil and half corn oil)
· lemon juice
· freshly ground pepper

Aioli garni:
1 pound dried chickpeas
1 bay leaf
1 large onion, peeled and stuck with 3 cloves
6-pound whole salmon, poached
2 pounds small French-style carrots, peeled
2 pounds small Finnish potatoes, not peeled
2½ pounds green beans, cut into 3-inch lengths
2 small cauliflowers, divided into flowerets
3 dozen canned snails, rinsed thoroughly under cold water

1 cup dry white vermouth or dry white wine
½ teaspoon fennel seeds
· few sprigs fresh thyme or ½ teaspoon dried thyme
1 bay leaf
2 to 3 pounds Hood Canal shrimp or other shrimp, cooked
2 fennel bulbs or 1 head celery, cut into thick strips
5 hardboiled eggs, peeled and cut in half lengthwise
5 tomatoes, cut into wedges
· parsley and lemon wedges

The night before, cover the chickpeas with cold water and allow to stand at room temperature.

The next day, first prepare the aioli: put the garlic cloves through a press into a large mortar. Add the egg yolks and beat them into the garlic with the pestle or a wire whisk until they are a light yellow in color. Add the pinch of salt and begin to beat in the oil, at first adding it very slowly drop by drop. This will take longer than a plain mayonnaise sauce because the garlic thins out the yolks. When half the oil has been added and the sauce is quite thick, add the lemon juice to taste and continue to beat in the remaining oil. When all the oil has been added, taste for seasoning, adding a bit more salt or lemon juice if necessary and a grinding or two of black pepper. Cover the sauce and refrigerate.

About 3 or 4 hours before serving, poach the salmon and allow it to cool in the court bouillon.

Two hours before serving, drain the chickpeas, place them in a large pot, and add the bay leaf, the onion stuck with cloves, and some salt. Cover them with water, bring them to a boil, reduce the heat, and simmer for about 1½ hours, until tender.

The simplest way of preparing the vegetables is to first steam the carrots for 10 to 15 minutes; then add the potatoes to the same pot and continue to steam for another 10 minutes, depending on the size of your potatoes. The green beans and cauliflower should each be boiled separately in their own pots until tender.

While the vegetables are cooking, combine the white vermouth or wine with the fennel seeds, thyme, and bay leaf in a saucepan. Add a quart of water and bring the court bouillon to a boil; add the snails, reduce the heat, and simmer them for about 15 minutes, until tender.

Place the salmon on a large serving platter; remove the skin if you wish. Surround the fish with the potatoes, carrots, and cauliflower. Garnish the platter with the tomato and egg wedges. Place the chickpeas in a bowl and surround them with the green beans and garnish with parsley.

Place the drained snails in a shallow serving dish and surround with the fennel or celery strips; garnish with parsley. Place the shrimps, still in their shells, on a serving platter and garnish with parsley and lemon wedges. Mound the aioli in the mortar or a deep serving bowl and place in the center of the table. Serve at once.

Cannoli
serves eight

A dessert immensely popular in Sicily: cylindrical pastry shells filled with a creamy mixture of ricotta cheese, candied fruit, and grated chocolate. In Seattle, the pastry shells are available readymade at DeLaurenti's in the Pike Place Market; filling them is a simple task with the aid of a pastry bag. These delicious pastries can be prepared hours in advance and chilled. I have chosen to flavor the cheese filling with toasted hazelnuts, orange rind, and rum.

8	cannoli shells
1	cup (½ pound) ricotta cheese
¼	cup confectioner's sugar
2	tablespoons dark rum
·	finely grated rind of two oranges
¼	cup toasted hazelnuts, coarsely chopped, or
¼	cup finely grated bitter chocolate

Put the ricotta cheese through a fine sieve into a bowl and beat in the sugar and the rum. Add the orange rind and hazelnuts, and blend well. Put this mixture into a 12- or 14-inch pastry bag (not fitted with a pastry tip) and pipe a bit of the mixture into each of the cannoli shells. Chill the cannoli for at least 1 hour before serving.

Tarte aux Pruneaux
serves eight

This rich prune tart can be prepared in any season but it is especially pleasing now, when there is only a limited selection of fresh fruit available.

1	cup pitted dried prunes
1	cup steaming hot tea
½	pound cream cheese
3	large eggs
¼	cup sugar
½	cup heavy cream
1	teaspoon pure vanilla extract
¼	teaspoon powdered cinnamon
·	pinch freshly grated nutmeg
·	finely grated rind of 1 small lemon
½	cup blanched almonds, finely ground
·	a partially baked (for 20 minutes at 400 degrees) pastry shell fitted into a 10-inch quiche pan
·	confectioner's sugar

Soak the prunes in the hot tea for about 45 minutes or until soft.

Beat together the cream cheese, eggs, sugar, and heavy cream until well blended. Stir in the vanilla, cinnamon, nutmeg, lemon rind, and the almonds. Bake the pastry shell as described at "Strawberry Tart."

Drain the prunes and chop them coarsely; stir them into the cream cheese mixture. After the partially baked pastry shell has cooled slightly, pour in the prune filling. Bake the tart in the center of the oven for 45 to 50 minutes until the filling has set. Remove tart from the oven, dust the top with confectioner's sugar, and allow to cool before serving.

Variation: substitute dried apricots for the prunes and grated orange rind for the lemon rind.

Mousse aux Mandarines
serves eight

The mousse has a tangy flavor because of the addition of lemon juice. It contains no gelatin, so it cannot be molded.

6   large eggs
⅔   cup finely granulated sugar
2½   tablespoons finely grated tangerine rind
·   juice of 2 tangerines
2   tablespoons freshly squeezed lemon juice
1   cup heavy cream

Separate the eggs. Place the whites in a copper or stainless-steel mixing bowl and set aside; put the yolks in a cast-iron enameled saucepan, add the sugar, grated rind, and tangerine and lemon juices, and blend thoroughly.

Put the saucepan over medium heat and beat the mixture constantly with a wire whisk until it thickens and is able to coat a wooden spoon, 5 to 8 minutes. Remove from heat immediately and allow to cool. (This method is much quicker than using a double boiler but you must not leave the yolk mixture unattended for a moment, and the saucepan must be heavy enough to conduct the heat evenly.)

Beat the egg whites until stiff but not dry. Stir a large spoonful of whites into the yolks to lighten them up; then pour the yolk mixture into the bowl of beaten whites. Fold in gently with a rubber spatula.

Whip the heavy cream until stiff, add to the mousse mixture, and fold together well. Chill for at least 2 hours before serving.

Chocolate Truffles Seville
makes about sixty-five pieces

A luscious marriage of dark chocolate, ground almonds, orange rind, and Grand Marnier.

1   pound semi-sweet chocolate
1/2   pound almonds, blanched (skins removed), toasted, and ground to a powder
1/4   pound sweet butter
11/2   tablespoons finely grated orange rind
¼   cup Grand Marnier
1   cup unsweetened cocoa powder mixed with
1   tablespoon powdered cinnamon and
1½   tablespoons powdered sugar

Cut the chocolate into small pieces. Place in a double boiler and mix in the ground almonds. Allow the chocolate to melt over simmering water. When no lumps are apparent, stir in the butter, cut into small pieces, and blend well. Remove from heat and add the orange rind and Grand Marnier and mix together. Place in the refrigerator and chill until firm, about 1 hour.

While the chocolate is cooling, mix the cocoa powder, cinnamon, and sugar in a wide soup plate. With 2 small spoons shape the chocolate mixture into irregular pieces about the size of a chestnut, roll them in the cocoa mixture to coat, and freeze. They will keep for weeks if put into a tin container fitted with a tight lid.

Chocolate Truffles Italienne
makes about sixty-five pieces

Here the truffles are flavored with ground Italian almond nougat and Amaretto liqueur. The nougat can be ground in a food processor.

1   pound semi-sweet chocolate
1/4   pound sweet butter, cut into small pieces
1   cup finely ground Italian Torrone almond nougat
1/3   cup Amaretto liqueur
1   cup unsweetened cocoa powder

Cut the chocolate into small pieces; place in the top half of a double boiler and allow to melt over simmering water. When no lumps are apparent, stir in the butter, little by little, until it is absorbed. Remove the mixture from the heat and stir in the ground nougat and the liqueur. Place in the refrigerator and chill until firm, about 1 hour.

Place the cocoa powder in a wide soup plate. Form the truffles with 2 dessert spoons into irregular pieces about the size of a chestnut and roll them in the cocoa powder to cover. Place them in a tin with a tightly fitting lid and freeze. When stored in this manner, the truffles will keep for weeks.

Zuccotto
serves eight

Zuccotto, a dessert dear to the hearts of the Florentines, is said to have been created by a pastry-maker to resemble the dome of the celebrated cathedral, Santa Maria del Fiore. In the Florentine dialect, the word "zucca" means a large squash (zucchini: small squash) or head. Any sponge cake baked in a sheet may be used to form the outside of the sweet. My favorite is the ladyfinger biscuit from Jacques Pepin's book, *La Technique.*

1 recipe ladyfinger biscuit or other sponge cake, baked and cooled.

Filling:

1 cup ricotta, sieved
2 cups heavy cream
¼ cup confectioner's sugar
1 teaspoon pure vanilla extract
1 cup Italian Torrone almond nougat, finely ground in food processor
1 tablespoon unsweetened cocoa powder
3 tablespoons dark rum or cognac

Garnish:

· unsweetened cocoa powder
· confectioner's sugar
1 to 1½ cups heavy cream, whipped

While the cake is baking, prepare the filling: beat the heavy cream, adding the confectioner's sugar and the vanilla extract. Fold in the ground nougat and the ricotta, sieved to remove its grainy texture.

Line a buttered, round-bottomed 2-quart bowl with waxed paper. Divide and cut the cooled cake into suitably sized squares; then cut the squares in half into triangular sections. Line the bowl with the triangular sections, fitting them in point side down, until the bowl's surface has been covered. Reserve any scraps for covering the top. Sprinkle the cake sections with the rum or cognac. Spread a thick layer of the cream and nougat mixture over the cake.

Mix the tablespoon of cocoa powder into the cream mixture remaining. Pour this into the bowl and smooth over the top with a spatula. Cover with the reserved pieces of cake. (Since this will be the bottom of the dessert, you needn't worry if it looks a bit irregular.) Cover the cake with a layer of waxed paper, place a plate on top, and weigh it down with one large or several small cans of food. Refrigerate overnight.

Remove and discard the waxed paper from the top of the bowl.

Place a serving plate over the top of the bowl and invert the zuccotto onto it. Remove the waxed paper and discard. The cake should be decorated in alternating sections of cocoa powder and confectioner's sugar, like a brown and white beach ball. This is most easily done with the aid of a small sieve and waxed paper to cover the sections not being sprinkled. Pipe the remaining whipped cream between the sections and around the bottom of the zuccotto.

INDEX

Herb paste, 146, 171
Hunter's stew, 20

Italian Bean and Tuna Salad, 35
Italian Rice Salad, 166

Jambalaya, 67
Juniper berries, sauteed with potatoes,
    204

Kidney beans, in chili, 25
Knackwurst, in choucroute, 27
Kulebiaka, 111

Lamb
    abbaccioalla cacciatoria, 90
    and bean soup, 10
    breast of, grilled, 150
        in soup, 10
    buying, 79
    ground, in moussaka, 189
    leg of, grilled, 151
    rack of, grilled, 150
    sauteed with artichoke hearts, 91
    shanks, braised, 26
    spit-roasted, 88
    steaks, pan-fried, 90
    stew, 191
    stuffed in grape leaves, 185
Lamb Riblets a la Grecque, 150
Lamb Shanks, Greek Style, 26
Lamb Shashlik, 151
Late Summer Bean Soup, 184
Leek and Sausage Tart, 188
Leeks
    about, 221
    and potato soup, 13
    cleaning, 229
    gratin, with ham, 228
    in vinaigrette, 228
    pureed, with beef in pastry, 231
    with sausage in tart, 188
Leeks in Vinaigrette, 228
Lemon
    and green bean saute, 119
    dessert ices, 177
    in sauce for pork, 174
    mousse, 128
    sauce, for lamb, 26
    sauce, with chicken, 46
    with blueberries in souffle, 195
Lemon Blueberry Souffle Glace, 195
Lemon Ices, 177
Lettuce, cream soup of, 84

Lima bean and lamb soup, 10
Lime marinade for seviche, 107
Linguini Primavera, 92
Linguini with Mussel Sauce, 72
Louisiana Crayfish Boil, 172

Marinades
    about, 139
    citrus, for fish, 107
    dill, for salmon, 105
    for grilled meats, 139
    for grilled pork, 144
    lemon and oregano, 150
    lemon, for lamb, 151
    lemon pepper, for fowl, 149
    lime, for salmon, 162
    orange juice and onion, for pork, 175
Matelote of Sturgeon, 59
Mayonnaise
    garlic, 249
    in sauce for pork, 174
    tomato, 163
Meats, grilled, 138-139
Medallions of Pork with Potatoes and
        Herbs, 109
Melon
    fool, 132
    honey dew, in anisette, 155
    in chicken curry, 126
    ripe, choosing, 154
    sherbet, 154
Melon in Anisette, 155
Meuniere, Sole, 42
Mint
    in salad dressing, 98
    with braised peas, 104
Moroccan Chicken, 146
Moroccan Lamb Tajin, 191
Moroccan Orange and Radish Salad,
        182
Moussaka, 189
Mousse
    chicken liver, 244
    cream cheese, 128
    lemon, 128
    tangerine, 253
Mousse aux Mandarines, 253
Mushrooms
    about, 200
    chanterelle soup, 205
    chanterelle stuffing for chicken, 208
    in pastry with salmon, 111
    salad, 81
Mussel Chowder, 72
Mussels
    chowder of, 72
    cleaning, 70-71